The Myths
Of
The New World

by

Daniel G. Brinton

Double9
BOOKS

The Myths Of
The New World
by Daniel G. Brinton

ISBN: 978-93-59320-75-5

Published by

DOUBLE 9 BOOKS

2/13-B, Ansari Road, Daryaganj
New Delhi – 110002
info@double9books.com
www.double9books.com
Tel. 011-40042856

ABOUT THE AUTHOR

Daniel Garrison Brinton (May 13, 1837 - July 31, 1899) was a surgeon, historian, archaeologist, and ethnologist from the United States. Brinton was born in Chester County, Pennsylvania, in Thornbury Township. Brinton graduated from Yale University in 1858 and spent the next year traveling in Europe after attending Jefferson Medical College for two years. He pursued his studies further in Paris and Heidelberg. During the American Civil War, he served as a surgeon in the Union army from 1862 to 1865, serving as surgeon-in-charge of the US Army general hospital in Quincy, Illinois, from 1864 to 1865. Brinton got sunburned at Missionary Ridge (the Third Battle of Chattanooga) and was never able to travel in extremely hot weather again. This handicap has an impact on his work as an ethnologist.

CONTENTS

CHAPTER XI

PREFACE

I have written this work more for the thoughtful general reader than the antiquary. It is a study of an obscure portion of the intellectual history of our species as exemplified in one of its varieties.

What are man's earliest ideas of a soul and a God, and of his own origin and destiny? Why do we find certain myths, such as of a creation, a flood, an after-world; certain symbols, as the bird, the serpent, the cross; certain numbers, as the three, the four, the seven—intimately associated with these ideas by every race? What are the laws of growth of natural religions? How do they acquire such an influence, and is this influence for good or evil? Such are some of the universally interesting questions which I attempt to solve by an analysis of the simple faiths of a savage race.

If in so doing I succeed in investing with a more general interest the fruitful theme of American ethnology, my objects will have been accomplished.

Philadelphia,
April, 1868.

CHAPTER I
GENERAL CONSIDERATIONS
ON THE RED RACE

Natural religions the unaided attempts of man to find out God, modified by peculiarities of race and nation. — The peculiarities of the red race: 1. Its languages unfriendly to abstract ideas. Native modes of writing by means of pictures, symbols, objects, and phonetic signs. These various methods compared in their influence on the intellectual faculties. 2. Its isolation, unique in the history of the world. 3. Beyond all others, a hunting race. — Principal linguistic subdivisions: 1. The Eskimos. 2. The Athapascas. 3. The Algonkins and Iroquois. 4. The Apalachian tribes. 5. The Dakotas. 6. The Aztecs. 7. The Mayas. 8. The Muyscas. 9. The Quichuas. 10. The Caribs and Tupis. 11. The Araucanians. — General course of migrations. — Age of man in America. — Unity of type in the red race.

WHEN Paul, at the request of the philosophers of Athens, explained to them his views on divine things, he asserted, among other startling novelties, that "God has made of one blood all nations of the earth, that they should seek the Lord, if haply they might feel after him and find him, though he is not far from every one of us."

Here was an orator advocating the unity of the human species, affirming that the chief end of man is to develop an innate idea of God, and that all religions, except the one he preached, were examples of more or less unsuccessful attempts to do so. No wonder the Athenians, who acknowledged no kinship to barbarians, who looked dubiously at the doctrine of innate ideas, and were divided in opinion as to whether their mythology was a shrewd device of legislators to keep the populace in subjection, a veiled natural philosophy, or the celestial reflex of their own history, mocked at such a babbler and went their ways. The generations of philosophers that followed them partook of their doubts and approved their opinions, quite down to our own times. But now, after weighing the question maturely, we are compelled to admit that the Apostle was not so wide of the mark after all — that, in fact, the latest and best authorities, with no bias in his favor, support his position and may almost be said to paraphrase his words. For according to a writer who ranks second to none in the science of ethnology, the severest and most recent investigations show that "not only do acknowledged facts permit the assumption of the unity of the human species, but this opinion is attended with fewer discrepancies, and has greater inner consistency than the opposite one of specific diversity." 2-1 And as to the religions of heathendom, the view of Saint Paul is but expressed with a more poetic turn by a distinguished living author when he calls them "not fables, but truths, though clothed in a garb woven by fancy, wherein the web is the notion of God, the ideal of reason in the soul of man, the thought of the Infinite." 2-2

Inspiration and science unite therefore to bid us dismiss the effete prejudice that natural religions either arise as the ancient philosophies taught, or that they are, as the Dark Ages imagined, subtle nets of the devil spread to catch human souls. They are rather the unaided attempts of man to find out God; they are the efforts of the reason struggling to define the infinite; they are the expressions of that "yearning after the gods" which the earliest of poets discerned in the hearts of all men. Studied in this sense they are rich in teachings. Would we estimate the intellectual and æsthetic culture of a people, would we generalize the laws of progress, would we appreciate the sublimity of Christianity, and read the seals of its authenticity: the natural conceptions of divinity reveal them. No mythologies are so crude, therefore, none so barbarous, but deserve the attention of the philosophic mind, for they are never the empty fictions of an idle fancy, but rather the utterances, however inarticulate, of an immortal and ubiquitous intuition.

These considerations embolden me to approach with some confidence even the aboriginal religions of America, so often stigmatized as incoherent fetichisms, so barren, it has been said, in grand or beautiful creations. The task bristles with difficulties. Carelessness, prepossessions, and ignorance have disfigured them with false colors and foreign additions without number. The first maxim, therefore, must be to sift and scrutinize authorities, and to reject whatever betrays the plastic hand of the European. For the religions developed by the red race, not those mixed creeds learned from foreign invaders, are to be the subjects of our study. Then will remain the formidable undertaking of reducing the authentic materials thus obtained to system and order, and this not by any preconceived theory of what they ought to conform to, but learning from them the very laws of religious growth they illustrate. The historian traces the birth of arts, science, and government to man's dependence on nature and his fellows for the means of self-preservation. Not that man receives these endowments from without, but that the stern step-mother, Nature, forces him by threats and stripes to develop his own inherent faculties. So with religion: The idea of God does not, and cannot, proceed from the external world, but, nevertheless, it finds its *historical* origin also in the desperate struggle for life, in the satisfaction of the animal wants and passions, in those vulgar aims and motives which possessed the mind of the primitive man to the exclusion of everything else.

There is an ever present embarrassment in such inquiries. In dealing with these matters beyond the cognizance of the senses, the mind is forced to express its meaning in terms transferred from sensuous perceptions, or under symbols borrowed from the material world. These transfers must be understood, these symbols explained, before the real meaning of a myth can be reached. He who fails to guess the riddle of the sphynx, need not hope to gain admittance to the shrine. With delicate ear the faint whispers of thought must be apprehended which prompt the intellect when it names the immaterial from the material; when it chooses from the infinity of visible forms those meet to shadow forth Divinity.

Two lights will guide us on this venturesome path. Mindful of the watchword of inductive science, to proceed from the known to the unknown, the inquiry will be put whether the aboriginal languages of America employ the same tropes to express such ideas as deity, spirit, and soul, as our own and kindred tongues. If the answer prove affirmative, then not only have we gained a firm foothold whence to survey the whole edifice of their mythology; but from an unexpected quarter arises evidence of the unity of our species far weightier than any mere anatomy can furnish, evidence from the living soul, not from the dead body. True that the science of American linguistics is still in its infancy, and that a proper handling of the materials it even now offers involves a more critical acquaintance with its innumerable dialects than I possess; but though the gleaning be sparse, it is enough that I break the ground. Secondly, religious rites are living commentaries on religious beliefs. At first they are rude representations of the supposed doings of the gods. The Indian rain-maker mounts to the roof of his hut, and rattling vigorously a dry gourd containing pebbles, to represent the thunder, scatters water through a reed on the ground beneath, as he imagines up above in the clouds do the spirits of the storm. Every spring in ancient Delphi was repeated in scenic ceremony the combat of Apollo and the Dragon, the victory of the lord of bright summer over the demon of chilling winter. Thus do forms and ceremonies reveal the meaning of mythology, and the origin of its fables.

Let it not be objected that this proposed method of analysis assumes that religions begin and develop under the operation of inflexible laws. The soul is shackled by no fatalism. Formative influences there are, deep seated, far reaching, escaped by few, but like those which of yore astrologers imputed to the stars, they potently incline, they do not coerce. Language, pursuits, habits, geographical position, and those subtle mental traits which make up the characteristics of races and nations, all tend to deflect from a given standard the religious life of the individual and the mass. It is essential to give these due weight, and a necessary preface therefore to an analysis of the myths of the red race is an enumeration of its peculiarities, and of its chief families as they were located when first known to the historian.

Of all such modifying circumstances none has greater importance than the means of expressing and transmitting intellectual action. The spoken and the written language of a nation reveal to us its prevailing, and to a certain degree its unavoidable mode of thought. Here the red race offers a striking phenomenon. There is no other trait that binds together its scattered clans, and brands them as members of one great family, so unmistakably as this of language. From the Frozen Ocean to the Land of Fire, without a single exception, the native dialects, though varying infinitely in words, are marked by a peculiarity in construction which is found nowhere else on the globe, 6-1 and which is so foreign to the genius of *our* tongue that it is no easy matter to explain it. It is called by philologists the *polysynthetic* construction. What it is will best appear by comparison. Every grammatical sentence conveys one leading idea with its modifications and relations. Now a Chinese would express these latter by unconnected syllables, the precise bearing of which could only be guessed by their position; a Greek or a German would use independent words, indicating their relations by terminations meaningless in themselves; an Englishman gains the same end chiefly by the use of particles and by position. Very different from all these is the spirit of a polysynthetic language. It seeks to unite in the most intimate manner all relations and modifications with the leading idea, to merge one in the other by altering the forms of the words themselves and welding them together, to express the whole in one word, and to banish any conception except as it arises in relation to others. Thus in many American tongues there is, in fact, no word for father, mother, brother, but only for my, your, his father, etc. This has advantages and defects. It offers marvellous facilities for defining the perceptions of the senses with the utmost accuracy, but regarding everything in the concrete, it is unfriendly to the nobler labors of the mind, to abstraction and generalization. In the numberless changes of these languages, their bewildering flexibility, their variable forms, and their rapid deterioration, they seem to betray a lack of individuality, and to resemble the vague and tumultuous history of the tribes who employ them. They exhibit an almost incredible laxity. It is nothing uncommon for the two sexes to use different names for the same object, and for nobles and vulgar, priests and people, the old and the young, nay, even the married and single, to observe what seem to the European ear quite different modes of expression. Families and whole villages suddenly drop words and manufacture others in their places out of mere caprice or superstition, and a few years' separation suffices to produce a marked dialectic difference. In their copious forms and facility of reproduction they remind one of those anomalous animals, in whom, when a limb is lopped, it rapidly grows again, or even if cut in pieces each part will enter on a separate life quite unconcerned about his fellows. But as the naturalist is far from regarding this superabundant vitality as a characteristic of ·a higher type, so the philologist justly assigns these tongues a low position in the linguistic scale. Fidelity to form, here as everywhere, is the test of excellence. At the outset, we divine there can be nothing very subtle in the mythologies of nations with such languages. Much there must be that will be obscure, much that is vague, an exhausting variety in repetition, and a strong tendency to lose the idea in the symbol.   ,

What definiteness of outline might be preserved must depend on the care with which the old stories of the gods were passed from one person and one generation to another. The fundamental myths of a race have a surprising tenacity of life. How many centuries had elapsed between the period the Germanic hordes left their ancient homes in Central Asia, and when Tacitus listened to their wild songs on the banks of the Rhine? Yet we know that through those unnumbered ages of barbarism and aimless roving, these songs, "their only sort of history or annals," says the historian, had preserved intact the story of Mannus, the Sanscrit Manu, and his three sons, and of the great god Tuisco, the Indian Dyu. 9-1 So much the more do all means invented by the red race to record and transmit thought merit our careful attention. Few and feeble they seem to us, mainly shifts to aid the memory. Of some such, perhaps, not a single tribe was destitute. The tattoo marks on the warrior's breast, his string of gristly scalps, the bear's claws around his neck, were not only trophies of his prowess, but records of his exploits, and to the contemplative mind contain the rudiments of the beneficent art of letters. Did he draw in rude outline on his skin tent figures of men transfixed with arrows as many as he had slain enemies, his education was rapidly advancing. He had mastered the elements of *picture writing*, beyond which hardly the wisest of his race progressed. Figures of the natural objects connected by symbols having fixed meanings make up the whole of this art. The relative frequency of the latter marks its advancement from a merely figurative to an ideographic notation. On what principle of mental association a given sign was adopted to express a certain idea, why, for instance, on the Chipeway scrolls a circle means *spirits*, and a horned snake *life*, it is often hard to guess. The difficulty grows when we find that to the initiated the same sign calls up quite different ideas, as the subject of the writer varies from war to love, or from the chase to religion. The connection is generally beyond the power of divination, and the key to ideographic writing once lost can never be recovered.

The number of such arbitrary characters in the Chipeway notation is said to be over two hundred, but if the distinction between a figure and a symbol were rigidly applied, it would be much reduced. This kind of writing, if it deserves the name, was common throughout the continent, and many specimens of it, scratched on the plane surfaces of stones, have been preserved to the present day. Such is the once celebrated inscription on Dighton Rock, Massachusetts, long supposed to be a record of the Northmen of Vinland; such those that mark the faces of the cliffs which overhang the waters of the Orinoco, and those that in Oregon, Peru, and La Plata have been the subject of much curious speculation. They are alike the mute and meaningless epitaphs of vanished generations.

I would it could be said that in favorable contrast to our ignorance of these inscriptions is our comprehension of the highly wrought pictography of the Aztecs. No nation ever reduced it more to a system. It was in constant use in the daily transactions of life. They manufactured for writing purposes a thick, coarse paper from the leaves of the agave plant by a process of maceration and pressure. An Aztec book closely resembles one of our quarto volumes. It is made of a single sheet, twelve to fifteen inches wide, and often sixty or seventy feet long, and is not rolled, but folded either in squares or zigzags in such a manner that on opening it there are two pages exposed to view. Thin wooden boards are fastened to each of the outer leaves, so that the whole presents as neat an appearance, remarks Peter Martyr, as if it had come from the shop of a skilful bookbinder. They also covered buildings, tapestries, and scrolls of parchment with these devices, and for trifling transactions were familiar with the use of *slates* of soft stone from which the figures could readily be erased with water. 11-1 What is still more astonishing, there is reason to believe, in some instances, their figures were not painted, but actually *printed* with movable blocks of wood on which the symbols were carved in relief, though this was probably confined to those intended for ornament only.

In these records we discern something higher than a mere symbolic notation. They contain the germ of a phonetic alphabet, and represent sounds of spoken language. The symbol is often not connected with the *idea* but with the *word*. The mode in which this is done corresponds precisely to that of the rebus. It is a simple method, readily suggesting itself. In the middle ages it was much in vogue in Europe for the same purpose for which it was chiefly employed in Mexico at the same time—the writing of proper names. For example, the English family Bolton was known in heraldry by a *tun* transfixed by a *bolt*. Precisely so the Mexican emperor Ixcoatl is mentioned in the Aztec manuscripts under the figure of a serpent *coatl*, pierced by obsidian knives *ixtli*, and Moquauhzoma by a mouse-trap *montli*, an eagle *quauhtli*, a lancet *zo*, and a hand *maitl*. As a syllable could be expressed by any object whose name commenced with it, as few words can be given the form of a rebus without some change, as the figures sometimes represent their full phonetic value, sometimes only that of their initial sound, and as universally the attention of the artist was directed less to the sound than to the idea, the didactic painting of the Mexicans, whatever it might have been to them, is a sealed book to us, and must remain so in great part. Moreover, it is entirely undetermined whether it should be read from the first to the last page, or *vice versa*, whether from right to left or from left to right, from bottom to top or from top to bottom, around the edges of the page toward the centre, or each line in the opposite direction from the preceding one. There are good authorities for all these methods, 12-1 and they may all be correct, for there is no evidence that any fixed rule had been laid down in this respect.

Immense masses of such documents were stored in the imperial archives of ancient Mexico. Torquemada asserts that five cities alone yielded to the Spanish governor on one requisition no less than sixteen thousand volumes or scrolls! Every leaf was destroyed. Indeed, so thorough and wholesale was the destruction of these memorials now so precious in our eyes that hardly enough remain to whet the wits of antiquaries. In the libraries of Paris, Dresden, Pesth, and the Vatican are, however, a sufficient number to make us despair of deciphering them had we for comparison all which the Spaniards destroyed.

Beyond all others the Mayas, resident on the peninsula of Yucatan, would seem to have approached nearest a true phonetic system. They had a regular and well understood alphabet of twenty seven elementary sounds, the letters of which are totally different from those of any other nation, and evidently original with themselves. But besides these they used a large number of purely conventional symbols, and moreover were accustomed constantly to employ the ancient pictographic method in addition as a sort of commentary on the sound represented. What is more curious, if the obscure explanation of an ancient writer can be depended upon, they not only aimed to employ an alphabet after the manner of ours, but to express the sound absolutely like our phonographic signs do. 13-1 With the aid of this alphabet, which has fortunately been preserved, we are enabled to spell out a few words on the Yucatecan manuscripts and façades, but thus far with no positive results. The loss of the ancient pronunciation is especially in the way of such studies.

In South America, also, there is said to have been a nation who cultivated the art of picture writing, the Panos, on the river Ucayale. A missionary, Narcisso Gilbar by name, once penetrated, with great toil, to one of their villages. As he approached he beheld a venerable man seated under the shade of a palm tree, with a great book open before him from which he was reading to an attentive circle of auditors the wars and wanderings of their forefathers. With difficulty the priest got a sight of the precious volume, and found it covered with figures and signs in marvellous symmetry and order. 14-1 No wonder such a romantic scene left a deep impression on his memory.

The Peruvians adopted a totally different and unique system of records, that by means of the *quipu*. This was a base cord, the thickness of the finger, of any required length, to which were attached numerous small strings of different colors, lengths, and textures, variously knotted and twisted one with another. Each of these peculiarities represented a certain number, a quality, quantity, or other idea, but *what*, not the most fluent *quipu* reader could tell unless he was acquainted with the general topic treated of. Therefore, whenever news was sent in this manner a person accompanied the bearer to serve as verbal commentator, and to prevent confusion the *quipus* relating to the various departments of knowledge were placed in separate storehouses, one for war, another for taxes, a third for history, and so forth. On what principle or mnemotechnics the ideas were connected with the knots and colors we are totally in the dark; it has even been doubted whether they had any application beyond the art of numeration. 14-2 Each combination had, however, a fixed ideographic value in a certain branch of knowledge, and thus the *quipu* differed essentially from the Catholic rosary, the Jewish phylactery, or the knotted strings of the natives of North America and Siberia, to all of which it has at times been compared.

The *wampum* used by the tribes of the north Atlantic coast was, in many respects, analogous to the quipu. In early times it was composed chiefly of bits of wood of equal size, but different colors. These were hung on strings which were woven into belts and bands, the hues, shapes, sizes, and combinations of the strings hinting their general significance. Thus the lighter shades were invariable harbingers of peaceful or pleasant tidings, while the darker portended war and danger. The substitution of beads or shells in place of wood, and the custom of embroidering figures in the belts were, probably, introduced by European influence.

Besides these, various simpler mnemonic aids were employed, such as parcels of reeds of different lengths, notched sticks, knots in cords, strings of pebbles or fruit-stones, circular pieces of wood or slabs pierced with different figures which the English liken to "cony holes," and at a victory, a treaty, or the founding of a village, sometimes a pillar or heap of stones was erected equalling in number the persons present at the occasion, or the number of the fallen.

This exhausts the list. All other methods of writing, the hieroglyphs of the Micmacs of Acadia, the syllabic alphabet of the Cherokees, the pretended traces of Greek, Hebrew, and Celtiberic letters which have from time to time been brought to the notice of the public, have been without exception the products of foreign civilization or simply frauds. Not a single coin, inscription, or memorial of any kind whatever, has been found on the American continent showing the existence, either generally or locally, of any other means of writing than those specified.

Poor as these substitutes for a developed phonetic system seem to us, they were of great value to the uncultivated man. In his legends their introduction is usually ascribed to some heaven-sent benefactor, the antique characters were jealously adhered to, and the pictured scroll of bark, the quipu ball, the belt of wampum, were treasured with provident care, and their import minutely expounded to the most intelligent of the rising generation. In all communities beyond the stage of barbarism a class of persons was set apart for this duty and no other. Thus, for example, in ancient Peru, one college of priests styled *amauta*, learned, had exclusive charge over the quipus containing the mythological and historical traditions; a second, the *haravecs*, singers, devoted themselves to those referring to the national ballads and dramas; while a third occupied their time solely with those pertaining to civil affairs. Such custodians preserved and prepared the archives, learned by heart with their aid what their fathers knew, and in some countries, as, for instance, among the Panos mentioned above, and the Quiches of Guatemala, 16-1 repeated portions of them at times to the assembled populace. It has even been averred by one of their converted chiefs, long a missionary to his fellows, that the Chipeways of Lake Superior have a college composed of ten "of the wisest and most venerable of their nation," who have in charge the pictured records containing the ancient history of their tribe. These are kept in an underground chamber, and are disinterred every fifteen years by the assembled guardians, that they may be repaired, and their contents explained to new members of the society. 17-1

In spite of these precautions, the end seems to have been very imperfectly attained. The most distinguished characters, the weightiest events in national history faded into oblivion after a few generations. The time and circumstances of the formation of the league of the Five Nations, the dispersion of the mound builders of the Ohio valley in the fifteenth century, the chronicles of Peru or Mexico beyond a century or two anterior to the conquest, are preserved in such a vague and contradictory manner that they have slight value as history. Their mythology fared somewhat better, for not only was it kept fresh in the memory by frequent repetition; but being itself founded in nature, it was constantly nourished by the truths which gave it birth. Nevertheless, we may profit by the warning to remember that their myths are myths only, and not the reflections of history or heroes.

Rising from these details to a general comparison of the symbolic and phonetic systems in their reactions on the mind, the most obvious are their contrasted effects on the faculty of memory. Letters represent elementary sounds, which are few in any language, while symbols stand for ideas, and they are numerically infinite. The transmission of knowledge by means of the latter is consequently attended with most disproportionate labor. It is almost as if we could quote nothing from an author unless we could recollect his exact words. We have a right to look for excellent memories where such a mode is in vogue, and in the present instance we are not disappointed. "These savages," exclaims La Hontan, "have the happiest memories in the world!" It was etiquette at their councils for each speaker to repeat verbatim all his predecessors had said, and the whites were often astonished and confused at the verbal fidelity with which the natives recalled the transactions of long past treaties. Their songs were inexhaustible. An instance is on record where an Indian sang two hundred on various subjects. 18-1 Such a fact reminds us of a beautiful expression of the elder Humboldt: "Man," he says, "regarded as an animal, belongs to one of the singing species; but his notes are always associated with ideas." The youth who were educated at the public schools of ancient Mexico — for that realm, so far from neglecting the cause of popular education, established houses for gratuitous instruction, and to a certain extent made the attendance upon them obligatory — learned by rote long orations, poems, and prayers with a facility astonishing to the conquerors, and surpassing anything they were accustomed to see in the universities of Old Spain. A phonetic system actually weakens the retentive powers of the mind by offering a more facile plan for preserving thought. "*Ce que je mets sur papier, je remets de ma mémoire*" is an expression of old Montaigne which he could never have used had he employed ideographic characters.

Memory, however, is of far less importance than a free activity of thought, untrammelled by forms or precedents, and ever alert to novel combinations of ideas. Give a race this and it will guide it to civilization as surely as the needle directs the ship to its haven. It is here that ideographic writing reveals its fatal inferiority. It is forever specifying, materializing, dealing in minutiæ. In the Egyptian symbolic alphabet there is a figure for a virgin, another for a married woman, for a widow without offspring, for a widow with one child, two children, and I know not in how many other circumstances, but for *woman* there is no sign. It must be so in the nature of things, for the symbol represents the object as it appears or is fancied to appear, and not as it is *thought*. Furthermore, the constant learning by heart infallibly leads to slavish repetition and mental servility.

A symbol when understood is independent of language, and is as universally current as an Arabic numeral. But this divorce of spoken and written language is of questionable advantage. It at once destroys all permanent improvement in a tongue through elegance of style, sonorous periods, or delicacy of expression, and the life of the language itself is weakened when its forms are left to fluctuate uncontrolled. Written poetry, grammar, rhetoric, all are impossible to the student who draws his knowledge from such a source.

Finally, it has been justly observed by the younger Humboldt that the painful fidelity to the antique figures transmitted from barbarous to polished generations is injurious to the æsthetic sense, and dulls the mind to the beautiful in art and nature.

The transmission of thought by figures and symbols would, on the whole, therefore, foster those narrow and material tendencies which the genius of polysynthetic languages would seem calculated to produce. Its one redeeming trait of strengthening the memory will serve to explain the strange tenacity with which certain myths have been preserved through widely dispersed families, as we shall hereafter see.

Besides this of language there are two traits in the history of the red man without parallel in that of any other variety of our species which has achieved any notable progress in civilization.

The one is his *isolation*. Cut off time out of mind from the rest of the world, he never underwent those crossings of blood and culture which so modified and on the whole promoted the growth of the old world nationalities. In his own way he worked out his own destiny, and what he won was his with a more than ordinary right of ownership. For all those old dreams of the advent of the Ten Lost Tribes, of Buddhist priests, of Welsh princes, or of Phenician merchants on American soil, and there exerting a permanent influence, have been consigned to the dustbin by every unbiased student, and when we see such men as Mr. Schoolcraft and the Abbé E. C. Brasseur essaying to resuscitate them, we regretfully look upon it in the light of a literary anachronism.

The second trait is the entire absence of the herdsman's life with its softening associations. Throughout the continent there is not a single authentic instance of a pastoral tribe, not one of an animal raised for its milk, 21-1 nor for the transportation of persons, and very few for their flesh. It was essentially a hunting race. The most civilized nations looked to the chase for their chief supply of meat, and the courts of Cuzco and Mexico enacted stringent game and forest laws, and at certain periods the whole population turned out for a general crusade against the denizens of the forest. In the most densely settled districts the conquerors found vast stretches of primitive woods.

If we consider the life of a hunter, pitting his skill and strength against the marvellous instincts and quick perceptions of the brute, training his senses to preternatural acuteness, but blunting his more tender feelings, his sole aim to shed blood and take life, dependent on luck for his food, exposed to deprivations, storms, and long wanderings, his chief diet flesh, we may more readily comprehend that conspicuous disregard of human suffering, those sanguinary rites, that vindictive spirit, that inappeasable restlessness, which we so often find in the chronicles of ancient America. The law with reason objects to accepting a butcher as a juror on a trial for life; here is a whole race of butchers.

The one mollifying element was agriculture. On the altar of Mixcoatl, god of hunting, the Aztec priest tore the heart from the human victim and smeared with the spouting blood the snake that coiled its lengths around the idol; flowers and fruits, yellow ears of maize and clusters of rich bananas decked the shrine of Centeotl, beneficent patroness of agriculture, and bloodless offerings alone were her appropriate dues. This shows how clear, even to the native mind, was the contrast between these two modes of subsistence. By substituting a sedentary for a wandering life, by supplying a fixed dependence for an uncertain contingency, and by admonishing man that in preservation, not in destruction, lies his most remunerative sphere of activity, we can hardly estimate too highly the wide distribution of the zea mays. This was their only cereal, and it was found in cultivation from the southern extremity of Chili to the fiftieth parallel of north latitude, beyond which limits the low temperature renders it an uncertain crop. In their legends it is represented as the gift of the Great Spirit (Chipeways), brought from the terrestrial Paradise by the sacred animals (Quiches), and symbolically the mother of the race (Nahuas), and the material from which was moulded the first of men (Quiches).

As the races, so the great families of man who speak dialects of the same tongue are, in a sense, individuals, bearing each its own physiognomy. When the whites first heard the uncouth gutturals of the Indians, they frequently proclaimed that hundreds of radically diverse languages, invented, it was piously suggested, by the Devil for the annoyance of missionaries, prevailed over the continent. Earnest students of such matters — Vater, Duponceau,

Gallatin, and Buschmann—have, however, demonstrated that nine-tenths of the area of America, at its discovery, were occupied by tribes using dialects traceable to ten or a dozen primitive stems. The names of these, their geographical position in the sixteenth century, and, so far as it is safe to do so, their individual character, I shall briefly mention.

Fringing the shores of the Northern Ocean from Mount St. Elias on the west to the Gulf of St. Lawrence on the east, rarely seen a hundred miles from the coast, were the Eskimos. 23-1 They are the connecting link between the races of the Old and New Worlds, in physical appearance and mental traits more allied to the former, but in language betraying their near kinship to the latter. An amphibious race, born fishermen, in their buoyant skin kayaks they brave fearlessly the tempests, make long voyages, and merit the sobriquet bestowed upon them by Von Baer, "the Phenicians of the north." Contrary to what one might suppose, they are, amid their snows, a contented, light-hearted people, knowing no longing for a sunnier clime, given to song, music, and merry tales. They are cunning handicraftsmen to a degree, but withal wholly ingulfed in a sensuous existence. The desperate struggle for life engrosses them, and their mythology is barren.

South of them, extending in a broad band across the continent from Hudson's Bay to the Pacific, and almost to the Great Lakes below, is the Athapascan stock. Its affiliated tribes rove far north to the mouth of the Mackenzie River, and wandering still more widely in an opposite direction along both declivities of the Rocky Mountains, people portions of the coast of Oregon south of the mouth of the Columbia, and spreading over the plains of New Mexico under the names of Apaches, Navajos, and Lipans, almost reach the tropics at the delta of the Rio Grande del Norte, and on the shores of the Gulf of California. No wonder they deserted their fatherland and forgot it altogether, for it is a very *terra damnata*, whose wretched inhabitants are cut off alike from the harvest of the sea and the harvest of the soil. The profitable culture of maize does not extend beyond the fiftieth parallel of latitude, and less than seven degrees farther north the mean annual temperature everywhere east of the mountains sinks below the freezing point. 25-1 Agriculture is impossible, and the only chance for life lies in the uncertain fortunes of the chase and the penurious gifts of an arctic flora. The denizens of these wilds are abject, slovenly, hopelessly savage, "at the bottom of the scale of humanity in North America," says Dr. Richardson, and their relatives who have wandered to the more genial climes of the south are as savage as they, as perversely hostile to a sedentary life, as gross and narrow in their moral notions. This wide-spread stock, scattered over forty-five degrees of latitude, covering thousands of square leagues, reaching from the Arctic Ocean to the confines of the empire of the

Montezumas, presents in all its subdivisions the same mental physiognomy and linguistic peculiarities. 25-2

Best known to us of all the Indians are the Algonkins and Iroquois, who, at the time of the discovery, were the sole possessors of the region now embraced by Canada and the eastern United States north of the thirty-fifth parallel. The latter, under the names of the Five Nations, Hurons, Tuscaroras, Susquehannocks, Nottoways and others, occupied much of the soil from the St. Lawrence and Lake Ontario to the Roanoke, and perhaps the Cherokees, whose homes were in the secluded vales of East Tennessee, were one of their early offshoots. 25-3 They were a race of warriors, courageous, cruel, unimaginative, but of rare political sagacity. They are more like ancient Romans than Indians, and are leading figures in the colonial wars.

The Algonkins surrounded them on every side, occupying the rest of the region mentioned and running westward to the base of the Rocky Mountains, where one of their famous bands, the Blackfeet, still hunts over the valley of the Saskatchewan. They were more genial than the Iroquois, of milder manners and more vivid fancy, and were regarded by these with a curious mixture of respect and contempt. Some writer has connected this difference with their preference for the open prairie country in contrast to the endless and sombre forests where were the homes of the Iroquois. Their history abounds in great men, whose ambitious plans were foiled by the levity of their allies and their want of persistence. They it was who under King Philip fought the Puritan fathers; who at the instigation of Pontiac doomed to death every white trespasser on their soil; who led by Tecumseh and Black Hawk gathered the clans of the forest and mountain for the last pitched battle of the races in the Mississippi valley. To them belonged the mild mannered Lenni Lenape, who little foreboded the hand of iron that grasped their own so softly under the elm tree of Shackamaxon, to them the restless Shawnee, the gypsy of the wilderness, the Chipeways of Lake Superior, and also to them the Indian girl Pocahontas, who in the legend averted from the head of the white man the blow which, rebounding, swept away her father and all his tribe. 27-1

Between their southernmost outposts and the Gulf of Mexico were a number of clans, mostly speaking the Muscogee tongue, Creeks, Choctaws, Chikasaws, and others, in later times summed up as Apalachian Indians, but by early writers sometimes referred to as "The Empire of the Natchez." For tradition says that long ago this small tribe, whose home was in the Big Black country, was at the head of a loose confederation embracing most of the nations from the Atlantic coast quite into Texas; and adds that the expedition of De Soto severed its lax bonds and shook it irremediably into fragments. Whether this is worth our credence or not, the comparative civilization of the Natchez, and the analogy their language bears to that of the Mayas of Yucatan, the builders of those ruined cities which Stephens and Catherwood have made so familiar to the world, attach to them a peculiar interest. 27-2

North of the Arkansas River on the right bank of the Mississippi, quite to its source, stretching over to Lake Michigan at Green Bay, and up the valley of the Missouri west to the mountains, resided the Dakotas, an erratic folk, averse to agriculture, but daring hunters and bold warriors, tall and strong of body. 28-1 Their religious notions have been carefully studied, and as they are remarkably primitive and transparent, they will often be referred to. The Sioux and the Winnebagoes are well-known branches of this family.

We have seen that Dr. Richardson assigned to a portion of the Athapascas the lowest place among North American tribes, but there are some in New Mexico who might contest the sad distinction, the Root Diggers, Comanches and others, members of the Snake or Shoshonee family, scattered extensively northwest of Mexico. It has been said of a part of these that they are "nearer the brutes than probably any other portion of the human race on the face of the globe." 28-2 Their habits in some respects are more brutish than those of any brute, for there is no limit to man's moral descent or ascent, and the observer might well be excused for doubting whether such a stock ever had a history in the past, or the possibility of one in the future. Yet these debased creatures speak a related dialect, and are beyond a doubt largely of the same blood as the famous Aztec race, who founded the empire of Anahuac, and raised architectural monuments rivalling the most famous structures of the ancient world. This great family, whose language has been traced from Nicaragua to Vancouver's Island, and whose bold intellects colored all the civilization of the northern continent, was composed in that division of it found in New Spain chiefly of two bands, the Toltecs, whose traditions point to the mountain ranges of Guatemala as their ancient seat, and the Nahuas, who claim to have come at a later period from the northwest coast, and together settled in and near the valley of Mexico. 29-1 Outlying colonies on the shore of Lake Nicaragua and in the mountains of Vera Paz rose to a civilization that rivalled that of the Montezumas, while others remained in utter barbarism in the far north.

The Aztecs not only conquered a Maya colony, and founded the empire of the Quiches in Central America, a complete body of whose mythology has been brought to light in late years, but seem to have made a marked imprint on the Mayas themselves. These possessed, as has already been said, the peninsula of Yucatan. There is some reason to suppose they came thither originally from the Greater Antilles, and none to doubt but that the

Huastecas who lived on the river Panuco and the Natchez of Louisiana were offshoots from them. Their language is radically distinct from that of the Aztecs, but their calendar and a portion of their mythology are common property. They seem an ancient race of mild manners and considerable polish. No American nation offers a more promising field for study. Their stone temples still bear testimony to their uncommon skill in the arts. A trustworthy tradition dates the close of the golden age of Yucatan a century anterior to its discovery by Europeans. Previously it had been one kingdom, under one ruler, and prolonged peace had fostered the growth of the fine arts; but when their capital Mayapan fell, internal dissensions ruined most of their cities.

No connection whatever has been shown between the civilization of North and South America. In the latter continent it was confined to two totally foreign tribes, the Muyscas, whose empire, called that of the Zacs, was in the neighborhood of Bogota, and the Peruvians, who in their two related divisions of Quichuas and Aymaras extended their language and race along the highlands of the Cordilleras from the equator to the thirtieth degree of south latitude. Lake Titicaca seems to have been the cradle of their civilization, offering another example how inland seas and well-watered plains favor the change from a hunting to an agricultural life. These four nations, the Aztecs, the Mayas, the Muyscas and the Peruvians, developed spontaneously and independently under the laws of human progress what civilization was found among the red race. They owed nothing to Asiatic or European teachers. The Incas it was long supposed spoke a language of their own, and this has been thought evidence of foreign extraction; but Wilhelm von Humboldt has shown conclusively that it was but a dialect of the common tongue of their country. 31-1

When Columbus first touched the island of Cuba, he was regaled with horrible stories of one-eyed monsters who dwelt on the other islands, but plundered indiscriminately on every hand. These turned out to be the notorious Caribs, whose other name, *Cannibals*, has descended as a common noun to our language, expressive of one of their inhuman practices. They had at that time seized many of the Antilles, and had gained a foothold on the coast of Honduras and Darien, but pointed for their home to the mainland of South America. This they possessed along the whole northern shore, inland at least as far as the south bank of the Amazon, and west nearly to the Cordilleras. It is still an open question whether the Tupis and Guaranis who inhabit the vast region between the Amazon and the Pampas of Buenos Ayres are affined to them. The traveller D'Orbigny zealously maintains the affirmative, and there is certainly some analogy of language, but withal an inexplicable contrast of character. The latter were, and are, in

the main, a peaceable, inoffensive, apathetic set, dull and unambitious, wh
the Caribs won a terrible renown as bold warriors, daring navigators, skil
in handicrafts; and their poisoned arrows, cruel and disgusting habits, a
enterprise, rendered them a terror and a by-word for generations. 32-1

Our information of the natives of the Pampas, Patagonia, and tl
Land of Fire, is too vague to permit their positive identification with tl
Araucanians of Chili; but there is much to render the view plausible. Certai
physical peculiarities, a common unconquerable love of freedom, and
delight in war, bring them together, and at the same time place them both ii
strong contrast to their northern neighbors. 33-1

There are many tribes whose affinities remain to be decided, especially
on the Pacific coast. The lack of inland water communication, the difficult
nature of the soil, and perhaps the greater antiquity of the population there,
seem to have isolated and split up beyond recognition the indigenous families
on that shore of the continent; while the great river systems and broad
plains of the Atlantic slope facilitated migration and intercommunication,
and thus preserved national distinctions over thousands of square leagues.

These natural features of the continent, compared with the actual
distribution of languages, offer our only guides in forming an opinion as to
the migrations of these various families in ancient times. Their traditions,
take even the most cultivated, are confused, contradictory, and in great
part manifestly fabulous. To construct from them by means of daring
combinations and forced interpretations a connected account of the race
during the centuries preceding Columbus were with the aid of a vivid fancy
an easy matter, but would be quite unworthy the name of history. The most
that can be said with certainty is that the general course of migrations in both
Americas was from the high latitudes toward the tropics, and from the great
western chain of mountains toward the east. No reasonable doubt exists
but that the Athapascas, Algonkins, Iroquois, Apalachians, and Aztecs all
migrated from the north and west to the regions they occupied. In South
America, curiously enough, the direction is reversed. If the Caribs belong
to the Tupi-Guaranay stem, and if the Quichuas belong to the Aymaras, as
there is strong likelihood, 34-1 then nine-tenths of the population of that
vast continent wandered forth from the steppes and valleys at the head
waters of the Rio de la Plata toward the Gulf of Mexico, where they came
in collision with that other wave of migration surging down from high
northern latitudes. For the banks of the river Paraguay and the steppes of
the Bolivian Cordilleras are unquestionably the earliest traditional homes of
both Tupis and Aymaras.

These movements took place not in large bodies under the stimulus of
a settled purpose, but step by step, family by family, as the older hunting

grounds became too thickly peopled. This fact hints unmistakably at the gray antiquity of the race. It were idle even to guess how great this must be, but it is possible to set limits to it in both directions. On the one hand, not a tittle of evidence is on record to carry the age of man in America beyond the present geological epoch. Dr. Lund examined in Brazil more than eight hundred caverns, out of which number only six contained human bones, and of these six only one had with the human bones those of animals now extinct. Even in that instance the original stratification had been disturbed, and probably the bones had been interred there. 35-1 This is strong negative evidence. So in every other example where an unbiased and competent geologist has made the examination, the alleged discoveries of human remains in the older strata have proved erroneous.

The cranial forms of the American aborigines have by some been supposed to present anomalies distinguishing their race from all others, and even its chief families from one another. This, too, falls to the ground before a rigid analysis. The last word of craniology, which at one time promised to revolutionize ethnology and even history, is that no one form of the skull is peculiar to the natives of the New World; that in the same linguistic family one glides into another by imperceptible degrees; and that there is as much diversity, and the same diversity among them in this respect as among the races of the Old Continent. 35-2 Peculiarities of structure, though they may pass as general truths, offer no firm foundation whereon to construct a scientific ethnology. Anatomy shows nothing unique in the Indian, nothing demanding for its development any special antiquity, still less an original diversity of type.

On the other hand, the remains of primeval art and the impress he made upon nature bespeak for man a residence in the New World coeval with the most distant events of history. By remains of art I do not so much refer to those desolate palaces which crumble forgotten in the gloom of tropical woods, nor even the enormous earthworks of the Mississippi valley covered with the mould of generations of forest trees, but rather to the humbler and less deceptive relics of his kitchens and his hunts. On the Atlantic coast one often sees the refuse of Indian villages, where generation after generation have passed their summers in fishing, and left the bones, shells, and charcoal as their only epitaph. How many such summers would it require for one or two hundred people to thus gradually accumulate a mound of offal eight or ten feet high and a hundred yards across, as is common enough? How many generations to heap up that at the mouth of the Altamaha River, examined and pronounced exclusively of this origin by Sir Charles Lyell, 36-1 which is about this height, and covers ten acres of ground? Those who, like myself, have tramped over many a ploughed field in search of arrow-heads must have sometimes been amazed at the numbers which are sown over the face of our country, betokening a most prolonged possession of the soil by their makers. For a hunting population is always sparse, and the collector finds only those arrow-heads which lie upon the surface.

Still more forcibly does nature herself bear witness to this antiquity of possession. Botanists declare that a very lengthy course of cultivation is required so to alter the form of a plant that it can no longer be identified with the wild species; and still more protracted must be the artificial propagation for it to lose its power of independent life, and to rely wholly on man to preserve it from extinction. Now this is precisely the condition of the maize, tobacco, cotton, quinoa, and mandioca plants, and of that species of palm called by botanists the *Gulielma speciosa*; all have been cultivated from immemorial time by the aborigines of America, and, except cotton, by no other race; all no longer are to be identified with any known wild species; several are sure to perish unless fostered by human care. 37-1 What numberless ages does this suggest? How many centuries elapsed ere man thought of cultivating Indian corn? How many more ere it had spread over nearly a hundred degrees of latitude, and lost all semblance to its original form? Who has the temerity to answer these questions? The judicious thinker will perceive in them satisfactory reasons for dropping once for all the vexed inquiry, "how America was peopled," and will smile at its imaginary solutions, whether they suggest Jews, Japanese, or, as the latest theory is, Egyptians.

While these and other considerations testify forcibly to that isolation I have already mentioned, they are almost equally positive for an extensive intercourse in very distant ages between the great families of the race, and for a prevalent unity of mental type, or perhaps they hint at a still visible oneness of descent. In their stage of culture, the maize, cotton, and tobacco could hardly have spread so widely by commerce alone. Then there are verbal similarities running through wide families of languages which, in the words of Professor Buschmann, are "calculated to fill us with bewildering amazement," 38-1 some of which will hereafter be pointed out; and lastly, passing to the psychological constitution of the race, we may quote the words of a sharp-sighted naturalist, whose monograph on one of its tribes is unsurpassed for profound reflections: "Not only do all the primitive inhabitants of America stand on one scale of related culture, but that mental condition of all in which humanity chiefly mirrors itself, to wit, their religious and moral consciousness, this source of all other inner and outer conditions, is one with all, however diverse the natural influences under which they live." 38-2

Penetrated with the truth of these views, all artificial divisions into tropical or temperate, civilized or barbarous, will in the present work, so far as possible, be avoided, and the race will be studied as a unit, its religion as the development of ideas common to all its members, and its myths as the garb thrown around these ideas by imaginations more or less fertile, but seeking everywhere to embody the same notions.

BIBLIOGRAPHICAL NOTE.

As the subject of American mythology is a new one to most readers, and as in its discussion everything depends on a careful selection of authorities, it is well at the outset to review very briefly what has already been written upon it, and to assign the relative amount of weight that in the following pages will be given to the works most frequently quoted. The conclusions I have arrived at are so different from those who have previously touched upon the topic that such a step seems doubly advisable.

The first who undertook a philosophical survey of American religions was Dr. Samuel Farmer Jarvis, in 1819 (A Discourse on the Religion of the Indian Tribes of North America, Collections of the New York Historical Society, vol. iii., New York, 1821). He confined himself to the tribes north of Mexico, a difficult portion of the field, and at that time not very well known. The notion of a state of primitive civilization prevented Dr. Jarvis from forming any correct estimate of the native religions, as it led him to look upon them as deteriorations from purer faiths instead of developments. Thus he speaks of them as having "departed less than among any other nation from the form of primeval truth," and also mentions their "wonderful uniformity" (pp. 219, 221).

The well-known American ethnologist, Mr. E. G. Squier, has also published a work on the subject, of wider scope than its title indicates (The Serpent Symbol in America, New York, 1851). Though written in a much more liberal spirit than the preceding, it is wholly in the interests of one school of mythology, and it the rather shallow physical one, so fashionable in Europe half a century ago. Thus, with a sweeping generalization, he says, "The religions or superstitions of the American nations, however different they may appear to the superficial glance, are rudimentally the same, and are only modifications of that primitive system which under its physical aspect has been denominated Sun or Fire worship" (p. 111). With this he combines the favorite and (may I add?) characteristic French doctrine, that the chief topic of mythology is the adoration of the generative power, and to rescue such views from their materializing tendencies, imagines to counterbalance them a clear, universal monotheism. "We claim to have shown," he says (p. 154), "that the grand conception of a Supreme Unity and the doctrine of the reciprocal principles existed in America in a well defined and clearly recognized form;" and elsewhere that "the monotheistic idea stands out clearly in *all* the religions of America" (p. 151).

If with a hope of other views we turn to our magnificent national work on the Indians (History, Conditions, and Prospects of the Indian Tribes of the United States: Washington, 1851-9), a great disappointment awaits us. That work was unfortunate in its editor. It is a monument of American extravagance and superficiality. Mr. Schoolcraft was a man of deficient education and narrow prejudices, pompous in style, and inaccurate in statements. The information from original observers it contains is often of real value, but the general views on aboriginal history and religion are shallow and untrustworthy in the extreme.

A German professor, Dr. J. G. Müller, has written quite a voluminous work on American Primitive Religions (*Geschichte der Amerikanischen Ur-religionen*, pp. 707: Basel, 1855). His theory is that "at the south a worship of nature with the adoration of the sun as its centre, at the north a fear of spirits combined with fetichism, made up the two fundamental divisions of the religion of the red race" (pp. 89, 90). This imaginary antithesis he traces out between the Algonkin and Apalachian tribes, and between the Toltecs of Guatemala and the Aztecs of Mexico. His quotations are nearly all at second hand, and so little does he criticize his facts as to confuse the Vaudoux worship of the Haitian negroes with that of Votan in Chiapa. His work can in no sense be considered an authority.

Very much better is the Anthropology of the late Dr. Theodore Waitz (*Anthropologie der Naturvœlker*: Leipzig, 1862-66). No more comprehensive, sound, and critical work on the indigenes of America has ever been written. But on their religions the author is unfortunately defective, being led astray by the hasty and groundless generalizations of others. His great anxiety, moreover, to subject all moral sciences to a realistic philosophy, was peculiarly fatal to any correct appreciation of religious growth, and his views are neither new nor tenable.

For a different reason I must condemn in the most unqualified manner the attempt recently made by the enthusiastic and meritorious antiquary, the Abbé E. Charles Brasseur (de Bourbourg), to explain American mythology after the example of Euhemerus, of Thessaly, as the apotheosis of history. This theory, which has been repeatedly applied to other mythologies with invariable failure, is now disowned by every distinguished student of European and Oriental antiquity; and to seek to introduce it into American religions is simply to render them still more obscure and unattractive, and to deprive them of the only general interest they now have, that of illustrating the gradual development of the religious ideas of humanity.

But while thus regretting the use he has made of them, all interested in American antiquity cannot too much thank this indefatigable explorer for the priceless materials he has unearthed in the neglected libraries of Spain and Central America, and laid before the public. For the present purpose the most significant of these is the Sacred National Book of the Quiches, a tribe of Guatemala. This contains their legends, written in the original tongue, and transcribed by Father Francisco Ximenes about 1725. The manuscripts of this missionary were used early in the present century, by Don Felix Cabrera, but were supposed to be entirely lost even by the Abbé Brasseur himself in 1850 (*Lettre à M. le Duc de Valmy*, Mexique, Oct. 15, 1850). Made aware of their importance by the expressions of regret used in the Abbé's letters, Dr. C. Sherzer, in 1854, was fortunate enough to discover them in the library of the University of San Carlos in the city of Guatemala. The legends were in Quiche with a Spanish translation and scholia. The Spanish was copied by Dr. Scherzer and published in Vienna, in 1856, under the title *Las Historias del Origen de los Indios de Guatemala, por el R. P. F. Francisco Ximenes*. In 1855 the Abbé Brasseur took a copy of the original which he brought out at Paris in 1861, with a translation of his own, under the title *Vuh Popol: Le Livre Sacré des Quichés et les Mythes de l'Antiquité Américaine*. Internal evidence proves that these legends were written down by a converted native some time in the seventeenth century. They carry the national history back about two centuries, beyond which all is professedly mythical. Although both translations are colored by the peculiar views of their makers, this is incomparably the most complete and valuable work on American mythology extant.

Another authority of inestimable value has been placed within the reach of scholars during the last few years. This is the *Relations de la Nouvelle France*, containing the annual reports of the Jesuit missionaries among the Iroquois and Algonkins from and after 1611. My references to this are always to the reprint at Quebec, 1858. Of not less excellence for another tribe, the Creeks, is the brief "Sketch of the Creek Country," by Col. Benjamin Hawkins, written about 1800, and first published in full by the Georgia Historical Society in 1848. Most of the other works to which I have referred are too well known to need any special examination here, or will be more particularly mentioned in the foot-notes when quoted.

FOOTNOTES:

2-1 Waitz, *Anthropologie der Naturvoelker*, i. p. 256.

2-2 Carriere, *Die Kunst im Zusammenhang der Culturentwickelung*, i. p. 66.

6-1 It is said indeed that the Yebus, a people on the west coast of Africa, speak a polysynthetic language, and *per contra*, that the Otomis of Mexico have a monosyllabic one like the Chinese. Max Mueller goes further, and asserts that what is called the process of agglutination in the Turanian languages is the same as what has been named polysynthesis in America. This is not to be conceded. In the former the root is unchangeable, the formative elements follow it, and prefixes are not used; in the latter prefixes are common, and the formative elements are blended with the root, both undergoing changes of structure. Very important differences.

9-1 Grimm, *Geschichte der Deutschen Sprache*, p. 571.

11-1 Peter Martyr, *De Insulis nuper Repertis*, p. 354: Colon. 1574.

12-1 They may be found in Waitz, *Anthrop. der Naturvoelker*, iv. p. 173.

13-1 The only authority is Diego de Landa, *Relacion de las Cosas de Yucatan*, ed. Brasseur, Paris, 1864, p. 318. The explanation is extremely obscure in the original. I have given it in the only sense in which the author's words seem to have any meaning.

14-1 Humboldt, *Vues des Cordillères*, p. 72.

14-2 Desjardins, *Le Pérou avant la Conquête Espagnole*, p. 122: Paris, 1858.

16-1 An instance is given by Ximenes, *Origen de los Indios de Guatemala*, p. 186: Vienna, 1856.

17-1 George Copway, *Traditional History of the Ojibway Nation*, p. 130: London, 1850.

18-1 Morse, *Report on the Indian Tribes*, App. p. 352.

21-1 Gomara states that De Ayllon found tribes on the Atlantic shore not far from Cape Hatteras keeping flocks of deer (*ciervos*) and from their milk making cheese (*Hist. de las Indias*, cap. 43). I attach no importance to this statement, and only mention it to connect it with some other curious notices of the tribe now extinct who occupied that locality. Both De Ayllon and Lawson mention their very light complexions, and the latter saw many with blonde hair, blue eyes, and a fair skin; they cultivated when first visited the potato (or the groundnut), tobacco, and cotton (Humboldt); they reckoned time by disks of wood divided into sixty segments (Lederer); and just in this latitude the most careful determination fixes the mysterious White-man's-land, or Great Ireland of the Icelandic Sagas (see the *American Hist. Mag.*, ix. p. 364), where the Scandinavian sea rovers in the eleventh century found men of their own color, clothed in long woven garments, and not less civilized than themselves.

23-1 The name Eskimo is from the Algonkin word *Eskimantick*, eaters of raw flesh. There is reason to believe that at one time they possessed the Atlantic coast considerably to the south. The Northmen, in the year 1000, found the natives of Vinland, probably near Rhode Island, of the same race as they were familiar with in Labrador. They call them *Skralingar*, chips, and describe them as numerous and short of stature (Eric Rothens Saga, in Mueller, *Sagænbibliothek*, p. 214). It is curious that the traditions of the Tuscaroras, who placed their arrival on the Virginian coast about 1300, spoke of the race they found there as eaters of raw flesh and ignorant of maize (Lederer, *Account of North America*, in Harris, Voyages).

25-1 Richardson, *Arctic Expedition*, p. 374.

25-2 The late Professor W. W. Turner of Washington, and Professor Buschmann of Berlin, are the two scholars who have traced the boundaries of this widely dispersed family. The name is drawn from Lake Athapasca in British America.

25-3 The Cherokee tongue has a limited number of words in common with the Iroquois, and its structural similarity is close. The name is of unknown origin. It should doubtless be spelled *Tsalakie*, a plural form, almost the same as that of the river Tellico, properly Tsaliko (Ramsey, *Annals of Tennessee*, p. 87), on the banks of which their principal towns were situated. Adair's derivation from *cheera*, fire, is worthless, as no such word exists in their language.

27-1 The term Algonkin may be a corruption of *agomeegwin*, people of the other shore. Algic, often used synonymously, is an adjective manufactured by Mr. Schoolcraft "from the words Alleghany and Atlantic" (Algic Researches, ii. p. 12). There is no occasion to accept it, as there is no objection to employing Algonkin both as substantive and adjective. Iroquois is a French compound of the native words *hiro*, I have said, and *kouè*, an interjection of assent or applause, terms constantly heard in their councils.

27-2 Apalachian, which should be spelt with one p, is formed of two Creek words, *apala*, the great sea, the ocean, and the suffix *chi*, people, and means those dwelling by the ocean. That the Natchez were offshoots of the Mayas I was the first to surmise and to prove by a careful comparison of one hundred Natchez words with their equivalents in the Maya dialects. Of these, *five* have affinities more or less marked to words peculiar to the Huastecas of the river Panuco (a Maya colony), *thirteen* to words common to Huasteca and Maya, and *thirty-nine* to words of similar meaning in the latter language. This resemblance may be exemplified by the numerals, one, two, four, seven, eight, twenty. In Natchez they are *hu, ah, gan, uk-woh, upku-tepish, oka-poo*: in Maya, *hu, ca, can, uk, uapxæ, hunkal*. (See the Am. Hist. Mag., New Series, vol. i. p. 16, Jan. 1867.)

28-1 Dakota, a native word, means friends or allies.

28-2 Rep. of the Commissioner of Indian Affairs, 1854, p. 209.

29-1 According to Professor Buschmann Aztec is probably from *iztac*, white, and Nahuatlacatl signifies those who speak the language *Nahuatl*, clear sounding, sonorous. The Abbé Brasseur (de Bourbourg), on the other hand, derives the latter from the Quiche *nawal*, intelligent, and adds the amazing information that this is identical with the English *know all*!! (*Hist. du Mexique*, etc., i. p. 102). For in his theory several languages of Central America are derived from the same old Indo-Germanic stock as the English, German, and cognate tongues. Toltec, from *Toltecatl*, means inhabitant of Tollan, which latter may be from *tolin*, rush, and signify the place of rushes. The signification *artificer*, often assigned to Toltecatl, is of later date, and was derived from the famed artistic skill of this early folk (Buschmann, *Aztek. Ortsnamen*, p. 682: Berlin, 1852). The Toltecs are usually spoken of as anterior to the Nahuas, but the Tlascaltecs and natives of Chololian or Cholula were in fact Toltecs, unless we assign to this latter name a merely mythical signification. The early migrations of the two Aztec bands and their relationship, it may be said in passing, are as yet extremely obscure. The Shoshonees when first known dwelt as far north as the head waters of the Missouri, and in the country now occupied by the Black Feet. Their language, which includes that of the Comanche, Wihinasht, Utah, and kindred bands, was first shown to have many and marked affinities with that of the Aztecs by Professor Buschmann in his great work, *Ueber die Spuren der Aztekischen Sprache im nördlichen Mexico und höheren Amerikanischen Norden*, p. 648: Berlin, 1854.

31-1 His opinion was founded on an analysis of fifteen words of the secret language of the Incas preserved in the Royal Commentaries of Garcilasso de la Vega. On examination, they all proved to be modified forms from the *lengua general* (Meyen, *Ueber die Ureinwohner von Peru*, p. 6). The Quichuas of Peru must not be confounded with the Quiches of Guatemala. Quiche is the name of a place, and means "many trees;" the derivation of Quichua is unknown. Muyscas means "men." This nation also called themselves Chibchas.

32-1   The significance of Carib is probably warrior. It may be the same word as Guarani, which also has this meaning. Tupi or Tupa is the name given the thunder, and can only be understood mythically.

33-1   The Araucanians probably obtained their name from two Quichua words, *ari auccan*, yes! they fight; an idiom very expressive of their warlike character. They had had long and terrible wars with the Incas before the arrival of Pizarro.

34-1 Since writing the text I have received the admirable work of Dr. von Martius, *Beiträge zur Ethnographie und Sprachenkunde Amerika's zumal Brasilians*, Leipzig, 1867, in which I observe that that profound student considers that there is no doubt but that the Island Caribs, and the Galibis of the main land are descendants from the same stock as the Tupis and Guaranis.

35-1 *Comptes Rendus*, vol. xxi. p. 1368 sqq.

35-2 The two best authorities are Daniel Wilson, *The American Cranial Type*, in *Ann. Rep. of the Smithson. Inst.*, 1862, p. 240, and J. A. Meigs, *Cranial Forms of the Amer. Aborigs.*: Phila. 1866. They accord in the views expressed in the text and in the rejection of those advocated by Dr. S. G. Morton in the Crania Americana.

36-1 *Second Visit to the United States*, i. p. 252.

37-1 Martius, *Von dem Rechtzustande unter den Ureinwohnern Brasiliens*, p. 80: Muenchen, 1832; recently republished in his *Beiträge zur Ethnographie und Sprachenkunde Amerika's*: Leipzig, 1867.

38-1 *Athapaskische Sprachstamm*, p. 164: Berlin, 1856.

38-2 Martius, *Von dem Rechtzustande unter den Ureinwohnern Brasiliens*, p. 77.

CHAPTER II
THE IDEA OF GOD

An intuition common to the species. — Words expressing it in American languages derived either from ideas of above in space, or of life manifested by breath. — Examples. — No conscious monotheism, and but little idea of immateriality discoverable. — Still less any moral dualism of deities, the Great Good Spirit and the Great Bad Spirit being alike terms and notions of foreign importation.

IF we accept the definition that mythology is the idea of God expressed in symbol, figure, and narrative, and always struggling toward a clearer utterance, it is well not only to trace this idea in its very earliest embodiment in language, but also, for the sake of comparison, to ask what is its latest and most approved expression. The reply to this is given us by Immanuel Kant. He has shown that our reason, dwelling on the facts of experience, constantly seeks the principles which connect them together, and only rests satisfied in the conviction that there is a highest and first principle which reconciles all their discrepancies and binds them into one. This he calls the Ideal of Reason. It must be true, for it is evolved from the laws of reason, our only test of truth. Furthermore, the sense of personality and the voice of conscience, analyzed to their sources, can only be explained by the assumption of an infinite personality and an absolute standard of right. Or, if to some all this appears but wire-drawn metaphysical subtlety, they are welcome to the definition of the realist, that the idea of God is the sum of those intelligent activities which the individual, reasoning from the analogy of his own actions, imagines to be behind and to bring about natural phenomena. 44-1 If either of these be correct, it were hard to conceive how any tribe or even any sane man could be without some notion of divinity.

Certainly in America no instance of its absence has been discovered. Obscure, grotesque, unworthy it often was, but everywhere man was oppressed with a *sensus numinis*, a feeling that invisible, powerful agencies were at work around him, who, as they willed, could help or hurt him. In every heart was an altar to the Unknown God. Not that it was customary to attach any idea of unity to these unseen powers. The supposition that in ancient times and in very unenlightened conditions, before mythology had grown, a monotheism prevailed, which afterwards at various times was revived by reformers, is a belief that should have passed away when the delights of savage life and the praises of a state of nature ceased to be the themes of philosophers. We are speaking of a people little capable of abstraction. The exhibitions of force in nature seemed to them the manifestations of that mysterious power felt by their self-consciousness; to combine these various manifestations and recognize them as the operations of one personality, was a step not easily taken. Yet He is not far from every one of us. "Whenever man thinks clearly, or feels deeply, he conceives God as self-conscious unity," says Carriere, with admirable insight; and elsewhere, "we have monotheism, not in contrast to polytheism, not clear to the thought, but in living intuition in the religious sentiments." 45-1

Thus it was among the Indians. Therefore a word is usually found in their languages analogous to none in any European tongue, a word comprehending all manifestations of the unseen world, yet conveying no sense of personal unity. It has been rendered spirit, demon, God, devil, mystery, magic, but commonly and rather absurdly by the English and French, "medicine." In the Algonkin dialects this word is *manito* and *oki*, in Iroquois *oki* and *otkon*, the Dakota has *wakan*, the Aztec *teotl*, the Quichua *huaca*, and the Maya *ku*. They all express in its most general form the idea of the supernatural. And as in this word, supernatural, we see a transfer of a conception of place, and that it literally means that which is *above* the natural world, so in such as we can analyze of these vague and primitive terms the same trope appears discoverable. *Wakan* as an adverb means *above*, *oki* is but another orthography for *oghee*, and *otkon* seems allied to *hetken*, both of which have the same signification. 46-1

The transfer is no mere figure of speech, but has its origin in the very texture of the human mind. The heavens, the upper regions, are in every religion the supposed abode of the divine. What is higher is always the stronger and the nobler; a *superior* is one who is better than we are, and therefore a chieftain in Algonkin is called *oghee-ma*, the higher one. There is, moreover, a naif and spontaneous instinct which leads man in his ecstasies of joy, and in his paroxysms of fear or pain, to lift his hands and eyes to the overhanging firmament. There the sun and bright stars sojourn, emblems of glory and stability. Its azure vault has a mysterious attraction which invites the eye to gaze longer and longer into its infinite depths. 46-2 Its color brings thoughts of serenity, peace, sunshine, and warmth. Even the rudest hunting tribes felt these sentiments, and as a metaphor in their speeches, and as a paint expressive of friendly design, blue was in wide use among them. 47-1

So it came to pass that the idea of God was linked to the heavens long ere man asked himself, are the heavens material and God spiritual, is He one, or is He many? Numerous languages bear trace of this. The Latin Deus, the Greek Zeus, the Sanscrit Dyaus, the Chinese Tien, all originally meant the sky above, and our own word heaven is often employed synonymously with God. There is at first no personification in these expressions. They embrace all unseen agencies, they are void of personality, and yet to the illogical primitive man there is nothing contradictory in making them the object of his prayers. The Mayas had legions of gods; "*ku*," says their historian, 47-2 "does not signify any particular god; yet their prayers are sometimes addressed to *kue*," which is the same word in the vocative case.

As the Latins called their united divinities *Superi*, those above, so Captain John Smith found that the Powhatans of Virginia employed the word *oki*, above, in the same sense, and it even had passed into a definite personification among them in the shape of an "idol of wood evil-favoredly carved." In purer dialects of the Algonkin it is always indefinite, as in the terms *nipoon oki*, spirit of summer, *pipoon oki*, spirit of winter. Perhaps the word was introduced into Iroquois by the Hurons, neighbors and associates of the Algonkins. The Hurons applied it to that demoniac power "who rules the seasons of the year, who holds the winds and the waves in leash, who can give fortune to their undertakings, and relieve all their wants." 48-1 In another and far distant branch of the Iroquois, the Nottoways of southern Virginia, it reappears under, the curious form *quaker*, doubtless a corruption of the Powhatan *qui-oki*, lesser gods. 48-2 The proper Iroquois name of him to whom they prayed was *garonhia*, which again turns out on examination to be their common word for *sky*, and again in all probability from the verbal root *gar*, to be above. 48-3 In the legends of the Aztecs and Quiches such phrases as "Heart of the Sky," "Lord of the Sky," "Prince of the Azure Planisphere," "He above all," are of frequent occurrence, and by a still bolder metaphor, the Araucanians, according to Molina, entitled their greatest god "The Soul of the Sky."

This last expression leads to another train of thought. As the philosopher, pondering on the workings of self-consciousness, recognizes that various pathways lead up to God, so the primitive man, in forming his language, sometimes trod one, sometimes another. Whatever else sceptics have questioned, no one has yet presumed to doubt that if a God and a soul exist at all, they are of like essence. This firm belief has left its impress on language in the names devised to express the supernal, the spiritual world. If we seek hints from languages more familiar to us than the tongues of the Indians, and take for example this word *spiritual*; we find it is from the Latin *spirare*, to blow, to breathe. If in Latin again we look for the derivation of *animus,* the mind, *anima,* the soul, they point to the Greek *anemos,* wind, and *aémi,* to blow. In Greek the words for soul or spirit, *psuche, pneuma, thumos,* all are directly from verbal roots expressing the motion of the wind or the breath. The Hebrew word *ruah* is translated in the Old Testament sometimes by wind, sometimes by spirit, sometimes by breath. Etymologically, in fact, ghosts and gusts, breaths and breezes, the Great Spirit and the Great Wind, are one and the same. It is easy to guess the reason of this. The soul is the life, the life is the breath. Invisible, imponderable, quickening with vigorous motion, slackening in rest and sleep, passing quite away in death, it is the most obvious sign of life. All nations grasped the analogy and identified the one with the other. But the breath is nothing but wind. How easy, therefore, to look upon the wind that moves up and down and to and fro upon the earth, that carries the clouds, itself unseen, that calls forth the terrible tempests and the various seasons, as the breath, the spirit of God, as God himself? So in the Mosaic record of creation, it is said "a mighty wind" passed over the formless sea and brought forth the world, and when the Almighty gave to the clay a living soul, he is said to have breathed into it "the wind of lives."

Armed with these analogies, we turn to the primitive tongues of America, and find them there as distinct as in the Old World. In Dakota *niya* is literally breath, figuratively life; in Netela *piuts* is life, breath, and soul; *silla,* in Eskimo, means air, it means wind, but it is also the word that conveys the highest idea of the world as a whole, and the reasoning faculty. The supreme existence they call *Sillam Innua,* Owner of the Air, or of the All; or *Sillam Nelega,* Lord of the Air or Wind. In the Yakama tongue of Oregon *wkrisha* signifies there is wind, *wkrishwit,* life; with the Aztecs, *ehecatl* expressed both air, life, and the soul, and personified in their myths it was said to have been born of the breath of Tezcatlipoca, their highest divinity, who himself is often called Yoalliehecatl, the Wind of Night. 50-1

The descent is, indeed, almost imperceptible which leads to the personification of the wind as God, which merges this manifestation of life and power in one with its unseen, unknown cause. Thus it was a worthy epithet which the Creeks applied to their supreme invisible ruler, when they addressed him as Esaugetuh Emissee, Master of Breath, and doubtless it was at first but a title of equivalent purport which the Cherokees, their neighbors, were wont to employ, Oonawleh unggi, Eldest of Winds, but rapidly leading to a complete identification of the divine with the natural phenomena of meteorology. This seems to have taken place in the same group of nations, for the original Choctaw word for Deity was Hushtoli, the Storm Wind. 51-1 The idea, indeed, was constantly being lost in the symbol. In the legends of the Quiches, the mysterious creative power is Hurakan, a name of no signification in their language, one which their remote ancestors brought with them from the Antilles, which finds its meaning in the ancient tongue of Haiti, and which, under the forms of *hurricane, ouragan, orkan,* was adopted into European marine languages as the native name of the terrible tornado of the Caribbean Sea. 51-2 Mixcohuatl, the Cloud Serpent, chief divinity of several tribes in ancient Mexico, is to this day the correct term in their language for the tropical whirlwind, and the natives of Panama worshipped the same phenomenon under the name Tuyra. 52-1 To kiss the air was in Peru the commonest and simplest sign of adoration to the collective divinities. 52-2

Many writers on mythology have commented on the prominence so frequently given to the winds. None have traced it to its true source. The facts of meteorology have been thought all sufficient for a solution. As if man ever did or ever could draw the idea of God from nature! In the identity of wind with breath, of breath with life, of life with soul, of soul with God, lies the far deeper and far truer reason, whose insensible development I have here traced, in outline indeed, but confirmed by the evidence of language itself.

Let none of these expressions, however, be construed to prove the distinct recognition of One Supreme Being. Of monotheism either as displayed in the one personal definite God of the Semitic races, or in the dim pantheistic sense of the Brahmins, there was not a single instance on the American continent. The missionaries found no word in any of their languages fit to interpret *Deus,* God. How could they expect it? The associations we attach to that name are the accumulated fruits of nigh two thousand years of Christianity. The phrases Good Spirit, Great Spirit, and similar ones, have occasioned endless discrepancies in the minds of travellers. In most instances they are entirely of modern origin, coined at the suggestion of missionaries, applied to the white man's God. Very rarely do they bring any conception of personality to the native mind, very rarely do they signify any object of worship, perhaps never did in the olden times. The Jesuit Relations state positively that there was no one immaterial god recognized by the Algonkin tribes, and that the title, the Great Manito, was introduced first by themselves in its personal sense. 53-1 The supreme Iroquois Deity Neo or Hawaneu, triumphantly adduced by many writers to show the monotheism underlying the native creeds, and upon whose name Mr. Schoolcraft has built some philological reveries, turns out on closer scrutiny to be the result of Christian instruction, and the words themselves to be but corruptions of the French *Dieu* and *le bon Dieu*! 53-2

Innumerable mysterious forces are in activity around the child of nature; he feels within him something that tells him they are not of his kind, and yet not altogether different from him; he sums them up in one word drawn from sensuous experience. Does he wish to express still more forcibly this sentiment, he doubles the word, or prefixes an adjective, or adds an affix, as the genius of his language may dictate. But it still remains to him but an unapplied abstraction, a mere category of thought, a frame for the All. It is never the object of veneration or sacrifice, no myth brings it down to his comprehension, it is not installed in his temples. Man cannot escape the belief that behind all form is one essence; but the moment he would seize and define it, it eludes his grasp, and by a sorcery more sadly ludicrous than that which blinded Titania, he worships not the Infinite he thinks but a base idol of his own making. As in the Zend Avesta behind the eternal struggle of Ormuzd and Ahriman looms up the undisturbed and infinite Zeruana Akerana, as in the pages of the Greek poets we here and there catch glimpses of a Zeus who is not he throned on Olympus, nor he who takes part in the wrangles of the gods, but stands far off and alone, one yet all, "who was, who is, who will be," so the belief in an Unseen Spirit, who asks neither supplication nor sacrifice, who, as the natives of Texas told Joutel in 1684, "does not concern himself about things here below," 54-1 who has no name to call him by, and is never a figure in mythology, was doubtless occasionally present to their minds. It was present not more but far less distinctly and often not at all in the more savage tribes, and no assertion can be more contrary to the laws of religious progress than that which pretends that a purer and more monotheistic religion exists among nations devoid of mythology. There are only two instances on the American continent where the worship of an immaterial God was definitely instituted, and these as the highest conquests of American natural religions deserve especial mention.

They occurred, as we might expect, in the two most civilized nations, the Quichuas of Peru, and the Nahuas of Tezcuco. It is related that about the year 1440, at a grand religious council held at the consecration of the newly-built temple of the Sun at Cuzco, the Inca Yupanqui rose before the assembled multitude and spoke somewhat as follows: —

"Many say that the Sun is the Maker of all things. But he who makes should abide by what he has made. Now many things happen when the Sun is absent; therefore he cannot be the universal creator. And that he is alive at all is doubtful, for his trips do not tire him. Were he a living thing, he would grow weary like ourselves; were he free, he would visit other parts of the heavens. He is like a tethered beast who makes a daily round under the eye of a master; he is like an arrow, which must go whither it is sent, not whither it wishes. I tell you that he, our Father and Master the Sun, must have a lord and master more powerful than himself, who constrains him to his daily circuit without pause or rest." 55-1

To express this greatest of all existences, a name was proclaimed, based upon that of the highest divinities known to the ancient Aymara race, Illatici Viracocha Pachacamac, literally, the thunder vase, the foam of the sea, animating the world, mysterious and symbolic names drawn from the deepest religious instincts of the soul, whose hidden meanings will be unravelled hereafter. A temple was constructed in a vale by the sea near Callao, wherein his worship was to be conducted without images or human sacrifices. The Inca was ahead of his age, however, and when the Spaniards visited the temple of Pachacamac in 1525, they found not only the walls adorned with hideous paintings, but an ugly idol of wood representing a man of colossal proportions set up therein, and receiving the prayers of the votaries. 56-1

No better success attended the attempt of Nezahuatl, lord of Tezcuco, which took place about the same time. He had long prayed to the gods of his forefathers for a son to inherit his kingdom, and the altars had smoked vainly with the blood of slaughtered victims. At length, in indignation and despair, the prince exclaimed, "Verily, these gods that I am adoring, what are they but idols of stone without speech or feeling? They could not have made the beauty of the heaven, the sun, the moon, and the stars which adorn it, and which light the earth, with its countless streams, its fountains and waters, its trees and plants, and its various inhabitants. There must be some god, invisible and unknown, who is the universal creator. He alone can console me in my affliction and take away my sorrow." Strengthened in this conviction by a timely fulfilment of his heart's desire, he erected a temple nine stories high to represent the nine heavens, which he dedicated "to the Unknown God, the Cause of Causes." This temple, he ordained, should never be polluted by blood, nor should any graven image ever be set up within its precincts. 57-1

In neither case, be it observed, was any attempt made to substitute another and purer religion for the popular one. The Inca continued to receive the homage of his subjects as a brother of the sun, and the regular services to that luminary were never interrupted. Nor did the prince of Tezcuco afterwards neglect the honors due his national gods, nor even refrain himself from plunging the knife into the breasts of captives on the altar of the god of war. 57-2 They were but expressions of that monotheism which is ever present, "not in contrast to polytheism, but in living intuition in the religious sentiments." If this subtle but true distinction be rightly understood, it will excite no surprise to find such epithets as "endless," "omnipotent," "invisible," "adorable," such appellations as "the Maker and Moulder of All," "the Mother and Father of Life," "the One God complete in perfection and unity," "the Creator of all that is," "the Soul of the World," in use and of undoubted indigenous origin not only among the civilized Aztecs, but even among the Haitians, the Araucanians, the Lenni Lenape, and others. 57-3 It will not seem contradictory to hear of them in a purely polytheistic worship; we shall be far from regarding them as familiar to the popular mind, and we shall never be led so far astray as to adduce them in evidence of a monotheism in either technical sense of that word. In point of fact they were not applied to any particular god even in the most enlightened nations, but were terms of laudation and magniloquence used by the priests and devotees of every several god to do him honor. They prove something in regard to a consciousness of divinity hedging us about, but nothing at all in favor of a recognition of one God; they exemplify how profound is the conviction of a highest and first principle, but they do not offer the least reason to surmise that this was a living reality in doctrine or practice.

The confusion of these distinct ideas has led to much misconception of the native creeds. But another and more fatal error was that which distorted them into a dualistic form, ranging on one hand the good spirit with his legions of angels, on the other the evil one with his swarms of fiends, representing the world as the scene of their unending conflict, man as the unlucky football who gets all the blows. This notion, which has its historical origin among the Parsees of ancient Iran, is unknown to savage nations. "The idea of the Devil," justly observes Jacob Grimm, "is foreign to all primitive religions." Yet Professor Mueller, in his voluminous work on those of America, after approvingly quoting this saying, complacently proceeds to classify the deities as good or bad spirits! 59-1

This view, which has obtained without question in every work on the native religions of America, has arisen partly from habits of thought difficult to break, partly from mistranslations of native words, partly from the foolish axiom of the early missionaries, "The gods of the gentiles are devils." Yet their own writings furnish conclusive proof that no such distinction existed out of their own fancies. The same word (*otkon*) which Father Bruyas employs to translate into Iroquois the term "devil," in the passage "the Devil took upon himself the figure of a serpent," he is obliged to use for "spirit" in the phrase, "at the resurrection we shall be spirits," 59-2 which is a rather amusing illustration how impossible it was by any native word to convey the idea of the spirit of evil. When, in 1570, Father Rogel commenced his labors among the tribes near the Savannah River, he told them that the deity they adored was a demon who loved all evil things, and they must hate him; whereupon his auditors replied, that so far from this being the case, whom he called a wicked being was the power that sent them all good things, and indignantly left the missionary to preach to the winds. 60-1

A passage often quoted in support of this mistaken view is one in Winslow's "Good News from New England," written in 1622. The author says that the Indians worship a good power called Kiehtan, and another "who, as farre as wee can conceive, is the Devill," named Hobbamock, or Hobbamoqui. The former of these names is merely the word "great," in their dialect of Algonkin, with a final *n*, and is probably an abbreviation of Kittanitowit, the great manito, a vague term mentioned by Roger Williams and other early writers, not the appellation of any personified deity. 60-2 The latter, so far from corresponding to the power of evil, was, according to Winslow's own statement, the kindly god who cured diseases, aided them in the chase, and appeared to them in dreams as their protector. Therefore, with great justice, Dr. Jarvis has explained it to mean "the *oke* or tutelary deity which each Indian worships," as the word itself signifies. 61-1

So in many instances it turns out that what has been reported to be the evil divinity of a nation, to whom they pray to the neglect of a better one, is in reality the highest power they recognize. Thus Juripari, worshipped by certain tribes of the Pampas of Buenos Ayres, and said to be their wicked spirit, is in fact the only name in their language for spiritual existence in general; and Aka-kanet, sometimes mentioned as the father of evil in the mythology of the Araucanians, is the benign power appealed to by their priests, who is throned in the Pleiades, who sends fruits and flowers to the earth, and is addressed as "grandfather." 61-2 The Çupay of the Peruvians never was, as Prescott would have us believe, "the shadowy embodiment of evil," but simply and solely their god of the dead, the Pluto of their pantheon, corresponding to the Mictla of the Mexicans.

The evidence on the point is indeed conclusive. The Jesuit missionaries very rarely distinguish between good and evil deities when speaking of the religion of the northern tribes; and the Moravian Brethren among the Algonkins and Iroquois place on record their unanimous testimony that "the idea of a devil, a prince of darkness, they first received in later times through the Europeans." 62-1 So the Cherokees, remarks an intelligent observer, "know nothing of the Evil One and his domains, except what they have learned from white men." 62-2 The term Great Spirit conveys, for instance, to the Chipeway just as much the idea of a bad as of a good spirit; he is unaware of any distinction until it is explained to him. 62-3 "I have never been able to discover from the Dakotas themselves," remarks the Rev. G. H. Pond, who had lived among them as a missionary for eighteen years, 62-4 "the least degree of evidence that they divide the gods into classes of good and evil, and am persuaded that those persons who represent them as doing so, do it inconsiderately, and because it is so natural to subscribe to a long cherished popular opinion."

Very soon after coming in contact with the whites, the Indians caught the notion of a bad and good spirit, pitted one against the other in eternal warfare, and engrafted it on their ancient traditions. Writers anxious to discover Jewish or Christian analogies, forcibly construed myths to suit their pet theories, and for indolent observers it was convenient to catalogue their gods in antithetical classes. In Mexican and Peruvian mythology this is so plainly false that historians no longer insist upon it, but as a popular error it still holds its ground with reference to the more barbarous and less known tribes.

Perhaps no myth has been so often quoted in its confirmation as that of the ancient Iroquois, which narrates the conflict between the first two brothers of our race. It is of undoubted native origin and venerable antiquity. The version given by the Tuscarora chief Cusic in 1825, relates that in the beginning of things there were two brothers, Enigorio and Enigohahetgea, names literally meaning the Good Mind and the Bad Mind. 63-1 The former went about the world furnishing it with gentle streams, fertile plains, and plenteous fruits, while the latter maliciously followed him creating rapids, thorns, and deserts. At length the Good Mind turned upon his brother in anger, and crushed him into the earth. He sank out of sight in its depths, but not to perish, for in the dark realms of the underworld he still lives, receiving the souls of the dead and being the author of all evil. Now when we compare this with the version of the same legend given by Father Brebeuf, missionary to the Hurons in 1636, we find its whole complexion altered; the moral dualism vanishes; the names Good Mind and Bad Mind do not appear; it is the struggle of Ioskeha, the White one, with his brother Tawiscara, the Dark one, and we at once perceive that Christian influence in the course of two centuries had given the tale a meaning foreign to its original intent.

So it is with the story the Algonkins tell of their hero Manibozho, who, in the opinion of a well-known writer, "is always placed in antagonism to a great serpent, a spirit of evil." 64-1 It is to the effect that after conquering many animals, this famous magician tried his arts on the prince of serpents. After a prolonged struggle, which brought on the general deluge and the destruction of the world, he won the victory. The first authority we have for this narrative is even later than Cusic; it is Mr. Schoolcraft in our own day; the legendary cause of the deluge as related by Father Le Jeune, in 1634, is quite dissimilar, and makes no mention of a serpent; and as we shall hereafter see, neither among the Algonkins nor any other Indians, was the serpent usually a type of evil, but quite the reverse. 64-2

The comparatively late introduction of such views into the native legends finds a remarkable proof in the myths of the Quiches, which were committed to writing in the seventeenth century. They narrate the struggles between the rulers of the upper and the nether world, the descent of the former into Xibalba, the Realm of Phantoms, and their victory over its lords, One Death and Seven Deaths. The writer adds of the latter, who clearly represent to his mind the Evil One and his adjutants, "in the old times they did not have much power; they were but annoyers and opposers of men, and in truth they were not regarded as gods. But when they appeared it was terrible. They were of evil, they were owls, fomenting trouble and discord." In this passage, which, be it said, seems to have impressed the translators very differently, the writer appears to compare the great power assigned by the Christian religion to Satan and his allies, with the very much less potency attributed to their analogues in heathendom, the rulers of the world of the dead. 65-1

A little reflection will convince the most incredulous that any such dualism as has been fancied to exist in the native religions, could not have been of indigenous growth. The gods of the primitive man are beings of thoroughly human physiognomy, painted with colors furnished by intercourse with his fellows. These are his enemies or his friends, as he conciliates or insults them. No mere man, least of all a savage, is kind and benevolent in spite of neglect and injury, nor is any man causelessly and ceaselessly malicious. Personal, family, or national feuds render some more inimical than others, but always from a desire to guard their own interests, never out of a delight in evil for its own sake. Thus the cruel gods of death, disease, and danger, were never of Satanic nature, while the kindliest divinities were disposed to punish, and that severely, any neglect of their ceremonies. Moral dualism can only arise in minds where the ideas of good and evil are not synonymous with those of pleasure and pain, for the conception of a wholly good or a wholly evil nature requires the use of these terms in their higher, ethical sense. The various deities of the Indians, it may safely be said in conclusion, present no stronger antithesis in this respect than those of ancient Greece and Rome.

FOOTNOTE:

44-1 But there is no ground for the most positive of philosophers to reject the doctrine of innate ideas when put in a certain way. The instincts and habits of the lower animals by which they obtain food, migrate, and perpetuate their kind, are in obedience to particular congenital impressions, and correspond to definite anatomical and morphological relations. No one pretends their knowledge is experimental. Just so the human cerebrum has received, by descent or otherwise, various sensory impressions peculiar to man as a species, which are just as certain to guide his thoughts, actions, and destiny, as is the cerebrum of the insectivorous aye-aye to lead it to hunt successfully for larvæ.

45-1 *Die Kunst im Zusammenhang der Culturentwickelung*, i. pp. 50, 252.

46-1 I offer these derivations with a certain degree of reserve, for such an extraordinary similarity in the sound of these words is discoverable in North and portions of South America, that one might almost be tempted to claim for them one original form. Thus in the Maya dialects it is *ku*, vocative *â kue*, in Natchez *kue-ya*, in the Uchee of West Florida *kauhwu*, in Otomi *okha*, in Mandan *okee*, Sioux *ogha*, *waughon*, *wakan*, in Quichua *waka*, *huaca*, in Iroquois *quaker*, *oki*, Algonkin *oki*, *okee*, Eskimo *aghatt*, which last has a singular likeness in sound to the German or Norse, *O Gott*, as some of the others have to the corresponding Finnish word *ukko*. *Ku* in the Carib tongue means *house*, especially a temple or house of the gods. The early Spanish explorers adopted the word with the orthography *cue*, and applied it to the sacred edifices of whatever nation they discovered. For instance, they speak of the great cemetery of Teotihuacan, near Tezcuco, as the *Llano de los Cues*.

46-2 "As the high heavens, the far-off mountains look to us blue, so a blue superficies seems to recede from us. As we would fain pursue an attractive object that flees from us, so we like to gaze at the blue, not that it urges itself upon us, but that it draws us after it." Goethe, *Farbenlehre*, secs. 780, 781.

47-1 Loskiel, *Geschichte der Mission der Evang. Brueder*, p. 63: Barby, 1789.

47-2 Cogolludo, *Historia de Yucathan*, lib. iv. cap. vii.

48-1 *Rel. de la Nouv. France*. An 1636, p. 107.

48-2 This word is found in Gallatin's vocabularies (*Transactions of the Am. Antiq. Soc.*, vol. ii.), and may have partially induced that distinguished ethnologist to ascribe, as he does in more than one place, whatever notions the eastern tribes had of a Supreme Being to the teachings of the Quakers.

48-3 Bruyas, *Radices Verborum Iroquæorum*, p. 84. This work is in Shea's Library of American Linguistics, and is a most valuable contribution to philology. The same etymology is given by Lafitau, *Mœurs des Sauvages*, etc., Germ. trans., p. 65.

50-1 My authorities are Riggs, *Dict. of the Dakota*, Boscana, *Account of New California*, Richardson's and Egede's Eskimo Vocabularies, Pandosy, *Gram. and Dict. of the Yakama* (Shea's Lib. of Am. Linguistics), and the Abbé Brasseur for the Aztec.

51-1 These terms are found in Gallatin's vocabularies. The last mentioned is not, as Adair thought, derived from *issto ulla* or *ishto hoollo*, great man, for in Choctaw the adjective cannot precede the noun it qualifies. Its true sense is visible in the analogous Creek words *ishtali*, the storm wind, and *hustolah*, the windy season.

51-2 Webster derives hurricane from the Latin *furio*. But Oviedo tells us in his description of Hispaniola that "Hurakan, in lingua di questa isola vuole dire propriamente fortuna tempestuosa molto eccessiva, perche en effetto non è altro que un grandissimo vento è pioggia insieme." *Historia dell' Indie*, lib. vi. cap. iii. It is a coincidence — perhaps something more — that in the Quichua language *huracan*, third person singular present indicative of the verbal noun *huraca*, means "a stream of water falls perpendicularly." (Markham, *Quichua Dictionary*, p. 132.)

52-1 Oviedo, *Rel. de la Prov. de Cueba*, p. 141, ed. Ternaux-Compans.

52-2 Garcia, *Origen de los Indios*, lib. iv. cap. xxii.

53-1 See the *Rel. de la Nouv. France pour l'An 1637*, p. 49.

53-2 Mr. Morgan, in his excellent work, *The League of the Iroquois*, has been led astray by an ignorance of the etymology of these terms. For Schoolcraft's views see his *Oneota*, p. 147. The matter is ably discussed in the *Etudes Philologiques sur Quelques Langues Sauvages de l'Amérique*, p. 14: Montreal, 1866; but comp. Shea, *Dict. Français-Onontagué*, preface.

54-1 "Qui ne prend aucun soin des choses icy bas." *Jour. Hist. d'un Voyage de l'Amérique*, p. 225: Paris, 1713.

55-1 In attributing this speech to the Inca Yupanqui, I have followed Balboa, who expressly says this was the general opinion of the Indians (*Hist. du Pérou*, p. 62, ed. Ternaux-Compans). Others assign it to other Incas. See Garcilasso de la Vega, *Hist.*

des Incas, lib. viii. chap. 8, and Acosta, *Nat. and Morall Hist. of the New World*, chap. 5. The fact and the approximate time are beyond question.

56-1 Xeres, *Rel. de la Conq. du Pérou*, p. 151, ed. Ternaux-Compans.

57-1 Prescott, *Conq. of Mexico*, i. pp. 192, 193, on the authority of Ixtlilxochitl.

57-2 Brasseur, *Hist. du Mexique*, iii. p. 297, note.

57-3 Of very many authorities that I have at hand, I shall only mention Heckewelder, Acc. of the   Inds.   p. 422, Duponceau, *Mém. sur les Langues de l'Amér. du Nord*, p. 310, Peter Martyr *De Rebus Oceanicis*, Dec. i., cap. 9, Molina, *Hist. of Chili*, ii. p. 75, Ximenes, *Origen de los Indios de Guatemala*, pp. 4, 5, Ixtlilxochitl, *Rel. des Conq. du Mexique*, p. 2. These terms bear the severest scrutiny. The Aztec appellation of the Supreme Being *Tloque nahuaque* is compounded of *tloc*, together, with, and *nahuac*, at, by, with, with possessive forms added, giving the signification, Lord of all existence and coexistence (alles Mitseyns und alles Beiseyns, bei welchem das Seyn aller Dinge ist. Buschmann, *Ueber die Aztekischen Ortsnamen*, p. 642). The Algonkin term *Kittanittowit* is derived from *kitta*, great, *manito*, spirit, *wit*, an adjective termination indicating a mode of existence, and means the Great Living Spirit (Duponceau, u. s.). Both these terms are undoubtedly of native origin. In the Quiche legends the Supreme Being is called *Bitol*, the substantive form of *bit*, to make pottery, to form, and *Tzakol*, substantive form of *tzak*, to build, the Creator, the Constructor. The Arowacks of Guyana applied the term *Aluberi* to their highest conception of a first cause, from the verbal form *alin*, he who makes (Martius, *Ethnographie und Sprachenkunde Amerika's*, i. p. 696).

59-1 *Geschichte der Amerikanischen Urreligionen*, p. 403.

59-2 Bruyas, *Rad. Verb. Iroquæorum*, p. 38.

60-1 Alcazar, *Chrono-historia de la Prov. de Toledo*, Dec. iii., Año viii., cap. iv: Madrid, 1710. This rare work contains the only faithful copies of Father Rogel's letters extant. Mr. Shea, in his History of Catholic Missions, calls him erroneously Roger.

60-2 It is fully analyzed by Duponceau, *Langues de l'Amérique du Nord*, p. 309.

61-1 *Discourse on the Religion of the Ind. Tribes of N. Am.*, p. 252 in the Trans. N. Y. Hist. Soc.

61-2 Mueller, *Amer. Urreligionen*, pp. 265, 272, 274. Well may he remark: "The dualism is not very striking among these tribes;" as a few pages previous he says of the Caribs, "The dualism of gods is anything but rigidly observed. The good gods do more evil than good. Fear is the ruling religious sentiment." To such a lame conclusion do these venerable prepossessions lead. "*Grau ist alle Theorie.*"

62-1 Loskiel, *Ges. der Miss. der evang. Brueder*, p. 46.

62-2 Whipple, *Report on the Ind. Tribes*, p. 33: Washington, 1855. Pacific Railroad Docs.

62-3 Schoolcraft, *Indian Tribes*, i. p. 359.

62-4 In Schoolcraft, *Ibid.*, iv. p. 642.

63-1 Or more exactly, the Beautiful Spirit, the Ugly Spirit. In Onondaga the radicals are *onigonra*, spirit, *hio* beautiful, *ahetken* ugly. *Dictionnaire Français-Onontagué, édité par Jean-Marie Shea*: New York, 1859.

64-1 Squier, *The Serpent Symbol in America*.

64-2 Both these legends will be analyzed in a subsequent chapter, and an attempt made not only to restore them their primitive form, but to explain their meaning.

65-1 Compare the translation and remarks of Ximenes, *Or. de los Indios de Guat.*, p. 76, with those of Brasseur, *Le Livre Sacré des Quichés*, p. 189.

CHAPTER III
THE SACRED NUMBER, ITS
ORIGIN AND APPLICATIONS

The number Four sacred in all American religions, and the key to their symbolism. — Derived from the Cardinal Points. — Appears constantly in government, arts, rites, and myths. — The Cardinal Points identified with the Four Winds, who in myths are the four ancestors of the human race, and the four celestial rivers watering the terrestrial Paradise. — Associations grouped around each Cardinal Point. — From the number four was derived the symbolic value of the number *Forty*, and the *Sign of the Cross*.

EVERY one familiar with the ancient religions of the world must have noticed the mystic power they attach to certain numbers, and how these numbers became the measures and formative quantities, as it were, of traditions and ceremonies, and had a symbolical meaning nowise connected with their arithmetical value. For instance, in many eastern religions, that of the Jews among the rest, *seven* was the most sacred number, and after it, *four* and *three*. The most cursory reader must have observed in how many connections the seven is used in the Hebrew Scriptures, occurring, in all, something over three hundred and sixty times, it is said. Why these numbers were chosen rather than others has not been clearly explained. Their sacred character dates beyond the earliest history, and must have been coeval with the first expressions of the religious sentiment. Only one of them, the FOUR, has any prominence in the religions of the red race, but this is so marked and so universal, that at a very early period in my studies I felt convinced that if the reason for its adoption could be discovered, much of the apparent confusion which reigns among them would be dispelled.

Such a reason must take its rise from some essential relation of man to nature, everywhere prominent, everywhere the same. It is found in the *adoration of the cardinal points*.

The red man, as I have said, was a hunter; he was ever wandering through pathless forests, coursing over boundless prairies. It seems to the white race not a faculty, but an instinct that guides him so unerringly. He is never at a loss. Says a writer who has deeply studied his character: "The Indian ever has the points of the compass present to his mind, and expresses himself accordingly in words, although it shall be of matters in his own house." 67-1

The assumption of precisely four cardinal points is not of chance; it is recognized in every language; it is rendered essential by the anatomical structure of the body; it is derived from the immutable laws of the universe. Whether we gaze at the sunset or the sunrise, or whether at night we look for guidance to the only star of the twinkling thousands that is constant to its place, the anterior and posterior planes of our bodies, our right hands and our left coincide with the parallels and meridians. Very early in his history did man take note of these four points, and recognizing in them his guides through the night and the wilderness, call them his gods. Long afterwards, when centuries of slow progress had taught him other secrets of nature—when he had discerned in the motions of the sun, the elements of matter, and the radicals of arithmetic a repetition of this number—they were to him further warrants of its sacredness. He adopted it as a regulating quantity in his institutions and his arts; he repeated it in its multiples and compounds; he imagined for it novel applications; he constantly magnified its mystic meaning; and finally, in his philosophical reveries, he called it the key to the secrets of the universe, "the source of ever-flowing nature." 68-1

In primitive geography the figure of the earth is a square plain; in the legend of the Quiché's it is "shaped as a square, divided into four parts, marked with lines, measured with cords, and suspended from the heavens by a cord to its four corners and its four sides." 68-2 The earliest divisions of territory were in conformity to this view. Thus it was with ancient Egypt, Syria, Mesopotamia, and China; 68-3 and in the new world, the states of Peru, Araucania, the Muyscas, the Quichés, and Tlascala were tetrarchies divided in accordance with, and in the first two instances named after, the cardinal points. So their chief cities—Cuzco, Quito, Tezcuco, Mexico, Cholula—were quartered by streets running north, south, east, and west. It was a necessary result of such a division that the chief officers of the government were four in number, that the inhabitants of town and country, that the whole social organization acquired a quadruplicate form. The official title of the Incas was "Lord of the four quarters of the earth," and the venerable formality in taking possession of land, both in their domain and that of the Aztecs, was to throw a stone, to shoot an arrow, or to hurl a firebrand to each of the cardinal points. 69-1 They carried out the idea in their architecture, building their palaces in squares with doors opening, their tombs with their angles pointing, their great causeways running in these directions. These architectural principles repeat themselves all over the continent; they recur in the sacred structures of Yucatan, in the ancient cemetery of Teo-tihuacan near Mexico, where the tombs are arranged along avenues corresponding exactly to the parallels and meridians of the central tumuli of the sun and moon; 69-2 and however ignorant we are about the mound builders of the Mississippi valley, we know that they constructed their earthworks with a constant regard to the quarters of the compass.

Nothing can be more natural than to take into consideration the regions of the heavens in the construction of buildings; I presume that at any time no one plans an edifice of pretensions without doing so. Yet this is one of those apparently trifling transactions which in their origin and applications have exerted a controlling influence on the history of the human race.

When we reflect how indissolubly the mind of the primitive man is welded to his superstitions, it were incredible that his social life and his architecture could thus be as it were in subjection to one idea, and his rites and myths escape its sway. As one might expect, it reappears in these latter more vividly than anywhere else. If there is one formula more frequently mentioned by travellers than another as an indispensable preliminary to all serious business, it is that of smoking, and the prescribed and traditional rule was that the first puff should be to the sky, and then one to each of the corners of the earth, or the cardinal points. 70-1 These were the spirits who made and governed the earth, and under whatever difference of guise the uncultivated fancy portrayed them, they were the leading figures in the tales and ceremonies of nearly every tribe of the red race. These were the divine powers summoned by the Chipeway magicians when initiating neophytes into the mysteries of the meda craft. They were asked to a lodge of four poles, to four stones that lay before its fire, there to remain four days, and attend four feasts. At every step of the proceeding this number or its multiples were repeated. 71-1 With their neighbors the Dakotas the number was also distinctly sacred; it was intimately inwoven in all their tales concerning the wakan power and the spirits of the air, and their religious rites. The artist Catlin has given a vivid description of the great annual festival of the Mandans, a Dakota tribe, and brings forward with emphasis the ceaseless reiteration of this number from first to last. 71-2 He did not detect its origin in the veneration of the cardinal points, but the information that has since been furnished of the myths of this stock leaves no doubt that such was the case. 71-3

Proximity of place had no part in this similarity of rite. In the grand commemorative festival of the Creeks called the Busk, which wiped out the memory of all crimes but murder, which reconciled the proscribed criminal to his nation and atoned for his guilt, when the new fire was kindled and the green corn served up, every dance, every invocation, every ceremony, was shaped and ruled by the application of the number four and its multiples in every imaginable relation. So it was at that solemn probation which the youth must undergo to prove himself worthy of the dignities of manhood and to ascertain his guardian spirit; here again his fasts, his seclusions, his trials, were all laid down in fourfold arrangement. 72-1

Not alone among these barbarous tribes were the cardinal points thus the foundation of the most solemn mysteries of religion. An excellent authority relates that the Aztecs of Micla, in Guatemala, celebrated their chief festival four times a year, and that four priests solemnized its rites. They commenced by invoking and offering incense to the sky and the four cardinal points; they conducted the human victim four times around the temple, then tore out his heart, and catching the blood in four vases scattered it in the same directions. 72-2 So also the Peruvians had four principal festivals annually, and at every new moon one of four days' duration. In fact the repetition of the number in all their religious ceremonies is so prominent that it has been a subject of comment by historians. They have attributed it to the knowledge of the solstices and equinoxes, but assuredly it is of more ancient date than this. The same explanation has been offered for its recurrence among the Nahuas of Mexico, whose whole lives were subjected to its operation. At birth the mother was held unclean for four days, a fire was kindled and kept burning for a like length of time, at the baptism of the child an arrow was shot to each of the cardinal points. Their prayers were offered four times a day, the greatest festivals were every fourth year, and their offerings of blood were to the four points of the compass. At death food was placed on the grave, as among the Eskimos, Creeks, and Algonkins, for four days (for all these nations supposed that the journey to the land of souls was accomplished in that time), and mourning for the dead was for four months or four years. 73-1

It were fatiguing and unnecessary to extend the catalogue much further. Yet it is not nearly exhausted. From tribes of both continents and all stages of culture, the Muyscas of Columbia and the Natchez of Louisiana, the Quichés of Guatemala and the Caribs of the Orinoko, instance after instance might be marshalled to illustrate how universally a sacred character was attached to this number, and how uniformly it is traceable to a veneration of the cardinal points. It is sufficient that it be displayed in some of its more unusual applications.

It is well known that the calendar common to the Aztecs and Mayas divides the month into four weeks, each containing a like number of secular days; that their indiction is divided into four periods; and that they believed the world had passed through four cycles. It has not been sufficiently emphasized that in many of the picture writings these days of the week are placed respectively north, south, east, and west, and that in the Maya language the quarters of the indiction still bear the names of the cardinal points, hinting the reason of their adoption. 74-1 This cannot be fortuitous. Again, the division of the year into four seasons—a division as devoid of foundation in nature as that of the ancient Aryans into three, and unknown among many tribes, yet obtained in very early times among Algonkins, Cherokees, Choctaws, Creeks, Aztecs, Muyscas, Peruvians, and Araucanians. They were supposed to be produced by the unending struggles and varying fortunes of the four aerial giants who rule the winds.

We must seek in mythology the key to the monotonous repetition and the sanctity of this number; and furthermore, we must seek it in those natural modes of expression of the religious sentiment which are above the power of blood or circumstance to control. One of these modes, we have seen, was that which led to the identification of the divinity with the wind, and this it is that solves the enigma in the present instance. Universally the spirits of the cardinal points were imagined to be in the winds that blew from them. The names of these directions and of the corresponding winds are often the same, and when not, there exists an intimate connection between them. For example, take the languages of the Mayas, Huastecas, and Moscos of Central America; in all of them the word for *north* is synonymous with *north wind*, and so on for the other three points of the compass. Or again, that of the Dakotas, and the word *tate-ouye-toba*, translated "the four quarters of the heavens," means literally, "whence the four winds come." 75-1 It were not difficult to extend the list; but illustrations are all that is required. Let it be remembered how closely the motions of the air are associated in thought and language with the operations of the soul and the idea of God; let it further be considered what support this association receives from the power of the winds on the weather, bringing as they do the lightning and the storm, the zephyr that cools the brow, and the tornado that levels the forest; how they summon the rain to fertilize the seed and refresh the shrivelled leaves; how they aid the hunter to stalk the game, and usher in the varying seasons; how, indeed, in a hundred ways, they intimately concern his comfort and his life; and it will not seem strange that they almost occupied the place of all other gods in the mind of the child of nature. Especially as those who gave or withheld the rains were they objects of his anxious solicitation. "Ye who dwell at the four corners of the earth—at the north, at the south, at the east, and at the west," commenced the Aztec prayer to the Tlalocs, gods of the showers. 75-2 For they, as it were, hold the food, the life of man in their power, garnered up on high, to grant or deny, as they see fit. It was from them that the prophet of old was directed to call back the spirits of the dead to the dry bones of the valley. "Prophesy unto the wind, prophesy, son of man, and say to the wind, thus saith the Lord God, come forth from the four winds, O breath, and breathe upon these slain, that they may live." (Ezek. xxxvii. 9.)

In the same spirit the priests of the Eskimos prayed to *Sillam Innua*, the Owner of the Winds, as the highest existence; the abode of the dead they called *Sillam Aipane*, the House of the Winds; and in their incantations, when they would summon a new soul to the sick, or order back to its home some troublesome spirit, their invocations were ever addressed to the winds from the cardinal points — to Pauna the East and Sauna the West, to Kauna the South and Auna the North. 76-1

As the rain-bringers, as the life-givers, it were no far-fetched metaphor to call them the fathers of our race. Hardly a nation on the continent but seems to have had some vague tradition of an origin from four brothers, to have at some time been led by four leaders or princes, or in some manner to have connected the appearance and action of four important personages with its earliest traditional history. Sometimes the myth defines clearly these fabled characters as the spirits of the winds, sometimes it clothes them in uncouth, grotesque metaphors, sometimes again it so weaves them into actual history that we are at a loss where to draw the line that divides fiction from truth.

I shall attempt to follow step by step the growth of this myth from its simplest expression, where the transparent drapery makes no pretence to conceal its true meaning, through the ever more elaborate narratives, the more strongly marked personifications of more cultivated nations, until it assumes the outlines of, and has palmed itself upon the world as actual history.

This simplest form is that which alone appears among the Algonkins and Dakotas. They both traced their lives back to four ancestors, personages concerned in various ways with the first things of time, not rightly distinguished as men or gods, but very positively identified with the four winds. Whether from one or all of these the world was peopled, whether by process of generation or some other more obscure way, the old people had not said, or saying, had not agreed. 77-1

It is a shade more complex when we come to the Creeks. They told of four men who came from the four corners of the earth, who brought them the sacred fire, and pointed out the seven sacred plants. They were called the Hi-you-yul-gee. Having rendered them this service, the kindly visitors disappeared in a cloud, returning whence they came. When another and more ancient legend informs us that the Creeks were at first divided into four clans, and alleged a descent from four female ancestors, it will hardly be venturing too far to recognize in these four ancestors the four friendly patrons from the cardinal points. 78-1

The ancient inhabitants of Haiti, when first discovered by the Spaniards, had a similar genealogical story, which Peter Martyr relates with various excuses for its silliness and exclamations at its absurdity. Perhaps the fault lay less in its lack of meaning than in his want of insight. It was to the effect that men lived in caves, and were destroyed by the parching rays of the sun, and were destitute of means to prolong their race, until they caught and subjected to their use four women who were swift of foot and slippery as eels. These were the mothers of the race of men. Or again, it was said that a certain king had a huge gourd which contained all the waters of the earth; four brothers, who coming into the world at one birth had cost their mother her life, ventured to the gourd to fish, picked it up, but frightened, by the old king's approach, dropped it on the ground, broke it into fragments, and scattered the waters over the earth, forming the seas, lakes, and rivers, as they now are. These brothers in time became the fathers of a nation, and to them they traced their lineage. 78-2 With the previous examples before our eyes, it asks no vivid fancy to see in these quaternions once more the four winds, the bringers of rain, so swift and so slippery.

The Navajos are a rude tribe north of Mexico. Yet even they have an allegory to the effect that when the first man came up from the ground under the figure of the moth-worm, the four spirits of the cardinal points were already there, and hailed him with the exclamation, "Lo, he is of our race." 79-1 It is a poor and feeble effort to tell the same old story.

The Haitians were probably relatives of the Mayas of Yucatan. Certainly the latter shared their ancestral legends, for in an ancient manuscript found by Mr. Stephens during his travels, it appears they looked back to four parents or leaders called the Tutul Xiu. But, indeed, this was a trait of all the civilized nations of Central America and Mexico. An author who would be very unwilling to admit any mythical interpretation of the coincidence, has adverted to it in tones of astonishment: "In all the Aztec and Toltec histories there are four characters who constantly reappear; either as priests or envoys of the gods, or of hidden and disguised majesty; or as guides and chieftains of tribes during their migrations; or as kings and rulers of monarchies after their foundation; and even to the time of the conquest, there are always four princes who compose the supreme government, whether in Guatemala, or in Mexico." 79-2 This fourfold division points not to a common history, but to a common nature. The ancient heroes and demigods, who, four in number, figure in all these antique traditions, were not men of flesh and blood, but the invisible currents of air who brought the fertilizing showers.

They corresponded to the four gods Bacab, who in the Yucatecan mythology were supposed to stand one at each corner of the world, supporting, like gigantic caryatides, the overhanging firmament. When at the general deluge all other gods and men were swallowed by the waters they alone escaped to people it anew. These four, known by the names of Kan, Muluc, Ix, and Cauac, represented respectively the east, north, west, and south, and as in Oriental symbolism, so here each quarter of the compass was distinguished by a color, the east by yellow, the south by red, the west by black, and the north by white. The names of these mysterious personages, employed somewhat as we do the Dominical letters, adjusted the calendar of the Mayas, and by their propitious or portentous combinations was arranged their system of judicial astrology. They were the gods of rain, and under the title Chac, the Red Ones, were the chief ministers of the highest power. As such they were represented in the religious ceremonies by four old men, constant attendants on the high priest in his official functions. 80-1 In this most civilized branch of the red race, as everywhere else, we thus find four mythological characters prominent beyond all others, giving a peculiar physiognomy to the national legends, arts, and sciences, and in them once more we recognize by signs infallible, personifications of the four cardinal points and the four winds.

They rarely lose altogether their true character. The Quiché legends tell us that the four men who were first created by the Heart of Heaven, Hurakan, the Air in Motion, were infinitely keen of eye and swift of foot, that "they measured and saw all that exists at the four corners and the four angles of the sky and the earth;" that they did not fulfil the design of their maker "to bring forth and produce when the season of harvest was near," until he blew into their eyes a cloud, "until their faces were obscured as when one breathes on a mirror." Then he gave them as wives the four mothers of our species, whose names were Falling Water, Beautiful Water, Water of Serpents, and Water of Birds. 81-1 Truly he who can see aught but a transparent myth in this recital, is a realist that would astonish Euhemerus himself.

There is in these Aztec legends a quaternion besides this of the first men, one that bears marks of a profound contemplation on the course of nature, one that answers to the former as the heavenly phase of the earthly conception. It is seen in the four personages, or perhaps we should say modes of action, that make up the one Supreme Cause of All, Hurakan, the breath, the wind, the Divine Spirit. They are He who creates, He who gives Form, He who gives Life, and He who reproduces. 82-1 This acute and extraordinary analysis of the origin and laws of organic life, clothed under the ancient belief in the action of the winds, reveals a depth of thought for which we were hardly prepared, and is perhaps the single instance of anything like metaphysics among the red race. It is clearly visible in the earlier portions of the legends of the Quichés, and is the more surely of native origin as it has been quite lost on both their translators.

Go where we will, the same story meets us. The empire of the Incas was attributed in the sacred chants of the Amautas, the priests assigned to take charge of the records, to four brothers and their wives. These mythical civilizers are said to have emerged from a cave called *Pacari tampu*, which may mean "the House of Subsistence," reminding us of the four heroes who in Aztec legend set forth to people the world from Tonacatepec, the mountain of our subsistence; or again it may mean—for like many of these mythical names it seems to have been designedly chosen to bear a double construction—the Lodgings of the Dawn, recalling another Aztec legend which points for the birthplace of the race to Tula in the distant orient. The cave itself suggests to the classical reader that of Eolus, or may be paralleled with that in which the Iroquois fabled the winds were imprisoned by their lord. 83-1 These brothers were of no common kin. Their voices could shake the earth and their hands heap up mountains. Like the thunder god, they stood on the hills and hurled their sling-stones to the four corners of the earth. When one was overpowered he fled upward to the heaven or was turned into stone, and it was by their aid and counsel that the savages who possessed the land renounced their barbarous habits and commenced to till the soil. There can be no doubt but that this in turn is but another transformation of the Protean myth we have so long pursued. 83-2

There are traces of the same legend among many other tribes of the continent, but the trustworthy reports we have of them are too scanty to permit analysis. Enough that they are mentioned in a note, for it is every way likely that could we resolve their meaning they too would carry us back to the four winds. 83-3

Let no one suppose, however, that this was the only myth of the origin of man. Far from it. It was but one of many, for, as I shall hereafter attempt to show, the laws that governed the formations of such myths not only allowed but enjoined great divergence of form. Equally far was it from being the only image which the inventive fancy hit upon to express the action of the winds as the rain bringers. They too were many, but may all be included in a twofold division, either as the winds were supposed to flow in from the corners of the earth or outward from its central point. Thus they are spoken of under such figures as four tortoises at the angles of the earthly plane who vomit forth the rains, 85-1 or four gigantic caryatides who sustain the heavens and blow the winds from their capacious lungs, 85-2 or more frequently as four rivers flowing from the broken calabash on high, as the Haitians, draining the waters of the primitive world, 85-3 as four animals who bring from heaven the maize, 85-4 as four messengers whom the god of air sends forth, or under a coarser trope as the spittle he ejects toward the cardinal points which is straightway transformed into wild rice, tobacco, and maize. 85-5

Constantly from the palace of the lord of the world, seated on the high hill of heaven, blow four winds, pour four streams, refreshing and fecundating the earth. Therefore, in the myths of ancient Iran there is mention of a celestial fountain, Arduisur, the virgin daughter of Ormuzd, whence four all nourishing rivers roll their waves toward the cardinal points; therefore the Thibetans believe that on the sacred mountain Himavata grows the tree of life Zampu, from whose foot once more flow the waters of life in four streams to the four quarters of the world; and therefore it is that the same tale is told by the Chinese of the mountain Kouantun, by the Brahmins of Mount Meru, and by the Parsees of Mount Albors in the Caucasus. 85-6 Each nation called their sacred mountain "the navel of the earth;" for not only was it the supposed centre of the habitable world, but through it, as the fœtus through the umbilical cord, the earth drew her increase. Beyond all other spots were they accounted fertile, scenes of joyous plaisance, of repose, and eternal youth; there rippled the waters of health, there blossomed the tree of life; they were fit trysting spots of gods and men. Hence came the tales of the terrestrial paradise, the rose garden of Feridun, the Eden gardens of the world. The name shows the origin, for paradise (in Sanscrit, *para desa*) means literally *high land*. There, in the unanimous opinion of the Orient, dwelt once in unalloyed delight the first of men; thence driven by untoward fate, no more anywhere could they find the path thither. Some thought that in the north among the fortunate Hyperboreans, others that in the mountains of the moon where dwelt the long lived Ethiopians, and others again that in the furthest east, underneath the dawn, was situate the seat of pristine happiness; but many were of opinion that somewhere in the western sea, beyond the pillars of Hercules and the waters of the Outer Ocean, lay the garden of the Hesperides, the Islands of the Blessed, the earthly Elysion.

It is not without design that I recall this early dream of the religious fancy. When Christopher Columbus, fired by the hope of discovering this terrestrial paradise, broke the enchantment of the cloudy sea and found a new world, it was but to light upon the same race of men, deluding themselves with the same hope of earthly joys, the same fiction of a long lost garden of their youth. They told him that still to the west, amid the mountains of Paria, was a spot whence flowed mighty streams over all lands, and which in sooth was the spot he sought; 87-1 and when that baseless fabric had vanished, there still remained the fabled island of Boiuca, or Bimini, hundreds of leagues north of Hispaniola, whose glebe was watered by a fountain of such noble virtue as to restore youth and vigor to the worn out and the aged. 87-2 This was no fiction of the natives to rid themselves of burdensome guests. Long before the white man approached their shores, families had started from Cuba, Yucatan, and Honduras in search of these renovating waters, and not returning, were supposed by their kindred to have been detained by the delights of that enchanted land, and to be revelling in its seductive joys, forgetful of former ties. 87-3

Perhaps it was but another rendering of the same belief that pointed to the impenetrable forests of the Orinoko, the ancient homes of the Caribs and Arowacks, and there located the famous realm of El Dorado with its imperial capital Manoa, abounding in precious metals and all manner of gems, peopled by a happy race, and governed by an equitable ruler.

The Aztec priests never chanted more regretful dirges than when they sang of Tulan, the cradle of their race, where once it dwelt in peaceful indolent happiness, whose groves were filled with birds of sweet voices and gay plumage, whose generous soil brought forth spontaneously maize, cocoa, aromatic gums, and fragrant flowers. "Land of riches and plenty, where the gourds grow an arm's length across, where an ear of corn is a load for a stout man, and its stalks are as high as trees; land where the cotton ripens of its own accord of all rich tints; land abounding with limpid emeralds, turquoises, gold, and silver." 88-1 This land was also called Tlalocan, from Tlaloc, the god of rain, who there had his dwelling place, and Tlapallan, the land of colors, or the red land, for the hues of the sky at sunrise floated over it. Its inhabitants were surnamed children of the air, or of Quetzalcoatl, and from its centre rose the holy mountain Tonacatepec, the mountain of our life or subsistence. Its supposed location was in the east, whence in that country blow the winds that bring mild rains, says Sahagun, and that missionary was himself asked, as coming from the east, whether his home was in Tlapallan; more definitely by some it was situated among the lofty peaks on the frontiers of Guatemala, and all the great rivers that water the earth were supposed to have their sources there. 88-2 But here, as elsewhere, its site was not determined. "There is a Tulan," says an ancient authority, "where the sun rises, and there is another in the land of shades, and another where the sun reposes, and thence came we; and still another where the sun reposes, and there dwells God." 89-1

The myth of the Quichés but changes the name of this pleasant land. With them it was *Pan-paxil-pa-cayala*, where the waters divide in falling, or between the waters parcelled out and mucky. This was "an excellent land, full of pleasant things, where was store of white corn and yellow corn, where one could not count the fruits, nor estimate the quantity of honey and food.". Over it ruled the lord of the air, and from it the four sacred animals carried the corn to make the flesh of men. 90-1

Once again, in the legends of the Mixtecas, we hear the old story repeated of the garden where the first two brothers dwelt. It lay between a meadow and that lofty peak which supports the heavens and the palaces of the gods. "Many trees were there, such as yield flowers and roses, very luscious fruits, divers herbs, and aromatic spices." The names of the brothers were the Wind of Nine Serpents and the Wind of Nine Caverns. The first was as an eagle, and flew aloft over the waters that poured around their enchanted garden; the second was as a serpent with wings, who proceeded with such velocity that he pierced rocks and walls. They were too swift to be seen by the sharpest eye, and were one near as they passed, he was only aware of a whisper and a rustling like that of the wind in the leaves. 90-2

Wherever, in short, the lust of gold lured the early adventurers, they were told of some nation a little further on, some wealthy and prosperous land, abundant and fertile, satisfying the desire of the heart. It was sometimes deceit, and it was sometimes the credited fiction of the earthly paradise, that in all ages has with a promise of perfect joy consoled the aching heart of man.

It is instructive to study the associations that naturally group themselves around each of the cardinal points, and watch how these are mirrored on the surface of language, and have directed the current of thought. Jacob Grimm has performed this task with fidelity and beauty as regards the Aryan race, but the means are wanting to apply his searching method to the indigenous tongues of America. Enough if in general terms their mythological value be determined.

When the day begins, man wakes from his slumbers, faces the rising sun, and prays. The east is before him; by it he learns all other directions; it is to him what the north is to the needle; with reference to it he assigns in his mind the position of the three other cardinal points. 91-1 There is the starting place of the celestial fires, the home of the sun, the womb of the morning. It represents in space the beginning of things in time, and as the bright and glorious creatures of the sky come forth thence, man conceits that his ancestors also in remote ages wandered from the orient; there in the opinion of many in both the old and new world was the cradle of the race;

there in Aztec legend was the fabled land of Tlapallan, and the wind from the east was called the wind of Paradise, Tlalocavitl.

From this direction came, according to the almost unanimous opinion of the Indian tribes, those hero gods who taught them arts and religion, thither they returned, and from thence they would again appear to resume their ancient sway. As the dawn brings light, and with light is associated in every human mind the ideas of knowledge, safety, protection, majesty, divinity, as it dispels the spectres of night, as it defines the cardinal points, and brings forth the sun and the day, it occupied the primitive mind to an extent that can hardly be magnified beyond the truth. It is in fact the central figure in most natural religions.

The west, as the grave of the heavenly luminaries, or rather as their goal and place of repose, brings with it thoughts of sleep, of death, of tranquillity, of rest from labor. When the evening of his days was come, when his course was run, and man had sunk from sight, he was supposed to follow the sun and find some spot of repose for his tired soul in the distant west. There, with general consent, the tribes north of the Gulf of Mexico supposed the happy hunting grounds; there, taught by the same analogy, the ancient Aryans placed the Nerriti, the exodus, the land of the dead. "The old notion among us," said on one occasion a distinguished chief of the Creek nation, "is that when we die, the spirit goes the way the sun goes, to the west, and there joins its family and friends who went before it." 92-1

In the northern hemisphere the shadows fall to the north, thence blow cold and furious winds, thence come the snow and early thunder. Perhaps all its primitive inhabitants, of whatever race, thought it the seat of the mighty gods. 92-2 A floe of ice in the Arctic Sea was the home of the guardian spirit of the Algonkins; 92-3 on a mountain near the north star the Dakotas thought Heyoka dwelt who rules the seasons; and the realm of Mictla, the Aztec god of death, lay where the shadows pointed. From that cheerless abode his sceptre reached over all creatures, even the gods themselves, for sooner or later all must fall before him. The great spirit of the dead, said the Ottawas, lives in the dark north, 93-1 and there, in the opinion of the Monquis of California, resided their chief god, Gumongo. 93-2

Unfortunately the makers of vocabularies have rarely included the words north, south, east, and west, in their lists, and the methods of expressing these ideas adopted by the Indians can only be partially discovered. The east and west were usually called from the rising and setting of the sun as in our words orient and occident, but occasionally from traditional notions. The Mayas named the west the greater, the east the lesser debarkation; believing that while their culture hero Zamna came from the east with a few attendants, the mass of the population arrived from the opposite direction. 93-3 The Aztecs spoke of the east as "the direction of Tlalocan," the terrestrial paradise. But for north and south there were no such natural appellations, and consequently the greatest diversity is exhibited in the plans adopted to express them. The north in the Caddo tongue is "the place of cold," in Dakota "the situation of the pines," in Creek "the abode of the (north) star," in Algonkin "the home of the soul," in Aztec "the direction of Mictla" the realm of death, in Quiché and Quichua, "to the right hand;" 93-4 while for the south we find such terms as in Dakota "the downward direction," in Algonkin "the place of warmth," in Quiché "to the left hand," while among the Eskimos, who look in this direction for the sun, its name implies "before one," just as does the Hebrew word *kedem*, which, however, this more southern tribe applied to the east.

We can trace the sacredness of the number four in other curious and unlooked-for developments. Multiplied into the number of the fingers—the arithmetic of every child and ignorant man—or by adding together the first four members of its arithmetical series (4 8 12 16), it gives the number forty. This was taken as a limit to the sacred dances of some Indian tribes, and by others as the highest number of chants to be employed in exorcising diseases. Consequently it came to be fixed as a limit in exercises of preparation or purification. The females of the Orinoko tribes fasted forty days before marriage, and those of the upper Mississippi were held unclean the same length of time after childbirth; such was the term of the Prince of Tezcuco's fast when he wished an heir to his throne, and such the number of days the Mandans supposed it required to wash clean the world at the deluge. 94-1

No one is ignorant how widely this belief was prevalent in the old world, nor how the quadrigesimal is still a sacred term with some denominations of Christianity. But a more striking parallelism awaits us. The symbol that beyond all others has fascinated the human mind, THE CROSS, finds here its source and meaning. Scholars have pointed out its sacredness in many natural religions, and have reverently accepted it as a mystery, or offered scores of conflicting and often debasing interpretations. It is but another symbol of the four cardinal points, the four winds of heaven. This will luminously appear by a study of its use and meaning in America.

The Catholic missionaries found it was no new object of adoration to the red race, and were in doubt whether to ascribe the fact to the pious labors of Saint Thomas or the sacrilegious subtlety of Satan. It was the central object in the great temple of Cozumel, and is still preserved on the bas-reliefs of the ruined city of Palenque. From time immemorial it had received the prayers and sacrifices of the Aztecs and Toltecs, and was suspended as an august emblem from the walls of temples in Popoyan and Cundinamarca.

In the Mexican tongue it bore the significant and worthy name "Tree of Our Life," or "Tree of our Flesh" (Tonacaquahuitl). It represented the god of rains and of health, and this was everywhere its simple meaning. "Those of Yucatan," say the chroniclers, "prayed to the cross as the god of rains when they needed water." The Aztec goddess of rains bore one in her hand, and at the feast celebrated to her honor in the early spring victims were nailed to a cross and shot with arrows. Quetzalcoatl, god of the winds, bore as his sign of office "a mace like the cross of a bishop;" his robe was covered with them strown like flowers, and its adoration was throughout connected with his worship. 96-1 When the Muyscas would sacrifice to the goddess of waters they extended cords across the tranquil depths of some lake, thus forming a gigantic cross, and at their point of intersection threw in their offerings of gold, emeralds, and precious oils. 96-2 The arms of the cross were designed to point to the cardinal points and represent the four winds, the rain bringers. To confirm this explanation, let us have recourse to the simpler ceremonies of the less cultivated tribes, and see the transparent meaning of the symbol as they employed it.

When the rain maker of the Lenni Lenape would exert his power, he retired to some secluded spot and drew upon the earth the figure of a cross (its arms toward the cardinal points?), placed upon it a piece of tobacco, a gourd, a bit of some red stuff, and commenced to cry aloud to the spirits of the rains. 96-3 The Creeks at the festival of the Busk, celebrated, as we have seen, to the four winds, and according to their legends instituted by them, commenced with making the new fire. The manner of this was "to place four logs in the centre of the square, end to end, forming a cross, the outer ends pointing to the cardinal points; in the centre of the cross the new fire is made." 97-1

As the emblem of the winds who dispense the fertilizing showers it is emphatically the tree of our life, our subsistence, and our health. It never had any other meaning in America, and if, as has been said, 97-2 the tombs of the Mexicans were cruciform, it was perhaps with reference to a resurrection and a future life as portrayed under this symbol, indicating that the buried body would rise by the action of the four spirits of the world, as the buried seed takes on a new existence when watered by the vernal showers. It frequently recurs in the ancient Egyptian writings, where it is interpreted *life*; doubtless, could we trace the hieroglyph to its source, it would likewise prove to be derived from the four winds.

While thus recognizing the natural origin of this consecrated symbol, while discovering that it is based on the sacredness of numbers, and this in turn on the structure and necessary relations of the human body, thus disowning the meaningless mysticism that Joseph de Maistre and his disciples have advocated, let us on the other hand be equally on our guard against accepting the material facts which underlie these beliefs as their deepest foundation and their exhaustive explanation. That were but withered fruit for our labors, and it might well be asked, where is here the divine idea said to be dimly prefigured in mythology? The universal belief in the sacredness of numbers is an instinctive faith in an immortal truth; it is a direct perception of the soul, akin to that which recognizes a God. The laws of chemical combination, of the various modes of motion, of all organic growth, show that simple numerical relations govern all the properties and are inherent to the very constitution of matter; more marvellous still, the most recent and severe inductions of physicists show that precisely those two numbers on whose symbolical value much of the edifice of ancient mythology was erected, the *four* and the *three*, regulate the molecular distribution of matter and preside over the symmetrical development of organic forms. This asks no faith, but only knowledge; it is science, not revelation. In view of such facts is it presumptuous to predict that experiment itself will prove the truth of Kepler's beautiful saying: "The universe is a harmonious whole, the soul of which is God; numbers, figures, the stars, all nature, indeed, are in unison with the mysteries of religion"?

FOOTNOTE:

67-1 Buckingham Smith, *Gram. Notices of the Heve Language*, p. 26 (Shea's Lib. Am. Linguistics).

68-1 I refer to the four "ultimate elementary particles" of Empedocles. The number was sacred to Hermes, and lay at the root of the physical philosophy of Pythagoras. The quotation in the text is from the "Golden Verses," given in Passow's lexicon under the word τετρακτὺς: ναι μα τον ἁμετερα ψυχᾳ παραδοντα τετρακτυν, παγαν αεναου φυσεως "The most sacred of all things," said this famous teacher, "is Number; and next to it, that which gives Names;" a truth that the lapse of three thousand years is just enabling us to appreciate.

68-2 Ximenes, *Or. de los Indios*, etc., p. 5.

68-3 See Sepp, *Heidenthum und dessen Bedeutung für das Christenthum*, i. p. 464 sqq., a work full of learning, but written in the wildest vein of Joseph de Maistre's school of Romanizing mythology.

69-1 Brasseur, *Hist. du Mexique*, ii. p. 227, *Le Livre Sacré des Quichés*, introd. p. ccxlii. The four provinces of Peru were Anti, Cunti, Chincha, and Colla. The meaning of these names has been lost, but to repeat them, says La Vega, was the same as to use our words, east, west, north, and south (*Hist. des Incas*, lib. ii. cap. 11).

69-2 Humboldt, *Polit. Essay on New Spain*, ii. p. 44.

70-1 This custom has been often mentioned among the Iroquois. Algonkins, Dakotas, Creeks, Natchez, Araucanians, and other tribes. Nuttall points out its recurrence among the Tartars of Siberia also. (*Travels*, p. 175.)

71-1 Schoolcraft, *Indian Tribes*, v. pp. 424 et seq.

71-2 *Letters on the North American Indians*, vol. i., Letter 22.

71-3 Schoolcraft, *Indian Tribes*, iv. p. 643 sq. "Four is their sacred number," says Mr. Pond (p. 646). Their neighbors, the Pawnees, though not the most remote affinity can be detected between their languages, coincide with them in this sacred number, and distinctly identified it with the cardinal points. See De Smet, *Oregon Missions*, pp. 360, 361.

72-1 Benj. Hawkins, *Sketch of the Creek Country*, pp. 75, 78: Savannah, 1848. The description he gives of the ceremonies of the Creeks was transcribed word for word and published in the first volume of the American Antiquarian Society's Transactions as of the Shawnees of Ohio. This literary theft has not before been noticed.

72-2 Palacios, *Des. de la Prov. de Guatemala*, pp. 31, 32, ed. Ternaux-Compans.

73-1 All familiar with Mexican antiquity will recall many such examples. I may particularly refer to Kingsborough, *Antiqs. of Mexico*, v. p. 480, Ternaux-Compans' *Recueil de pièces rel. à la Conq. du Mexique*, pp. 307, 310, and Gama, *Des. de las dos Piedras que se hallaron en la plaza principal de Mexico*, ii. sec. 126 (Mexico, 1832), who gives numerous instances beyond those I have cited, and directs with emphasis the attention of the reader to this constant repetition.

74-1 Albert Gallatin, *Trans. Am. Ethnol. Soc.*, ii. p. 316, from the Codex Vaticanus, No. 3738.

75-1 Riggs, *Gram. and Dict. of the Dakota Lang.*, s. v.

75-2 Sahagun, *Hist. de la Nueva España*, in Kingsborough, v. p. 375.

76-1 Egede, *Nachrichten von Grönland*, pp. 137, 173, 285. (Kopenhagen, 1790.)

77-1 Schoolcraft, *Algic Researches*, i. p. 139, and *Indian Tribes*, iv. p. 229.

78-1 Hawkins, *Sketch of the Creek Country*, pp. 81, 82, and Blomes, *Acc. of his Majesty's Colonies*, p. 156, London, 1687, in Castiglioni, *Viaggi nelle Stati Uniti*, i. p. 294.

78-2 Peter Martyr, *De Reb. Ocean.*, Dec. i. lib. ix. The story is also told more at length by the Brother Romain Pane, in the essay on the ancient histories of the natives he drew up by the order of Columbus. It has been reprinted with notes by the Abbé Brasseur, Paris, 1864, p. 438 sqq.

79-1 Schoolcraft, *Ind. Tribes*, iv. p. 89.

79-2 Brasseur, *Le Liv. Sac.*, Introd., p. cxvii.

80-1 Diego de Landa, *Rel. de las Cosas de Yucatan*, pp. 160, 206, 208, ed. Brasseur. The learned editor, in a note to p. 208, states erroneously the disposition of the colors, as may be seen by comparing the document on p. 395. This dedication of colors to the cardinal points is universal in Central Asia. The geographical names of the Red Sea, the Black Sea, the Yellow Sea or Persian Gulf, and the White Sea or the Mediterranean, are derived from this association. The cities of China, many of them at least, have their gates which open toward the cardinal points painted of certain colors, and precisely these four, the white, the black, the red, and the yellow, are those which in Oriental myth the mountain in the centre of Paradise shows to the different cardinal points. (Sepp, *Heidenthum und Christenthum*, i. p. 177.) The coincidence furnishes food for reflection.

81-1 *Le Livre Sacré des Quichés*, pp. 203-5, note.

82-1 The analogy is remarkable between these and the "quatre actes de la puissance generatrice jusqu'à l'entier developpément des corps organisés," portrayed by four globes in the Mycenean bas-reliefs. See Guigniaut, *Religions de l'Antiquité*, i. p. 374. It were easy to multiply the instances of such parallelism in the growth of religious thought in the Old and New World, but I designedly refrain from doing so. They have already given rise to false theories enough, and moreover my purpose in this work is not "comparative mythology."

83-1 Müller, *Amer. Urreligionen*, p. 105, after Strahlheim, who is, however, no authority.

83-2 Müller, *ubi supra*, pp. 308 sqq., gives a good résumé of the different versions of the myth of the four brothers in Peru.

83-3 The Tupis of Brazil claim a descent from four brothers, three of whose names are given by Hans Staden, a prisoner among them about 1550, as Krimen, Hermittan, and Coem; the latter he explains to mean the morning, the east (*le matin*, printed by mistake *le mutin*, *Relation de Hans Staden de Homberg*, p. 274, ed. Ternaux-Compans, compare Dias, *Dicc. da Lingua Tupy*, p. 47). Their southern relatives, the Guaranis of Paraguay, also spoke of the four brothers and gave two of their names as Tupi and Guarani, respectively parents of the tribes called after them (Guevara, *Hist. del Paraguay*, lib. i. cap. ii., in Waitz). The fourfold division of the Muyscas of Bogota was traced back to four chieftains created by their hero god Nemqueteba (A. von Humboldt, *Vues des Cordillères*, p. 246). The Nahuas of Mexico much more frequently spoke of themselves as descendants of four or eight original families than of seven (Humboldt, *ibid.*, p. 317, and others in Waitz, *Anthropologie*, iv. pp. 36, 37). The Sacs or Sauks of the Upper Mississippi supposed that two men and two women were first created, and from these four sprang all men (Morse, *Rep. on Ind. Affairs*, App. p. 138). The Ottoes, Pawnees, "and other Indians," had a tradition that from eight ancestors all nations and races were descended (Id., p. 249). This duplication of the number probably arose from assigning the first four men four women as wives. The division into clans or totems which prevails in most northern tribes rests theoretically on descent from different ancestors. The Shawnees and Natchez were divided into four such clans, the Choctaws, Navajos, and Iroquois into eight, thus proving that in those tribes also the myth I have been discussing was recognized.

85-1 Mandans in Catlin, *Letts. and Notes*, i. p. 181.

85-2 The Mayas, Cogolludo, *Hist. de Yucathan*, lib. iv. cap. 8.

85-3 The Navajos, Schoolcraft, *Ind. Tribes*, iv. p. 89.

85-4 The Quichés, Ximenes, *Or. de los Indios*, p. 79.

85-5 The Iroquois, Müller, *Amer. Urreligionen*, p. 109.

85-6 For these myths see Sepp, *Das Heidenthum und dessen Bedeutung für das Christenthum*, i. p. 111 sqq. The interpretation is of course my own.

87-1 Peter Martyr, *De Reb. Ocean.*, Dec. iii., lib. ix. p. 195; Colon, 1574.

87-2 Ibid., Dec. iii., lib. x. p. 202.

87-3 Florida was also long supposed to be the site of this wondrous spring, and it is notorious that both Juan Ponce de Leon and De Soto had some lurking hope of discovering it in their expeditions thither. I have examined the myth somewhat at length in *Notes on the Floridian Peninsula, its Literary History, Indian Tribes, and Antiquities*, pp. 99, 100: Philadelphia, 1859.

88-1 Sahagun, *Hist. de la Nueva España*, lib. iii. cap. iii.

88-2 *Le Livre Sacré des Quichés*, Introd., p. clviii.

89-1 Memorial de Tecpan Atitlan, in Brasseur, *Hist. du Mexique*, i. p. 167. The derivation of Tulan, or Tula, is extremely uncertain. The Abbé Brasseur sees in it the *ultima Thule* of the ancient geographers, which suits his idea of early American history. Hernando De Soto found a village of this name on the Mississippi, or near it. But on looking into Gallatin's vocabularies, *tulla* turns out to be the Choctaw word for *stone*, and as De Soto was then in the Choctaw country, the coincidence is explained at once. Buschmann, who spells it *Tollan*, takes it from *tolin*, a rush, and translates, *juncetum*, Ort der Binsen. Ueber die Aztekischen Orstnamen , p. 682. Those who have attempted to make history from these mythological fables have been much puzzled about the location of this mystic land. Humboldt has placed it on the northwest coast, Cabrera at Palenque, Clavigero north of Anahuac, etc. etc. Aztlan, literally, the White Land, is another name of wholly mythical purport, which it would be equally vain to seek on the terrestrial globe. In the extract in the text, the word translated God is *Qabavil*, an old word for the highest god, either from a root meaning to open, to disclose, or from one of similar form signifying to wonder, to marvel; literally, therefore, the Revealer, or the Wondrous One (*Vocab. de la Lengua Quiché*, p. 209: Paris, 1862).

90-1 Ximenes, *Or. de los Indios*, p. 80, *Le Livre Sacré*, p. 195.

90-2 Garcia, *Origen de los Indios*, lib. iv. cap. 4.

91-1 Compare the German expression *sich orientiren*, to right oneself by the east, to understand one's surroundings.

92-1 Hawkins, *Sketch of the Creek Country*, p. 80.

92-2 See Jacob Grimm, *Geschichte der Deutschen Sprache*, p. 681

92-3 De Smet, Oregon Missions, p. 352.

93-1 Bressani, *Relation Abrégé*, p. 93.

93-2 Venegas, *Hist. of California*, i. p. 91: London, 1759.

93-3 Cogolludo, *Hist. de Yucathan*, lib. iv. cap. iii.

93-4 Alexander von Humboldt has asserted that the Quichuas had other and very circumstantial terms to express the cardinal points drawn from the positions of the son (*Ansichten der Natur*, ii. p. 368). But the distinguished naturalist overlooked the literal meaning of the phrases he quotes for north and south, *intip chaututa chayananpata* and *intip chaupunchau chayananpata*, literally, the sun arriving toward the midnight, the sun arriving toward the midday. These are evidently translations of the Spanish *hacia la media noche, hacia el medio dia*, for they could not have originated among a people under or south of the equatorial line.

94-1 Catlin, *Letters and Notes*, i., Letter 22; La Hontan, *Mémoires*, ii. p. 151; Gumilla, *Hist. del Orinoco*, p. 159

96-1 On the worship of the cross in Mexico and Yucatan and its invariable meaning as representing the gods of rain, consult Ixtlilxochitl, *Hist. des Chichimeques*, p. 5; Sahagun, *Hist. de la Nueva España*, lib. i. cap. ii.; Garcia, *Or. de los Indios*, lib. iii. cap. vi. p. 109; Palacios, *Des. de la Prov. de Guatemala*, p. 29; Cogolludo, *Hist. de Yucathan*, lib. iv. cap. ix.; Villagutierre Sotomayor, *Hist. de el Itza y de el Lacandon*, lib. iii. cap. 8; and many others might be mentioned.

96-2 Rivero and Tschudi, *Peruvian Antiquities*, p. 162, after J. Acosta.

96-3 Loskiel, *Ges. der Miss. der evang. Brüder*, p. 60.

97-1 Hawkins, *Sketch of the Creek Country*, p. 75. Lapham and Pidgeon mention that in the State of Wisconsin many low mounds are found in the form of a cross with the arms directed to the cardinal points. They contain no remains. Were they not altars built to the Four Winds? In the mythology of the Dakotas, who inhabited that region, the winds were always conceived as birds, and for the cross they have a native name literally signifying "the musquito hawk spread out" (Riggs, *Dict. of the Dakota*, s. v.). Its Maya name is *vahom che*, the tree erected or set up, the adjective being drawn from the military language and implying as a defence or protection, as the warrior lifts his lance or shield (Landa, *Rel. de las Cosas de Yucatan*, p. 65).

97-2 Squier, *The Serpent Symbol in America*, p. 98.

CHAPTER IV
THE SYMBOLS OF THE BIRD
AND THE SERPENT

Relations of man to the lower animals. — Two of these, the Bird and the Serpent, chosen as symbols beyond all others. — The Bird throughout America the symbol of the Clouds and Winds. — Meaning of certain species. — The symbolic meaning of the Serpent derived from its mode of locomotion, its poisonous bite, and its power of charming. — Usually the symbol of the Lightning and the Waters. — The Rattlesnake the symbolic species in America. — The war charm. — The Cross of Palenque. — The god of riches. — Both symbols devoid of moral significance.

THOSE stories which the Germans call *Thierfabeln*, wherein the actors are different kinds of brutes, seem to have a particular relish for children and uncultivated nations. Who cannot recall with what delight he nourished his childish fancy on the pranks of Reynard the Fox, or the tragic adventures of Little Red Riding Hood and the Wolf? Every nation has a congeries of such tales, and it is curious to mark how the same animal reappears with the same imputed physiognomy in all of them. The fox is always cunning, the wolf ravenous, the owl wise, and the ass foolish. The question has been raised whether such traits were at first actually ascribed to animals, or whether their introduction in story was intended merely as an agreeable figure of speech for classes of men. We cannot doubt but that the former was the case. Going back to the dawn of civilization, we find these relations not as amusing fictions, but as myths, embodying religious tenets, and the brute heroes held up as the ancestors of mankind, even as rightful claimants of man's prayers and praises.

Man, the paragon of animals, praying to the beast, is a spectacle so humiliating that, for the sake of our common humanity, we may seek the explanation of it least degrading to the dignity of our race. We must remember that as a hunter the primitive man was always matched against the wild creatures of the woods, so superior to him in their dumb certainty of instinct, their swift motion, their muscular force, their permanent and sufficient clothing. Their ways were guided by a wit beyond his divination, and they gained a living with little toil or trouble. They did not mind the darkness so terrible to him, but through the night called one to the other in a tongue whose meaning he could not fathom, but which, he doubted not, was as full of purport as his own. He did not recognize in himself those god-like qualities destined to endow him with the royalty of the world, while far more clearly than we do he saw the sly and strange faculties of his antagonists. They were to him, therefore, not inferiors, but equals— even superiors. He doubted not that once upon a time he had possessed their instinct, they his language, but that some necromantic spell had been flung on them both to keep them asunder. None but a potent sorcerer could break this charm, but such an one could understand the chants of birds and the howls of savage beasts, and on occasion transform himself into one or another animal, and course the forest, the air, or the waters, as he saw fit. Therefore, it was not the beast that he worshipped, but that share of the omnipresent deity which he thought he perceived under its form. 101-1

Beyond all others, two subdivisions of the animal kingdom have so riveted the attention of men by their unusual powers, and enter so frequently into the myths of every nation of the globe, that a right understanding of their symbolic value is an essential preliminary to the discussion of the divine legends. They are the Bird and the Serpent. We shall not go amiss if we seek the reasons of their pre-eminence in the facility with which their peculiarities offered sensuous images under which to convey the idea of divinity, ever present in the soul of man, ever striving at articulate expression.

The bird has the incomprehensible power of flight; it floats in the atmosphere, it rides on the winds, it soars toward heaven where dwell the gods; its plumage is stained with the hues of the rainbow and the sunset; its song was man's first hint of music; it spurns the clods that impede his footsteps, and flies proudly over the mountains and moors where he toils wearily along. He sees no more enviable creature; he conceives the gods and angels must also have wings; and pleases himself with the fancy that he, too, some day will shake off this coil of clay, and rise on pinions to the heavenly mansions. All living beings, say the Eskimos, have the faculty of soul (*tarrak*), but especially the birds. 101-2 As messengers from the upper world and interpreters of its decrees, the flight and the note of birds have ever been anxiously observed as omens of grave import. "There is one bird especially," remarks the traveller Coreal, of the natives of Brazil, "which they regard as of good augury. Its mournful chant is heard rather by night than day. The savages say it is sent by their deceased friends to bring them news from the other world, and to encourage them against their enemies." 102-1 In Peru and in Mexico there was a College of Augurs, corresponding in purpose to the auspices of ancient Rome, who practised no other means of divination than watching the course and professing to interpret the songs of fowls. So natural and so general is such a superstition, and so widespread is the respect it still obtains in civilized and Christian lands, that it is not worth while to summon witnesses to show that it prevailed universally among the red race also. What imprinted it with redoubled force on their imagination was the common belief that birds were not only divine nuncios, but the visible spirits of their departed friends. The Powhatans held that a certain small wood bird received the souls of their princes at death, and they refrained religiously from doing it harm; 102-2 while the Aztecs and various other nations thought that all good people, as a reward of merit, were metamorphosed at the close of life into feathered songsters of the grove, and in this form passed a certain term in the umbrageous bowers of Paradise.

But the usual meaning of the bird as a symbol looks to a different analogy—to that which appears in such familiar expressions as "the wings of the wind," "the flying clouds." Like the wind, the bird sweeps through the aerial spaces, sings in the forests, and rustles on its course; like the cloud, it floats in mid-air and casts its shadow on the earth; like the lightning, it darts from heaven to earth to strike its unsuspecting prey. These tropes were truths to savage nations, and led on by that law of language which forced them to conceive everything as animate or inanimate, itself the product of a deeper law of thought which urges us to ascribe life to whatever has motion, they found no animal so appropriate for their purpose here as the bird. Therefore the Algonkins say that birds always make the winds, that they create the water spouts, and that the clouds are the spreading and agitation of their wings; 103-1 the Navajos, that at each cardinal point stands a white swan, who is the spirit of the blasts which blow from its dwelling; and the Dakotas, that in the west is the house of the Wakinyan, the Flyers, the breezes that send the storms. So, also, they frequently explain the thunder as the sound of the cloud-bird flapping his wings, and the lightning as the fire that flashes from his tracks, like the sparks which the buffalo scatters when he scours over a stony plain. 103-2 The thunder cloud was also a bird to the Caribs, and they imagined it produced the lightning in true Carib fashion by blowing it through a hollow reed, just as they to this day hurl their poisoned darts. 104-1 Tupis, Iroquois, Athapascas, for certain, perhaps all the families of the red race, were the subject pursued, partook of this persuasion; among them all it would probably be found that the same figures of speech were used in comparing clouds and winds with the feathered species as among us, with however this most significant difference, that whereas among us they are figures and nothing more, to them they expressed literal facts.

How important a symbol did they thus become! For the winds, the clouds, producing the thunder and the changes that take place in the ever-shifting panorama of the sky, the rain bringers, lords of the seasons, and not this only, but the primary type of the soul, the life, the breath of man and the world, these in their role in mythology are second to nothing. Therefore as the symbol of these august powers, as messenger of the gods, and as the embodiment of departed spirits, no one will be surprised if they find the bird figure most prominently in the myths of the red race.

Sometimes some particular species seems to have been chosen as most befitting these dignified attributes. No citizen of the United States will be apt to assert that their instinct led the indigenes of our territory astray when they chose with nigh unanimous consent the great American eagle as that fowl beyond all others proper to typify the supreme control and the most admirable qualities. Its feathers composed the war flag of the Creeks, and its images carved in wood or its stuffed skin surmounted their council lodges (Bartram); none but an approved warrior dare wear it among the Cherokees (Timberlake); and the Dakotas allowed such an honor only to him who had first touched the corpse of the common foe (De Smet). The Natchez and Akanzas seem to have paid it even religious honors, and to have installed it in their most sacred shrines (Sieur de Tonty, Du Pratz); and very clearly it was not so much for ornament as for a mark of dignity and a recognized sign of worth that its plumes were so highly prized. The natives of Zuñi, in New Mexico, employed four of its feathers to represent the four winds in their invocations for rain (Whipple), and probably it was the eagle which a tribe in Upper California (the Acagchemem) worshipped under the name Panes. Father Geronimo Boscana describes it as a species of vulture, and relates that one of them was immolated yearly, with solemn ceremony, in the temple of each village. Not a drop of blood was spilled, and the body burned. Yet with an amount of faith that staggered even the Romanist, the natives maintained and believed that it was the same individual bird they sacrificed each year; more than this, that the same bird was slain by each of the villages! 105-1

The owl was regarded by Aztecs, Quichés, Mayas, Peruvians, Araucanians, and Algonkins as sacred to the lord of the dead. "The Owl" was one of the names of the Mexican Pluto, whose realm was in the north, 106-1 and the wind from that quarter was supposed by the Chipeways to be made by the owl as the south by the butterfly. 106-2 As the bird of night, it was the fit emissary of him who rules the darkness of the grave. Something in the looks of the creature as it sapiently stares and blinks in the light, or perhaps that it works while others sleep, got for it the character of wisdom. So the Creek priests carried with them as the badge of their learned profession the stuffed skin of one of these birds, thus modestly hinting their erudite turn of mind, 106-3 and the culture hero of the Monquis of California was represented, like Pallas Athene, having one as his inseparable companion (Venegas).

As the associate of the god of light and air, and as the antithesis therefore of the owl, the Aztecs reverenced a bird called *quetzal*, which I believe is a species of parroquet. Its plumage is of a bright green hue, and was prized extravagantly as a decoration. It was one of the symbols and part of the name of Quetzalcoatl, their mythical civilizer, and the prince of all sorts of singing birds, myriads of whom were fabled to accompany him on his journeys.

The tender and hallowed associations that have so widely shielded the dove from harm, which for instance Xenophon mentions among the ancient Persians, were not altogether unknown to the tribes of the New World. Neither the Hurons nor Mandans would kill them, for they believed they were inhabited by the souls of the departed, 107-1 and it is said, but on less satisfactory authority, that they enjoyed similar immunity among the Mexicans. Their soft and plaintive note and sober russet hue widely enlisted the sympathy of man, and linked them with his more tender feelings.

"As wise as the serpent, as harmless as the dove," is an antithesis that might pass current in any human language. They are the emblems of complementary, often contrasted qualities. Of all animals, the serpent is the most mysterious. No wonder it possessed the fancy of the observant child of nature. Alone of creatures it swiftly progresses without feet, fins, or wings. "There be three things which are too wonderful for me, yea, four which I know not," said wise King Solomon; and the chief of them were, "the way of an eagle in the air, the way of a serpent upon a rock."

Its sinuous course is like to nothing so much as that of a winding river, which therefore we often call serpentine. So did the Indians. Kennebec, a stream in Maine, in the Algonkin means snake, and Antietam, the creek in Maryland of tragic celebrity, in an Iroquois dialect has the same significance. How easily would savages, construing the figure literally, make the serpent a river or water god! Many species being amphibious would confirm the idea. A lake watered by innumerable tortuous rills wriggling into it, is well calculated for the fabled abode of the king of the snakes. Thus doubtless it happened that both Algonkins and Iroquois had a myth that in the great lakes dwelt a monster serpent, of irascible temper, who unless appeased by meet offerings raised a tempest or broke the ice beneath the feet of those venturing on his domain, and swallowed them down. 108-1

The rattlesnake was the species almost exclusively honored by the red race. It is slow to attack, but venomous in the extreme, and possesses the power of the basilisk to attract within reach of its spring small birds and squirrels. Probably this much talked of fascination is nothing more than by its presence near their nests to incite them to attack, and to hazard near and nearer approaches to their enemy in hope to force him to retreat, until once within the compass of his fell swoop they fall victims to their temerity. I have often watched a cat act thus. Whatever explanation may be received, the fact cannot be questioned, and is ever attributed by the unreflecting, to some diabolic spell cast upon them by the animal. They have the same strange susceptibility to the influence of certain sounds as the vipers, in which lies the secret of snake charming. Most of the Indian magicians were familiar with this singularity. They employed it with telling effect to put beyond question their intercourse with the unseen powers, and to vindicate the potency of their own guardian spirits who thus enabled them to handle with impunity the most venomous of reptiles. 109-1 . The well-known antipathy of these serpents to certain plants, for instance the hazel, which bound around the ankles is an efficient protection against their attacks, and perhaps some antidote to their poison used by the magicians, led to their frequent introduction in religious ceremonies. Such exhibitions must have made a profound impression on the spectators, and redounded in a corresponding degree to the glory of the performer. "Who is a manito?" asks the mystic meda chant of the Algonkins. "He," is the reply, "he who walketh with a serpent, walking on the ground, he is a manito." 109-2 And the intimate alliance of this symbol with the most sacred mysteries of religion, the darkest riddles of the Unknown, is reflected in their language, and also in that of their neighbors the Dakotas, in both of which the same words *manito*, *wakan*, which express divinity in its broadest sense, are also used as generic terms signifying this species of animals! This strange fact is not without a parallel, for in both Arabic and Hebrew, the word for serpent has many derivatives, meaning to have intercourse with demoniac powers, to practise magic, and to consult familiar spirits. 110-1

The pious founder of the Moravian brotherhood, the Count of Zinzendorf, owed his life on one occasion to this deeply rooted superstition. He was visiting a missionary station among the Shawnees, in the Wyoming valley. Recent quarrels with the whites had unusually irritated this unruly folk, and they resolved to make him their first victim. After he had retired to his secluded hut, several of their braves crept upon him, and cautiously lifting the corner of the lodge, peered in. The venerable man was seated before a little fire, a volume of the Scriptures on his knees, lost in the perusal of the sacred words. While they gazed, a huge rattlesnake, unnoticed by him, trailed across his feet, and rolled itself into a coil in the comfortable warmth of the fire. Immediately the would-be murderers forsook their purpose and noiselessly retired, convinced that this was indeed a man of God.

A more unique trait than any of these is its habit of casting its skin every spring, thus as it were renewing its life. In temperate latitudes the rattlesnake, like the leaves and flowers, retires from sight during the cold season, and at the return of kindly warmth puts on a new and brilliant coat. Its cast-off skin was carefully collected by the savages and stored in the medicine bag as possessing remedial powers of high excellence. Itself thus immortal, they thought it could impart its vitality to them. So when the mother was travailing in sore pain, and the danger neared that the child would be born silent, the attending women hastened to catch some serpent and give her its blood to drink. 111-1

It is well known that in ancient art this animal was the symbol of Æsculapius, and to this day, Professor Agassiz found that the Maues Indians, who live between the upper Tapajos and Madeira Rivers in Brazil, whenever they assign a form to any "remedio," give it that of a serpent. 111-2

Probably this notion that it was annually rejuvenated led to its adoption as a symbol of Time among the Aztecs; or, perchance, as they reckoned by suns, and the figure of the sun, a circle, corresponds to nothing animate but a serpent with its tail in its mouth, eating itself, as it were, this may have been its origin. Either of them is more likely than that the symbol arose from the recondite reflection that time is "never ending, still beginning, still creating, still destroying," as has been suggested.

Only, however, within the last few years has the significance of the serpent symbol in its length and breadth been satisfactorily explained, and its frequent recurrence accounted for. By a searching analysis of Greek and German mythology, Dr. Schwarz, of Berlin, has shown that the meaning which is paramount to all others in this emblem is *the lightning*; a meaning drawn from the close analogy which the serpent in its motion, its quick spring, and mortal bite, has to the zigzag course, the rapid flash, and sudden stroke of the electric discharge. He even goes so far as to imagine that by this resemblance the serpent first acquired the veneration of men. But this is an extravagance not supported by more thorough research. He has further shown with great aptness of illustration how, by its dread effects, the lightning, the heavenly serpent, became the god of terror and the opponent of such heroes as Beowulf, St. George, Thor, Perseus, and others, mythical representations of the fearful war of the elements in the thunder storm; how from its connection with the advancing summer and fertilizing showers it bore the opposite character of the deity of fruitfulness, riches, and plenty; how, as occasionally kindling the woods where it strikes, it was associated with the myths of the descent of fire from heaven, and as in popular imagination where it falls it scatters the thunderbolts in all directions, the flint-stones which flash when struck were supposed to be these fragments, and gave rise to the stone worship so frequent in the old world; and how, finally, the prevalent myth of a king of serpents crowned with a glittering stone or wearing a horn is but another type of the lightning. 113-1 Without accepting unreservedly all these conclusions, I shall show how correct they are in the main when applied to the myths of the New World, and thereby illustrate how the red race is of one blood and one faith with our own remote ancestors in heathen Europe and Central Asia.

It asks no elaborate effort of the imagination to liken the lightning to a serpent. It does not require any remarkable acuteness to guess the conundrum of Schiller: —

"Unter allen Schlangen ist eine
Auf Erden nicht gezeugt,
Mit der an Schnelle keine,
An Wuth sich keine vergleicht."

When Father Buteux was a missionary among the Algonkins, in 1637, he asked them their opinion of the nature of lightning. "It is an immense serpent," they replied, "which the Manito is vomiting forth; you can see the twists and folds that he leaves on the trees which he strikes; and underneath such trees we have often found huge snakes." "Here is a novel philosophy for you!" exclaims the Father. 113-2 So the Shawnees called the thunder "the hissing of the great snake;" 113-3 and Tlaloc, the Toltec thunder god, held in his hand a serpent of gold to represent the lightning. 114-1 For this reason the Caribs spoke of the god of the thunder storm as a great serpent dwelling in the fruit forests, 114-2 and in the Quiché legends other names for Hurakan, the hurricane or thunder-storm, are the Strong Serpent, He who hurls below, referring to the lightning. 114-3

Among the Hurons, in 1648, the Jesuits found a legend current that there existed somewhere a monster serpent called Onniont, who wore on his head a horn that pierced rocks, trees, hills, in short everything he encountered. Whoever could get a piece of this horn was a fortunate man, for it was a sovereign charm and bringer of good luck. The Hurons confessed that none of them had had the good hap to find the monster and break his horn, nor indeed had they any idea of his whereabouts; but their neighbors, the Algonkins, furnished them at times small fragments for a large consideration. 114-4 Clearly the myth had been taught them for venal purposes by their trafficking visitors. Now among the Algonkins, the Shawnee tribe did more than all others combined to introduce and carry about religious legends and ceremonies. From the earliest times they seem to have had peculiar aptitude for the ecstasies, deceits, and fancies that made up the spiritual life of their associates. Their constantly roving life brought them in contact with the myths of many nations. And it is extremely probable that they first brought the tale of the horned serpent from the Creeks and Cherokees. It figured extensively in the legends of both these tribes.

The latter related that once upon a time among the glens of their mountains dwelt the prince of rattlesnakes. Obedient subjects guarded his palace, and on his head glittered in place of a crown a gem of marvellous magic virtues. Many warriors and magicians tried to get possession of this precious talisman, but were destroyed by the poisoned fangs of its defenders. Finally, one more inventive than the rest hit upon the bright idea of encasing himself in leather, and by this device marched unharmed through the hissing and snapping court, tore off the shining jewel, and bore it in triumph to his nation. They preserved it with religious care, brought it forth on state occasions with solemn ceremony, and about the middle of the last century, when Captain Timberlake penetrated to their towns, told him its origin. 115-1

The charm which the Creeks presented their young men when they set out on the war path was of very similar character. It was composed of the bones of the panther and the horn of the fabulous horned snake. According to a legend taken down by an unimpeachable authority toward the close of the last century, the great snake dwelt in the waters; the old people went to the brink and sang the sacred songs. The monster rose to the surface. The sages recommenced the mystic chants. He rose a little out o the water. Again they repeated the songs. This time he showed his horns and they cut one off. Still a fourth time did they sing, and as he rose to listen cut off the remaining horn. A fragment of these in the "war physic" protected from inimical arrows and gave success in the conflict. 116-1

In these myths, which attribute good fortune to the horn of the snake, that horn which pierces trees and rocks, which rises from the waters, which glitters as a gem, which descends from the ravines of the mountains, we shall not overstep the bounds of prudent reasoning if we see the thunderbolt, sign of the fructifying rain, symbol of the strength of the lightning, horn of the heavenly serpent. They are strictly meteorological in their meaning. And when in later Algonkin tradition the hero Michabo appears in conflict with the shining prince of serpents who lives in the lake and floods the earth with its waters, and destroys the reptile with a dart, and further when the conqueror clothes himself with the skin of his foe and drives the rest of the serpents to the south where in that latitude the lightnings are last seen in the autumn; 116-2 or when in the traditional history of the Iroquois we hear of another great horned serpent rising out of the lake and preying upon the people until a similar hero-god destroys it with a thunderbolt, 116-3 we cannot be wrong in rejecting any historical or ethical interpretation, and in construing them as allegories which at first represented the atmospheric changes which accompany the advancing seasons and the ripening harvests. They are narratives conveying under agreeable personifications the tidings of that unending combat which the Dakotas said was being waged with varying fortunes by Unktahe against Wauhkeon, the God of Waters against the Thunder Bird. 117-1 They are the same stories which in the old world have been elaborated into the struggles of Ormuzd and Ahriman, of Thor and Midgard, of St. George and the Dragon, and a thousand others.

Yet it were but a narrow theory of natural religion that allowed no other meaning to these myths. Many another elemental warfare is being waged around us, and applications as various as nature herself lie in these primitive creations of the human fancy. Let it only be remembered that there was never any moral, never any historical purport in them in the infancy of religious life.

In snake charming as a proof of proficiency in magic, and in the symbol of the lightning, which brings both fire and water, which in its might controls victory in war, and in its frequency, plenteous crops at home, lies the secret of the serpent symbol. As the "war physic" among the tribes of the United States was a fragment of a serpent, and as thus signifying his incomparable skill in war, the Iroquois represent their mythical king Atatarho clothed in nothing but black snakes; so that when he wished to don a new suit he simply drove away one set and ordered another to take their places, 118-1 so, by a precisely similar mental process, the myth of the Nahuas assigns as a mother to their war god Huitzilapochtli, Coatlicue, the robe of serpents; her dwelling place Coatepec, the hill of serpents; and at her lying-in say that she brought forth a serpent. Her son's image was surrounded by serpents, his sceptre was in the shape of one, his great drum was of serpents' skins, and his statue rested on four vermiform caryatides.

As the symbol of the fertilizing summer showers the lightning serpent was the god of fruitfulness. Born in the atmospheric waters, it was an appropriate attribute of the ruler of the winds. But we have already seen that the winds were often spoken of as great birds. Hence the union of these two emblems in such names as Quetzalcoatl, Gucumatz, Kukulkan, all titles of the god of the air in the languages of Central America, all signifying the "Bird-serpent." Here also we see the solution of that monument which has so puzzled American antiquaries, the cross at Palenque. It is a tablet on the wall of an altar representing a cross surmounted by a bird and supported by the head of a serpent. The latter is not well defined in the plate in Mr. Stephens' Travels, but is very distinct in the photographs taken by M. Charnay, which that gentleman was kind enough to show me. The cross I have previously shown was the symbol of the four winds, and the bird and serpent are simply the rebus of the air god, their ruler. 119-1 Quetzalcoatl, called also Yolcuat, the rattlesnake, was no less intimately associated with serpents than with birds. The entrance to his temple at Mexico represented the jaws of one of these reptiles, and he finally disappeared in the province of Coatzacoalco, the hiding place of the serpent, sailing towards the east in a bark of serpents' skins. All this refers to his power over the lightning serpent.

He was also said to be the god of riches and the patron consequently of merchants. For with the summer lightning come the harvest and the ripening fruits, come riches and traffic. Moreover "the golden color of the liquid fire," as Lucretius expresses it, naturally led where this metal was known, to its being deemed the product of the lightning. Thus originated many of those tales of a dragon who watches a treasure in the earth, and of a serpent who is the dispenser of riches, such as were found among the Greeks and ancient Germans. 119-2 So it was in Peru where the god of riches was worshipped under the image of a rattlesnake horned and hairy, with a tail of gold. It was said to have descended from the heavens in the sight of all the people, and to have been seen by the whole army of the Inca. 119-3 Whether it was in reference to it, or as emblems of their prowess, that the Incas themselves chose as their arms two serpents with their tails interlaced, is uncertain; possibly one for each of these significations.

Because the rattlesnake, the lightning serpent, is thus connected with the food of man, and itself seems never to die but annually to renew its youth, the Algonkins called it "grandfather" and "king of snakes;" they feared to injure it; they believed it could grant prosperous breezes, or raise disastrous tempests; crowned with the lunar crescent it was the constant symbol of life in their picture writing; and in the meda signs the mythical grandmother of mankind *me suk kum me go kwa* was indifferently represented by an old woman or a serpent. 120-1 For like reasons Cihuacoatl, the Serpent Woman, in the myths of the Nahuas was also called Tonantzin, our mother. 120-2

The serpent symbol in America has, however, been brought into undue prominence. It had such an ominous significance in Christian art, and one which chimed so well with the favorite proverb of the early missionaries — "the gods of the heathens are devils" — that wherever they saw a carving or picture of a serpent they at once recognized the sign manual of the Prince of Darkness, and inscribed the fact in their note-books as proof positive of their cherished theory. After going over the whole ground, I am convinced that none of the tribes of the red race attached to this symbol any ethical significance whatever, and that as employed to express atmospheric phenomena, and the recognition of divinity in natural occurrences, it far more frequently typified what was favorable and agreeable than the reverse.

FOOTNOTE:

101-1 That these were the real views entertained by the Indians in regard to the brute creation, see Heckewelder, *Acc. of the Ind. Nations*, p. 247; Schoolcraft, *Ind. Tribes*, iii. p. 520.

101-2 Egede, *Nachrichten von Grönland*, p. 156.

102-1 *Voiages aux Indes Occidentales*, pt. ii. p. 203: Amst. 1722.

102-2 Beverly, *Hist. de la Virginie*, liv. iii. chap. viii.

103-1 Schoolcraft, *Ind. Tribes*, v. p. 420.

103-2 Mrs. Eastman, *Legends of the Sioux*, p. 191: New York, 1849. This is a trustworthy and meritorious book, which can be said of very few collections of Indian traditions. They were collected during a residence of seven years in our northwestern territories, and are usually verbally faithful to the native narrations.

104-1 Müller, *Amer. Urreligionen*, p. 222, after De la Borde.

105-1 *Acc. of the Inds. of California*, ch. ix. Eng. trans. by Robinson: New York, 1847. The Acagchemem were a branch of the Netela tribe, who dwelt near the mission San Juan

Capistrano (see Buschmann, *Spuren der Aztek. Sprache*, etc., p. 548).

106-1 Called in the Aztec tongue *Tecolotl*, night owl; literally, the stone scorpion. The transfer was mythological. The Christians prefixed to this word *tlaca*, man, and thus formed a name for Satan, which Prescott and others have translated "rational owl." No such deity existed in ancient Anahuac (see Buschmann, *Die Voelker und Sprachen Neu Mexico's*, p. 262).

106-2 Schoolcraft, *Ind. Tribes*, v. p. 420.

106-3 William Bartram, Travels, p. 504. Columbus found the natives of the Antilles wearing tunics with figures of these birds embroidered upon them. Prescott, *Conq. of Mexico*, i. p. 58, note.

107-1 *Rel. de la Nouv. France*, An 1636, ch. ix. Catlin, *Letters and notes*, Lett. 22.

108-1 *Rel. de la Nouv. France*, An 1648, p. 75; Cusic, *Trad. Hist. of the Six Nations*, pt. iii. The latter is the work of a native Tuscarora chief. It is republished in Schoolcraft's Indian Tribes, but is of little value.

109-1 For example, in Brazil, Müller, *Amer. Urrelig.*, p. 277; in Yucatan, Cogolludo, *Hist. de Yucathan*, lib. iv. cap. 4; among the western Algonkins, *Hennepin, Decouverte dans l'Amer. Septen.* chap. 33. Dr. Hammond has expressed the opinion that the North American Indians enjoy the same immunity from the virus of the rattlesnake, that certain African tribes do from some vegetable poisons (*Hygiene*, p. 73). But his observation must be at fault, for many travellers mention the dread these serpents inspired, and the frequency of death from their bites, e. g. *Rel. Nouv. France*. 1667, p. 22.

109-2 *Narrative of the Captivity and Adventures of John Tanner*, p. 356.

110-1 See Gallatin's vocabularies in the second volume of the *Trans. Am. Antiq. Soc.* under the word *Snake*. In Arabic *dzann* is serpent; *dzanan* a spirit, a soul, or the heart. So in Hebrew *nachas*, serpent, has many derivatives signifying to hold intercourse with demons, to conjure, a magician, etc. See Noldeke in the *Zeitschrift für Voelkerpsychologie und Sprachwissenschaft*, i. p. 413.

111-1 Alexander Henry, *Travels*, p. 117.

111-2 *Bost. Med. and Surg. Journal*, vol. 76, p. 21.

113-1 Schwarz, *Der Ursprung der Mythologie dargelegt an Griechischer und Deutscher Sage*: Berlin, 1860, *passim*.

113-2 *Rel. de la Nouv. France*: An 1637, p. 53.

113-3 *Sagen der Nord-Amer. Indianer*, p. 21. This is a German translation of part of Jones's *Legends of the N. Am. Inds.*: London, 1820. Their value as mythological material is very small.

114-1 Torquemada, *Monarquia Indiana*, lib. vi. cap. 37.

114-2 Müller, *Amer. Urrelig.*, 221, after De la Borde.

114-3 *Le Livre Sacré des Quichés*, p. 3.

114-4 *Rel. de la Nouv. France*, 1648, p. 75.

115-1 *Memoirs of Lieut. Henry Timberlake*, p. 48: London, 1765. This little book gives an account of the Cherokees at an earlier date than is elsewhere found.

116-1 Hawkins, *Sketch of the Creek Country*, p. 80.

116-2 Schoolcraft, *Algic Researches*, i. p. 179 sq.; compare ii. p. 117.

116-3 Morgan, *League of the Iroquois*, p. 159; Cusic, *Trad. Hist. of the Six Nations*, pt. ii.

117-1 Mrs. Eastman, *Legends of the Sioux*, pp. 161, 212. In this explanation I depart from Prof. Schwarz, who has collected various legends almost identical with these of the Indians (with which he was not acquainted), and interpreted the precious crown or horn to be the summer sun, brought forth by the early vernal lightning. *Ursprung der Mythologie*, p. 27, note.

118-1 Cusic, u. s., pt. ii.

119-1 This remarkable relic has been the subject of a long and able article in the *Revue Américaine* (tom. ii. p. 69), by the venerable traveller De Waldeck. Like myself—and I had not seen his opinion until after the above was written—he explains the cruciform design as indicating the four cardinal points, but offers the explanation merely as a suggestion, and without referring to these symbols as they appear in so many other connections.

119-2 Schwarz, *Ursprung der Mythologie*, pp. 62 sqq.

119-3 "I have examined many Indians in reference to these details," says the narrator, an Augustin monk writing in 1554, "and they have all confirmed them as eye-witnesses" (*Lettre sur les Superstitions du Pérou*, p. 106, ed. Ternaux-Compans. This document is very valuable).

120-1 *Narrative of John Tanner*, p. 355; Henry, *Travels*, p. 176.

120-2 Torquemada, *Monarquia Indiana*, lib. vi. cap. 31.

CHAPTER V
THE MYTHS OF WATER, FIRE, AND THE THUNDER-STORM

Water the oldest element.—Its use in purification.—Holy water.—The Rite of Baptism.—The Water of Life.—Its symbols.—The Vase.—The Moon.—The latter the goddess of love and agriculture, but also of sickness, night, and pain.—Often represented by a dog.—Fire worship under the form of Sun worship.—The perpetual fire.—The new fire—Burning the dead.—A worship of the passions, but no sexual dualism in myths, nor any phallic worship in America.—Synthesis of the worship of Fire, Water, and the Winds in the Thunder-storm, personified as Haokah, Tupa, Catequil, Contici, Heno, Tlaloc, Mixcoatl, and other deities, many of them triune.

THE primitive man was a brute in everything but the susceptibility to culture; the chief market of his time was to sleep, fight, and feed; his bodily comfort alone had any importance in his eyes; and his gods were nothing, unless they touched him here. Cold, hunger, thirst, these were the hounds that were ever on his track; these were the fell powers he saw constantly snatching away his fellows, constantly aiming their invisible shafts at himself. Fire, food, and water were the gods that fought on his side; they were the chief figures in his pantheon, his kindliest, perhaps his earliest, divinities.

With a nearly unanimous voice mythologies assign the priority to water. It was the first of all things, the parent of all things. Even the gods themselves were born of water, said the Greeks and the Aztecs. Cosmogonies reach no further than the primeval ocean that rolled its shoreless waves through a timeless night.

"Omnia pontus erant, deerant quoque litora ponto."

Earth, sun, stars, lay concealed in its fathomless abysses. "All of us," ran the Mexican baptismal formula, "are children of Chalchihuitlycue, Goddess of Water," and the like was said by the Peruvians of Mama Cocha, by the Botocudos of Taru, by the natives of Darien of Dobayba, by the Iroquois of Ataensic—all of them mothers of mankind, all personifications of water.

How account for such unanimity? Not by supposing some ancient intercourse between remote tribes, but by the uses of water as the originator and supporter, the essential prerequisite of life. Leaving aside the analogy presented by the motherly waters which nourish the unborn child, nor emphasizing how indispensable it is as a beverage, the many offices this element performs in nature lead easily to the supposition that it must have preceded all else. By quenching thirst, it quickens life; as the dew and the rain it feeds the plant, and when withheld the seed perishes in the ground and forests and flowers alike wither away; as the fountain, the river, and the lake, it enriches the valley, offers safe retreats, and provides store of fishes; as the ocean, it presents the most fitting type of the infinite. It cleanses, it purifies; it produces, it preserves. "Bodies, unless dissolved, cannot act," is a maxim of the earliest chemistry. Very plausibly, therefore, was it assumed as the source of all things.

The adoration of streams, springs, and lakes, or rather of the spirits their rulers, prevailed everywhere; sometimes avowedly because they provided food, as was the case with the Moxos, who called themselves children of the lake or river on which their village was, and were afraid to migrate lest their parent should be vexed; 124-1 sometimes because they were the means of irrigation, as in Peru, or on more general mythical grounds. A grove by a fountain is in all nature worship the ready-made shrine of the sylphs who live in its limpid waves and chatter mysteriously in its shallows. On such a spot in our Gulf States one rarely fails to find the sacrificial mound of the ancient inhabitants, and on such the natives of Central America were wont to erect their altars (Ximenes). Lakes are the natural centres of civilization. Like the lacustrine villages which the Swiss erected in ante-historic times, like ancient Venice, the city of Mexico was first built on piles in a lake, and for the same reason — protection from attack. Security once obtained, growth and power followed. Thus we can trace the earliest rays of Aztec civilization rising from lake Tezcuco, of the Peruvian from Lake Titicaca, of the Muyscas from Lake Guatavita. These are the centres of legendary cycles. Their waters were hallowed by venerable reminiscences. From the depths of Titicaca rose Viracocha, mythical civilizer of Peru. Guatavita was the bourne of many a foot-sore pilgrim in the ancient empire of the Zac. Once a year the high priest poured the collective offerings of the multitude into its waves, and anointed with oils and glittering with gold dust, dived deep in its midst, professing to hold communion with the goddess who there had her home. 125-1

Not only does the life of man but his well-being depends on water. As an ablution it invigorates him bodily and mentally. No institution was in higher honor among the North American Indians than the sweat-bath followed by the cold douche. It was popular not only as a remedy in every and any disease, but as a preliminary to a council or an important transaction. Its real value in cold climates is proven by the sustained fondness for the Russian bath in the north of Europe. The Indians, however, with their usual superstition attributed its good effects to some mysterious healing power in water itself. Therefore, when the patient was not able to undergo the usual process, or when his medical attendant was above the vulgar and routine practice of his profession, it was administered on the infinitesimal system. The quack muttered a formula over a gourd filled from a neighboring spring and sprinkled it on his patient, or washed the diseased part, or sucked out the evil spirit and blew it into a bowl of water, and then scattered the liquid on the fire or earth. 125-2

The use of such "holy water" astonished the Romanist missionaries, and they at once detected Satan parodying the Scriptures. But their astonishment rose to horror when they discovered among various nations a rite of baptism of appalling similarity to their own, connected with the imposing of a name, done avowedly for the purpose of freeing from inherent sin, believed to produce a regeneration of the spiritual nature, nay, in more than one instance called by an indigenous word signifying "to be born again." 126-1 Such a rite was of immemorial antiquity among the Cherokees, Aztecs, Mayas, and Peruvians. Had the missionaries remembered that it was practised in Asia with all these meanings long before it was chosen as the sign of the new covenant, they need have invoked neither Satan nor Saint Thomas to explain its presence in America.

As corporeal is near akin to spiritual pollution, and cleanliness to godliness, ablution preparatory to engaging in religious acts came early to have an emblematic as well as a real significance. The water freed the soul from sin as it did the skin from stain. We should come to God with clean hands and a clean heart. As Pilate washed his hands before the multitude to indicate that he would not accept the moral responsibility of their acts, so from a similar motive a Natchez chief, who had been persuaded against his sense of duty not to sacrifice himself on the pyre of his ruler, took clean water, washed his hands, and threw it upon live coals. 126-2 When an ancient Peruvian had laid bare his guilt by confession, he bathed himself in a neighboring river and repeated this formula: —

"O thou River, receive the sins I have this day confessed unto the Sun, carry them down to the sea, and let them never more appear." 127-1

The Navajo who has been deputed to carry a dead body to burial, holds himself unclean until he has thoroughly washed himself in water prepared for the purpose by certain ceremonies. 127-2 A bath was an indispensable step in the mysteries of Mithras, the initiation at Eleusis, the meda worship of the Algonkins, the Busk of the Creeks, the ceremonials of religion everywhere. Baptism was at first always immersion. It was a bath meant to solemnize the reception of the child into the guild of mankind, drawn from the prior custom of ablution at any solemn occasion. In both the object is greater purity, bodily and spiritual. As certainly as there is a law of conscience, as certainly as our actions fall short of our volitions, so certainly is man painfully aware of various imperfections and shortcomings. What he feels he attributes to the infant. Avowedly to free themselves from this sense of guilt the Delawares used an emetic (Loskiel), the Cherokees a potion cooked up by an order of female warriors (Timberlake), the Takahlies of Washington Territory, the Aztecs, Mayas, and Peruvians, auricular confession. Formulize these feelings and we have the dogmas of "original sin," and of "spiritual regeneration." The order of baptism among the Aztecs commenced, "O child, receive the water of the Lord of the world, which is our life; it is to wash and to purify; may these drops remove the sin which was given to thee before the creation of the world, since all of us are under its power;" and concluded, "Now he liveth anew and is born anew, now is he purified and cleansed, now our mother the Water again bringeth him into the world." 128-1

A name was then assigned to the child, usually that of some ancestor, who it was supposed would thus be induced to exercise a kindly supervision over the little one's future. In after life should the person desire admittance to a superior class of the population and had the wealth to purchase it — for here as in more enlightened lands nobility was a matter of money — he underwent a second baptism and received another name, but still ostensibly from the goddess of water. 128-2

In Peru the child was immersed in the fluid, the priest exorcised the evil and bade it enter the water, which was then buried in the ground. 128-3 In either country sprinkling could take the place of immersion. The Cherokees believe that unless the rite is punctually performed when the child is three days old, it will inevitably die. 128-4

As thus curative and preservative, it was imagined that there was water of which whoever should drink would not die, but live forever. I have already alluded to the Fountain of Youth, supposed long before Columbus saw the surf of San Salvador to exist in the Bahama Islands or Florida. It seems to have lingered long on that peninsula. Not many years ago, Coacooche, a Seminole chieftain, related a vision which had nerved him to a desperate escape from the Castle of St. Augustine. "In my dream," said he, "I visited the happy hunting grounds and saw my twin sister, long since gone. She offered me a cup of pure water, which she said came from the spring of the Great Spirit, and if I should drink of it, I should return and live with her forever." 129-1 Some such mystical respect for the element, rather than as a mere outfit for his spirit home, probably induced the earlier tribes of the same territory to place the conch-shell which the deceased had used for a cup conspicuously on his grave, 129-2 and the Mexicans and Peruvians to inter a vase filled with water with the corpse, or to sprinkle it with the liquid, baptizing it, as it were, into its new associations. 130-1 It was an emblem of the hope that should cheer the dwellings of the dead, a symbol of the resurrection which is in store for those who have gone down to the grave.

The vase or the gourd as a symbol of water, the source and preserver of life, is a conspicuous figure in the myths of ancient America. As Akbal or Huecomitl, the great or original vase, in Aztec and Maya legends it plays important parts in the drama of creation; as Tici (Ticcu) in Peru it is the symbol of the rains, and as a gourd it is often mentioned by the Caribs and Tupis as the parent of the atmospheric waters.

As the Moon is associated with the dampness and dews of night, an ancient and wide-spread myth identified her with the Goddess of Water. Moreover, in spite of the expostulations of the learned, the common people the world over persist in attributing to her a marked influence on the rains. Whether false or true, this familiar opinion is of great antiquity, and was decidedly approved by the Indians, who were all, in the words of an old author, "great observers of the weather by the moon." 130-2 They looked upon her not only as forewarning them by her appearance of the approach of rains and fogs, but as being their actual cause.

Isis, her Egyptian title, literally means moisture; Ataensic, whom the Hurons said was the moon, is derived from the word for water; and Citatli and Atl, moon and water, are constantly confounded in Aztec theology. Their attributes were strikingly alike. They were both the mythical mothers of the race, and both protect women in child-birth, the babe in the cradle, the husbandman in the field, and the youth and maiden in their tender affections. As the transfer of legends was nearly always from the water to its lunar goddess, by bringing them in at this point their true meaning will not fail to be apparent.

We must ever bear in mind that the course of mythology is from many gods toward one, that it is a synthesis not an analysis, and that in this process the tendency is to blend in one the traits and stories of originally separate divinities. As has justly been observed by the Mexican antiquarian Gama: "It was a common trait among the Indians to worship many gods under the figure of one, principally those whose activities lay in the same direction, or those in some way related among themselves." 131-1

The time of full moon was chosen both in Mexico and Peru to celebrate the festival of the deities of water, the patrons of agriculture, 131-2 and very generally the ceremonies connected with the crops were regulated by her phases. The Nicaraguans said that the god of rains, Quiateot, rose in the east, 131-3 thus hinting how this connection originated. At a lunar eclipse the Orinoko Indians seized their hoes and labored with exemplary vigor on their growing corn, saying the moon was veiling herself in anger at their habitual laziness; 132-1 and a description of the New Netherlands, written about 1650, remarks that the savages of that land "ascribe great influence to the moon over crops." 132-2 This venerable superstition, common to all races, still lingers among our own farmers, many of whom continue to observe "the signs of the moon" in sowing grain, setting out trees, cutting timber, and other rural avocations.

As representing water, the universal mother, the moon was the protectress of women in child-birth, the goddess of love and babes, the patroness of marriage. To her the mother called in travail, whether by the name of "Diana, diva triformis" in pagan Rome, by that of Mama Quilla in Peru, or of Meztli in Anahuac. Under the title of Yohualticitl, the Lady of Night, she was also in this latter country the guardian of babes, and as Teczistecatl, the cause of generation. 132-3

Very different is another aspect of the moon goddess, and well might the Mexicans paint her with two colors. The beneficent dispenser of harvests and offspring, she nevertheless has a portentous and terrific phase. She is also the goddess of the night, the dampness, and the cold; she engenders the miasmatic poisons that rack our bones; she conceals in her mantle the foe who takes us unawares; she rules those vague shapes which fright us in the dim light; the causeless sounds of night or its more oppressive silence are familiar to her; she it is who sends dreams wherein gods and devils have their sport with man, and slumber, the twin brother of the grave. In the occult philosophy of the middle ages she was "Chief over the Night, Darkness, Rest, Death, and the Waters;" 133-1 in the language of the Algonkins, her name is identical with the words for night, death, cold, sleep, and water. 133-2

She is the evil minded woman who thus brings diseases upon men, who at the outset introduced pain and death in the world—our common mother, yet the cruel cause of our present woes. Sometimes it is the moon, sometimes water, of whom this is said: "We are all of us under the power of evil and sin, *because* we are children of the Water," says the Mexican baptismal formula. That Unktahe, spirit of water, is the master of dreams and witchcraft, is the belief of the Dakotas. 133-3 A female spirit, wife of the great manito whose heart is the sun, the ancient Algonkins believed brought death and disease to the race; "it is she who kills men, otherwise they would never die; she eats their flesh and knaws their vitals, till they fall away and miserably perish." 134-1 Who is this woman? In the legend of the Muyscas it is Chia, the moon, who was also goddess of water and flooded the earth out of spite. 134-2 Her reputation was notoriously bad. The Brazilian mother carefully shielded her infant from the lunar rays, believing that they would produce sickness; 134-3 the hunting tribes of our own country will not sleep in its light, nor leave their game exposed to its action. We ourselves have not outgrown such words as lunatic, moon-struck, and the like. Where did we get these ideas? The philosophical historian of medicine, Kurt Sprengel, traces them to the primitive and popular medical theories of ancient Egypt, in accordance with which all maladies were the effects of the anger of the goddess Isis, the Moisture, the Moon. 134-4

We have here the key to many myths. Take that of Centeotl, the Aztec goddess of Maize. She was said at times to appear as a woman of surpassing beauty, and allure some unfortunate to her embraces, destined to pay with his life for his brief moments of pleasure. Even to see her in this shape was a fatal omen. She was also said to belong to a class of gods whose home was in the west, and who produced sickness and pains. 134-5 Here we see the evil aspect of the moon reflected on another goddess, who was at first solely the patroness of agriculture.

As the goddess of sickness, it was supposed that persons afflicted with certain diseases had been set apart by the moon for her peculiar service. These diseases were those of a humoral type, especially such as are characterized by issues and ulcers. As in Hebrew the word *accursed* is derived from a root meaning *consecrated to God*, so in the Aztec, Quiché, and other tongues, the word for *leprous, eczematous,* or *syphilitic,* means also *divine.* This bizarre change of meaning is illustrated in a very ancient myth of their family. It is said that in the absence of the sun all mankind lingered in darkness. Nothing but a human sacrifice could hasten his arrival. Then Metzli, the moon, led forth one Nanahuatl, the leprous, and building a pyre, the victim threw himself in its midst. Straightway Metzli followed his example, and as she disappeared in the bright flames the sun rose over the horizon. 135-1 Is not this a reference to the kindling rays of the aurora, in which the dark and baleful night is sacrificed, and in whose light the moon presently fades away, and the sun comes forth?

Another reaction in the mythological laboratory is here disclosed. As the good qualities of water were attributed to the goddess of night, sleep, and death, so her malevolent traits were in turn reflected back on this element. Other thoughts aided the transfer. In primitive geography the Ocean Stream coils its infinite folds around the speck of land we inhabit, biding its time to swallow it wholly. Unwillingly did it yield the earth from its bosom, daily does it steal it away piece by piece. Every evening it hides the light in its depths, and Night and the Waters resume their ancient sway. The word for ocean (*mare*) in the Latin tongue means by derivation a desert, and the Greeks spoke of it as "the barren brine." Water is a treacherous element. Man treads boldly on the solid earth, but the rivers and lakes constantly strive to swallow those who venture within their reach. As streams run in tortuous channels, and as rains accompany the lightning serpent, this animal was occasionally the symbol of the waters in their dangerous manifestations. The Huron magicians fabled that in the lakes and rivers dwelt one of vast size called *Angont*, who sent sickness, death, and other mishaps, and the least mite of whose flesh was a deadly poison. They added—and this was the point of the tale—that they always kept on hand portions of the monster for the benefit of any who opposed their designs. 136-1 The legends of the Algonkins mention a rivalry between Michabo, creator of the earth, and the Spirit of the Waters, who was unfriendly to the project. 136-2 In later tales this antagonism becomes more and more pronounced, and borrows an ethical significance which it did not have at first. Taking, however, American religions as a whole, water is far more frequently represented as producing beneficent effects than the reverse.

Dogs were supposed to stand in some peculiar relation to the moon, probably because they howl at it and run at night, uncanny practices which have cost them dear in reputation. The custom prevailed among tribes so widely asunder as Peruvians, Tupis, Creeks, Iroquois, Algonkins, and Greenland Eskimos to thrash the curs most soundly during an eclipse. 137-1 The Creeks explained this by saying that the big dog was swallowing the sun, and that by whipping the little ones they could make him desist. What the big dog was they were not prepared to say. We know. It was the night goddess, represented by the dog, who was thus shrouding the world at midday. The ancient Romans sacrificed dogs to Hecate and Diana, in Egypt they were sacred to Isis, and thus as traditionally connected with night and its terrors, the Prince of Darkness, in the superstition of the middle ages, preferably appeared under the form of a cur, as that famous poodle which accompanied Cornelius Agrippa, or that which grew to such enormous size behind the stove of Dr. Faustus. In a better sense, they represented the more agreeable characteristics of the lunar goddess. Xochiquetzal, most fecund of Aztec divinities, patroness of love, of sexual pleasure, and of childbirth, was likewise called *Itzcuinan*, which, literally translated, is *bitch-mother*. This strange and to us so repugnant title for a goddess was not without parallel elsewhere. When in his wars the Inca Pachacutec carried his arms into the province of Huanca, he found its inhabitants had installed in their temples the figure of a dog as their highest deity. They were accustomed also to select one as his living representative, to pray to it and offer it sacrifice, and when well fattened, to serve it up with solemn ceremonies at a great feast, eating their god *substantialiter*. The priests in this province summoned their attendants to the temples by blowing through an instrument fashioned from a dog's skull. 138-1 This canine canonization explains why in some parts of Peru a priest was called by way of honor *allco*, dog! 138-2 And why in many tombs both there and in Mexico their skeletons are found carefully interred with the human remains. Wherever the Aztec race extended they seem to have carried the adoration of a wild species, the coyote, the *canis latrans* of naturalists. The Shoshonees of New Mexico call it their progenitor, 138-3 and with the Nahuas it was in such high honor that it had a temple of its own, a congregation of priests devoted to its service, statues carved in stone, an elaborate tomb at death, and is said to be meant by the god Chantico, whose audacity caused the destruction of the world. The story was that he made a sacrifice to the gods without observing a preparatory fast, for which he was punished by being changed into a dog. He then invoked the god of death to deliver him, which attempt to evade a just punishment so enraged the divinities that they immersed the world in water. 139-1

During a storm on our northern lakes the Indians think no offering so likely to appease the angry water god who is raising the tempest as a dog. Therefore they hasten to tie the feet of one and toss him overboard. 139-2 One meets constantly in their tales and superstitions the mysterious powers of the animals, and the distinguished actions he has at times performed bear usually a close parallelism to those attributed to water and the moon.

Hunger and thirst were thus alleviated by water. Cold remained, and against this *fire* was the shield. It gives man light in darkness and warmth in winter; it shows him his friends and warns him of his foes; the flames point toward heaven and the smoke makes the clouds. Around it social life begins. For his home and his hearth the savage has but one word, and what of tender emotion his breast can feel, is linked to the circle that gathers around his fire. The council fire, the camp fire, and the war fire, are so many epochs in his history. By its aid many arts become possible, and it is a civilizer in more ways than one. In the figurative language of the red race, it is constantly used as "an emblem of peace, happiness, and abundance." 140-1 To extingish an enemy's fire is to slay him; to light a visitor's fire is to bid him welcome. Fire worship was closely related to that of the sun, and so much has been said of sun worship among the aborigines of America that it is well at once to assign it its true position.

A generation ago it was a fashion very much approved to explain all symbols and myths by the action of this orb on nature. This short and easy method with mythology has, in Carlylian phrase, had its bottom pulled from under it in these later times. Nowhere has it manifested its inefficiency more palpably than in America. One writer, while thus explaining the religions of the tribes of colder regions and higher latitudes, denies sun worship among the natives of hot climates; another asserts that only among the latter did it exist at all; while a third lays down the maxim that the religion of the red race everywhere "was but a modification of Sun or Fire worship." 141-1 All such sweeping generalizations are untrue, and must be so. No one key can open all the arcana of symbolism. Man devised means as varied as nature herself to express the idea of God within him. The sun was but one of these, and not the first nor the most important. Fear, said the wise Epicurean, first made the gods. The sun with its regular course, its kindly warmth, its beneficent action, no wise inspires that sentiment. It conjures no phantasms to appal the superstitious fancy, and its place in primitive mythology is conformably inferior. The myths of the Eskimos and northern Athapascas omit its action altogether. The Algonkins by no means imagined it the highest god, and at most but one of his emblems. 142-1 That it often appears in their prayers is true, but this arose from the fact that in many of their dialects, as well as in the language of the Mayas and others, the word for heaven or sky was identical with that for sun, and the former, as I have shown, was the supposed abode of deity, "the wigwam of the Great Spirit." 142-2 The alleged sun worship of the Cherokees rests on testimony modern, doubtful, and unsupported. 142-3 In North America the Natchez alone were avowed worshippers of this luminary. Yet they adored it under the name Great Fire (*wah sil*), clearly pointing to a prior adoration of that element. The heliolatry organized principally for political ends by the Incas of Peru, stands alone in the religions of the red race. Those shrewd legislators at an early date officially announced that Inti, the sun, their own elder brother, was ruler of the cohorts of heaven by like divine right that they were of the four corners of the earth. This scheme ignominiously failed, as every attempt to fetter the liberty of conscience must and should. The later Incas finally indulged publicly in heterodox remarks, and compromised the matter by acknowledging a divinity superior even to their brother, the sun, as we have seen in a previous chapter.

The myths of creation never represent the sun as anterior to the world, but as manufactured by the "old people" (Navajos), as kindled and set going by the first of men (Algonkins), or as freed from some cave by a kindly deity (Haitians). It is always spoken of as a fire; only in Peru and Mexico had the precession. of the equinoxes been observed, and without danger of error we can merge the consideration of its worship almost altogether in that of this element. 143-1

The institutions of a perpetual fire, of obtaining new fire, and of burning the dead, prevailed extensively in the New World. In the present discussion the origin of such practices, rather than the ceremonies with which they were attended, have an interest. The savage knew that fire was necessary to his life. Were it lost, he justly foreboded dire calamities and the ruin of his race. Therefore at stated times with due solemnity he produced it anew by friction or the flint, or else was careful to keep one fire constantly alive. These not unwise precautions soon fell to mere superstitions. If the Aztec priest at the stated time failed to obtain a spark from his pieces of wood, if the sacred fire by chance became extinguished, the end of the world or the destruction of mankind was apprehended. "You know it was a saying among our ancestors," said an Iroquois chief in 1753, "that when the fire at Onondaga goes out, we shall no longer be a people." 144-1 So deeply rooted was this notion, that the Catholic missionaries in New Mexico were fain to wink at it, and perform the sacrifice of the mass in the same building where the flames were perpetually burning, that were not to be allowed to die until Montezuma and the fabled glories of ancient Anahuac with its heathenism should return. 144-2 Thus fire became the type of life. "Know that the life in your body and the fire on your hearth are one and the same thing, and that both proceed from one source," said a Shawnee prophet. 144-3 Such an expression was wholly in the spirit of his race. The greatest feast of the Delawares was that to their "grandfather, the fire." 144-4 "Their fire burns forever," was the Algonkin figure of speech to express the immortality of their gods. 144-5 "The ancient God, the Father and Mother of all Gods," says an Aztec prayer, "is the God of the Fire which is in the centre of the court with four walls, and which is covered with gleaming feathers like unto wings;" 144-6 dark sayings of the priests, referring to the glittering lightning fire borne from the four sides of the earth.

As the path to a higher life hereafter, the burning of the dead was first instituted. It was a privilege usually confined to a select few. Among the Algonkin-Ottawas, only, those of the distinguished totem of the Great Hare, among the Nicaraguans none but the caciques, among the Caribs exclusively the priestly caste, were entitled to this peculiar honor. 145-1 The first gave as the reason for such an exceptional custom, that the members of such an illustrious clan as that of Michabo, the Great Hare, should not rot in the ground as common folks, but rise to the heavens on the flames and smoke. Those of Nicaragua seemed to think it the sole path to immortality, holding that only such as offered themselves on the pyre of their chieftain would escape annihilation at death; 145-2 and the tribes of upper California were persuaded that such as were not burned at death were liable to be transformed into the lower orders of brutes. 145-3 Strangely, enough, we thus find a sort of baptism by fire deemed essential to a higher life beyond the grave.

Another analogy strengthened the symbolic force of fire as life. This is that which exists between the sensation of warmth and those passions whose physiological end is the perpetuation of the species. We see how native it is to the mind from such coarse expressions as "hot lust," "to burn," "to be in heat," "stews," and the like, figures not of the poetic, but the vulgar tongue. They occur in all languages, and hint how readily the worship of fire glided into that of the reproductive principle, into extravagances of chastity and lewdness, into the shocking orgies of the so-called phallic worship.

Some have supposed that a sexual dualism pervades all natural religions and this too has been assumed as the solution of all their myths. It has been said that the action of heat upon moisture, of the sun on the waters, the mysteries of reproduction, and the satisfaction of the sexual instincts, are the unvarying themes of primitive mythology. So far as the red race is concerned, this is a most gratuitous assumption. The facts that have been eagerly collated by Dulaure and others to bolster such a detestable theory lend themselves fairly to no such interpretation.

There existed, indeed, a worship of the passions. Apparently it was grafted upon or rose out of that of fire by the analogy I have pointed out. Thus the Mexican god of fire was supposed to govern the generative proclivities, 146-1 and there is good reason to believe that the sacred fire watched by unspotted virgins among the Mayas had decidedly such a signification. Certainly it was so, if we can depend upon the authority of a ballad translated from the original immediately after the conquest, cited by the venerable traveller and artist Count de Waldeck. It purports to be from the lover of one of these vestals, and referring to her occupation asks with a fine allusion to its mystic meaning—

"Ovièrge,quandpourrai-jeteposséderpourmacompagnecherie?
Combien de temps faut-il encore que tes vœux soient accomplis?
Dis-moi le jour qui doit devancer la belle nuit où tous deux,
Alimenterons le feu qui nous fit naitre et que nous devons perpetuer." 147-1

There is a bright as well as a dark side even to such a worship. In Mexico, Peru, and Yucatan, the women who watched the flames must be undoubted virgins; they were usually of noble blood, and must vow eternal chastity, or at least were free to none but the ruler of the realm. As long as they were consecrated to the fire, so long any carnal ardor was degrading to their lofty duties. The sentiment of shame, one of the first we find developed, led to the belief that to forego fleshly pleasures was a meritorious sacrifice in the eyes of the gods. In this persuasion certain of the Aztec priests practised complete abscission or entire discerption of the virile parts, and a mutilation of females was not unknown similar to that immemorially a custom in Egypt. 147-2 Such enforced celibacy was, however, neither common nor popular. Circumcision, if it can be proven to have existed among the red race—and though there are plenty of assertions to that effect, they are not satisfactory to an anatomist—was probably a symbolic renunciation of the lusts of the flesh. The same cannot be said of the very common custom with the Aztec race of anointing their idols with blood drawn from the genitals, the tongue, and the ears. This was simply a form of those voluntary scarifications, universally employed to mark contrition or grief by savage tribes, and nowhere more in vogue than with the red race.

There was an ancient Christian heresy which taught that the true way to conquer the passions was to satiate them, and therefore preached unbounded licentiousness. Whether this agreeable doctrine was known to the Indians I cannot say, but it is certainly the most creditable explanation that can be suggested for the miscellaneous congress which very often terminated their dances and ceremonies. Such orgies were of common occurrence among the Algonkins and Iroquois at a very early date, and are often mentioned in the Jesuit Relations; Venegas describes them as frequent among the tribes of Lower California; and Oviedo refers to certain festivals of the Nicaraguans, during which the women of all rank extended to whosoever wished just such privileges as the matrons of ancient Babylon, that mother of harlots and all abominations, used to grant even to slaves and strangers in the temple of Melitta, as one of the duties of religion. But in fact there is no ground whatever to invest these debauches with any recondite meaning. They are simply indications of the thorough and utter immorality which prevailed throughout the race. And a still more disgusting proof of it is seen in the frequent appearance among diverse tribes of men dressed as women and yielding themselves to indescribable vices. 149-1 There was at first nothing of a religious nature in such exhibitions. Lascivious priests chose at times to invest them with some such meaning for their own sensual gratification, just as in Brazil they still claim the *jus primæ noctis*. 149-2 The pretended phallic worship of the Natchez and of Culhuacan, cited by the Abbé Brasseur, rests on no good authority, and if true, is like that of the Huastecas of Panuco, nothing but an unrestrained and boundless profligacy which it were an absurdity to call a religion. 149-3 That which Mr. Stephens attempts to show existed once in Yucatan, 149-4 rests entirely by his own statement on a fancied resemblance of no value whatever, and the arguments of Lafitau to the same effect are quite insufficient. There is a decided indecency in the remains of ancient American art, especially in Peru (Meyen), and great lubricity in many ceremonies, but the proof is altogether wanting to bind these with the recognition of a fecundating principle throughout nature, or, indeed, to suppose for them any other origin than the promptings of an impure fancy. I even doubt whether they often referred to fire as the deity of sexual love.

By a flight of fancy inspired by a study of oriental mythology, the worship of the reciprocal principle in America has been connected with that of the sun and moon, as the primitive pair from whose fecund union all creatures proceeded. It is sufficient to say if such a myth exists among the Indians—which is questionable—it justifies no such deduction; that the moon is often mentioned in their languages merely as the "night sun;" and that in such important stocks as the Iroquois, Athapascas, Cherokees, and Tupis, the sun is said to be a feminine noun; while the myths represent them more frequently as brother and sister than as man and wife; nor did at least the northern tribes regard the sun as the cause of fecundity in nature at all, but solely as giving light and warmth. 150-1

In contrast to this, so much the more positive was their association of the THUNDER-STORM as that which brings both warmth and rain with the renewed vernal life of vegetation. The impressive phenomena which characterize it, the prodigious noise, the awful flash, the portentous gloom, the blast, the rain, have left a profound impression on the myths of every land. Fire from water, warmth and moisture from the destructive breath of the tempest, this was the riddle of riddles to the untutored mind. "Out of the eater came forth meat, out of the strong came forth sweetness." It was the visible synthesis of all the divine manifestations, the winds, the waters, and the flames.

The Dakotas conceived it as a struggle between the god of waters and the thunder bird for the command of their nation, 150-2 and as a bird, one of those which make a whirring sound with their wings, the turkey, the pheasant, or the nighthawk, it was very generally depicted by their neighbors, the Athapascas, Iroquois, and Algonkins. 151-1 As the herald of the summer it was to them a good omen and a friendly power. It was the voice of the Great Spirit of the four winds speaking from the clouds and admonishing them that the time of corn planting was at hand. 151-2 The flames kindled by the lightning were of a sacred nature, proper to be employed in lighting the fires of the religious rites, but on no account to be profaned by the base uses of daily life. When the flash entered the ground it scattered in all directions those stones, such as the flint, which betray their supernal origin by a gleam of fire when struck. These were the thunderbolts, and from such an one, significantly painted red, the Dakotas averred their race had proceeded. 151-3 For are we not all in a sense indebted for our lives to fire? "There is no end to the fancies entertained by the Sioux concerning thunder," observes Mrs. Eastman. They typified the paradoxical nature of the storm under the character of the giant Haokah. To him cold was heat, and heat cold; when sad he laughed, when merry groaned; the sides of his face and his eyes were of different colors and expressions; he wore horns or a forked headdress to represent the lightning, and with his hands he hurled the meteors. His manifestations were fourfold, and one of the four winds was the drum-stick he used to produce the thunder. 152-1

Omitting many others, enough that the sameness of this conception is illustrated by the myth of Tupa, highest god and first man of the Tupis of Brazil. During his incarnation, he taught them agriculture, gave them fire, the cane, and the pisang, and now in the form of a huge bird sweeps over the heavens, watching his children and watering their crops, admonishing them of his presence by the mighty sound of his voice, the rustling of his wings, and the flash of his eye. These are the thunder, the lightning, and the roar of the tempest. He is depicted with horns; he was one of four brothers, and only after a desperate struggle did he drive his fraternal rivals from the field. In his worship, the priests place pebbles in a dry gourd, deck it with feathers and arrows, and rattling it vigorously, reproduce in miniature the tremendous drama of the storm. 152-2

As nations rose in civilization these fancies put on a more complex form and a more poetic fulness. Throughout the realm of the Incas the Peruvians venerated as creator of all things, maker of heaven and earth, and ruler of the firmament, the god Ataguju. The legend was that from him proceeded the first of mortals, the man Guamansuri, who descended to the earth and there seduced the sister of certain Guachemines, rayless ones, or Darklings, who then possessed it. For this crime they destroyed him, but their sister proved pregnant, and died in her labor, giving birth to two eggs. From these emerged the twin brothers, Apocatequil and Piguerao. The former was the more powerful. By touching the corpse of his mother he brought her to life, he drove off and slew the Guachemines, and, directed by Ataguju, released the race of Indians from the soil by turning it up with a spade of gold. For this reason they adored him as their maker. He it was, they thought, who produced the thunder and the lightning by hurling stones with his sling; and the thunderbolts that fall, said they, are his children. Few villages were willing to be without one or more of these. They were in appearance small, round, smooth stones, but had the admirable properties of securing fertility to the fields, protecting from lightning, and, by a transition easy to understand, were also adored as gods of the Fire, as well material as of the passions, and were capable of kindling the dangerous flames of desire in the most frigid bosom. Therefore they were in great esteem as love charms.

Apocatequil's statue was erected on the mountains, with that of his mother on one hand, and his brother on the other. "He was Prince of Evil and the most respected god of the Peruvians. From Quito to Cuzco not an Indian but would give all he possessed to conciliate him. Five priests, two stewards, and a crowd of slaves served his image. And his chief temple was surrounded by a very considerable village whose inhabitants had no other occupation than to wait on him." In memory of these brothers, twins in Peru were deemed always sacred to the lightning, and when a woman or even a llama brought them forth, a fast was held and sacrifices offered to the two pristine brothers, with a chant commencing: *A chuchu cachiqui*, O Thou who causest twins, words mistaken by the Spaniards for the name of a deity. 154-1

Garcilasso de la Vega, a descendant of the Incas, has preserved an ancient indigenous poem of his nation, presenting the storm myth in a different form, which as undoubtedly authentic and not devoid of poetic beauty I translate, preserving as much as possible the trochaic tetrasyllabic verse of the original Quichua: —

> "Beauteous princess,
> Lo, thy brother
> Breaks thy vessel
> Now in fragments.
> From the blow come
> Thunder, lightning,
> Strokes of lightning.
> And thou, princess,
> Tak'st the water,
> With it rainest,

And the hail, or
Snow dispensest.
Viracocha,
World constructor,
World enliv'ner,
To this office
Thee appointed,
Thee created." 155-1

In this pretty waif that has floated down to us from the wreck of a literature now forever lost, there is more than one point to attract the notice of the antiquary. He may find in it a hint to decipher those names of divinities so common in Peruvian legends, Contici and Illatici. Both mean "the Thunder Vase," and both doubtless refer to the conception here displayed of the phenomena of the thunder-storm. 155-2

Again, twice in this poem is the triple nature of the storm adverted to. This is observable in many of the religions of America. It constitutes a sort of Trinity, not in any point resembling that of Christianity, nor yet the Trimurti of India, but the only one in the New World the least degree authenticated, and which, as half seen by ignorant monks, has caused its due amount of sterile astonishment. Thus, in the Quiché legends we read: "The first of Hurakan is the lightning, the second the track of the lightning, and the third the stroke of the lightning; and these three are Hurakan, the Heart of the Sky." 156-1 It reappears with characteristic uniformity of outline in Iroquois mythology. Heno, the thunder, gathers the clouds and pours out the warm rains. Therefore he was the patron of husbandry. He was invoked at seed time and harvest; and as purveyor of nourishment he was addressed as grandfather, and his worshippers styled themselves his grandchildren. He rode through the heavens on the clouds, and the thunderbolts which split the forest trees were the stones he hurled at his enemies. *Three* assistants were assigned him, whose names have unfortunately not been recorded, and whose offices were apparently similar to those of the three companions of Hurakan. 156-2

So also the Aztecs supposed that Tlaloc, god of rains and the waters, ruler of the terrestrial paradise and the season of summer, manifested himself under the three attributes of the flash, the thunderbolt, and the thunder. 157-1

But this conception of three in one was above the comprehension of the masses, and consequently these deities were also spoken of as fourfold in nature, three *and* one. Moreover, as has already been pointed out, the thunder god was usually ruler of the winds, and thus another reason for his quadruplicate nature was suggested. Hurakan, Haokah, Tlaloc, and probably Heno, are plural as well as singular nouns, and are used as nominatives to verbs in both numbers. Tlaloc was appealed to as inhabiting each of the cardinal points and every mountain top. His statue rested on a square stone pedestal, facing the east, and had in one hand a serpent of gold. Ribbons of silver, crossing to form squares, covered the robe, and the shield was composed of feathers of four colors, yellow, green, red, and blue. Before it was a vase containing all sorts of grain; and the clouds were called his companions, the winds his messengers. 157-2 As elsewhere, the thunderbolts were believed to be flints, and thus, as the emblem of fire and the storm, this stone figures conspicuously in their myths. Tohil, the god who gave the Quichés fire by shaking his sandals, was represented by a flint-stone. He is distinctly said to be the same as Quetzalcoatl, one of whose commonest symbols was a flint (tecpatl). Such a stone, in the beginning of things, fell from heaven to earth, and broke into 1600 pieces, each of which sprang up a god; 158-1 an ancient legend, which shadows forth the subjection of all things to him who gathers the clouds from the four corners of the earth, who thunders with his voice, who satisfies with his rain "the desolate and waste ground, and causes the tender herb to spring forth." This is the germ of the adoration of stones as emblems of the fecundating rains. This is why, for example, the Navajos use as their charm for rain certain long round stones, which they think fall from the cloud when it thunders. 158-2

Mixcoatl, the Cloud Serpent, or Iztac-Mixcoatl, the White or Gleaming Cloud Serpent, said to have been the only divinity of the ancient Chichimecs, held in high honor by the Nahuas, Nicaraguans, and Otomis, and identical with Taras, supreme god of the Tarascos and Camaxtli, god of the Teo-Chichimecs, is another personification of the thunder-storm. To this day this is the familiar name of the tropical tornado in the Mexican language. 158-3 He was represented, like Jove, with a bundle of arrows in his hand, the thunderbolts. Both the Nahuas and Tarascos related legends in which he figured as father of the race of man. Like other lords of the lightning he was worshipped as the dispenser of riches and the patron of traffic; and in Nicaragua his image is described as being "engraved stones," 158-4 probably the supposed products of the thunder.

FOOTNOTE:

124-1 A. D'Orbigny, *L'Homme Américain*, i. p. 240.

125-1 Rivero and Tschudi, *Peruvian Antiquities*, 162, after J. Acosta.

125-2 Narrative of *Oceola Nikkanoche, Prince of Econchatti*, p. 141; Schoolcraft, *Ind. Tribes*, iv. p. 650.

126-1 The term in Maya is *caput zihil,* corresponding exactly to the Latin *renasci,* to be re-born, Landa, *Rel. de Yucatan,* p. 144.

126-2 Dumont, *Mems. Hist. sur la Louisiane,* i. p. 233.

127-1 Acosta, *Hist. of the New World,* lib. v. cap. 25.

127-2 *Senate Report on Condition of Indian Tribes,* p. 358: Washington, 1867.

128-1 Sahagun, *Hist. de la Nueva España,* lib. vi. cap. 37.

128-2 Ternaux-Compans, *Pièces rel. à la Conq. du Mexique,* p. 233.

128-3 Velasco, *Hist. de la Royaume de Quito,* p. 106, and others.

128-4 Whipple, *Rep. on the Indian Tribes,* p. 35. I am not sure that this practice was of native growth to the Cherokees. This people have many customs and traditions strangely similar to those of Christians and Jews. Their cosmogony is a paraphrase of that of Genesis (Squier, *Serp. Symbol,* from Payne's MSS.); the number seven is as sacred with them as it was with the Chaldeans (Whipple, u. s.); and they have improved and increased by contact with the whites. Significant in this connection is the remark of Bartram, who visited them in 1773, that some of their females were "nearly as fair and blooming as European women," and generally that their complexion was lighter than their neighbors (*Travels,* p. 485). Two explanations of these facts may be suggested. They may be descendants in part of the ancient white race near Cape Hatteras, to whom I have referred in a previous note. More probably they derived their peculiarities from the Spaniards of Florida. Mr. Shea is of opinion that missions were established among them as early as 1566 and 1643 (*Hist. of Catholic Missions in the U. S.,* pp. 58, 73). Certainly in the latter half of the seventeenth century the Spaniards were prosecuting mining operations in their territory (See *Am. Hist. Mag.,* x. p. 137).

129-1 Sprague, *Hist. of the Florida War,* p. 328.

129-2 Basanier, *Histoire Notable de la Floride,* p. 10.

130-1 Sahagun, *Hist. de la Nueva España,* lib. iii. app. cap. i.; Meyen, *Ueber die Ureinwohner von Peru,* p. 29.

130-2 Gabriel Thomas, *Hist. of West New Jersey,* p. 6: London, 1698.

131-1 Gama, *Des. de las dos Piedras,* etc., i. p. 36.

131-2 Garcia, *Or. de los Indios,* p. 109.

131-3 Oviedo, *Rel. de la Prov. de Nicaragua,* p. 41. The name is a corruption of the Aztec *Quiauhteotl,* Rain-God.

132-1 Gumilla, *Hist. del Orinoco*, ii. cap. 23.

132-2 *Doc. Hist. of New York*, iv. p. 130.

132-3 Gama, *Des. de las dos Piedras*, ii. p. 41; Gallatin, *Trans. Am. Ethnol. Soc.*, i. p. 343.

133-1 Adrian Van Helmont, *Workes*, p. 142, fol.: London, 1662.

133-2 The moon is *nipa* or *nipaz*; *nipa*, I sleep; *nipawi*, night; *nip*, I die; *nepua*, dead; *nipanoue*, cold. This odd relationship was first pointed out by Volney (Duponceau, *Langues de l'Amérique du Nord*, p. 317). But the kinship of these words to that for water, *nip, nipi, nepi*, has not before been noticed. This proves the association of ideas on which I lay so much stress in mythology. A somewhat similar relationship exists in the Aztec and cognate languages, *miqui*, to die, *micqui*, dead, *mictlan*, the realm of death, *te-miqui*, to dream, *cec-miqui*, to freeze. Would it be going too far to connect these with *metzli*, moon? (See Buschmann, *Spuren der Aztekischen Sprache im Nördlichen Mexico*, p. 80.)

133-3 Schoolcraft, *Ind. Tribes*, vol. iii. p. 485.

134-1 *Rel. de la Nouv. France*, 1634, p. 16.

134-2 Humboldt, *Vues des Cordillères*, p. 21.

134-3 Spix and Martius, *Travels in Brazil*, ii. p. 247.

134-4 *Hist. de la Médecine*, i. p. 34.

134-5 Gama, *Des. de las dos Piedras*, etc., ii. pp. 100-102. Compare Sahagun, *Hist. de la Nueva España*, lib. i. cap. vi.

135-1 Codex Chimalpopoca, in Brasseur, *Hist. du Mexique*, i. p. 183. Gama and others translate Nanahuatl by *el buboso*, Brasseur by *le syphilitique*, and the latter founds certain medical speculations on the word. It is entirely unnecessary to say to a surgeon that it could not possibly have had the latter meaning, inasmuch as the diagnosis between secondary or tertiary syphilis and other similar diseases was unknown. That it is so employed now is nothing to the purpose. The same or a similar myth was found in Central America and on the Island of Haiti.

136-1 *Rel. de la Nouv. France*, 1648, p. 75.

136-2 Charlevoix is in error when he identifies Michabo with the Spirit of the Waters, and may be corrected from his own statements elsewhere. Compare his *Journal Historique*, pp. 281 and 344: ed. Paris, 1740.

137-1 Bradford, *American Antiquities*, p. 833; Martius, *Von dem Rechtszustande unter den Ureinwohnern Brasiliens*, p. 32; Schoolcraft, *Ind. Tribes*, i. p. 271.

138-1 La Vega, *Hist. des Incas,* liv. vi. cap. 9.

138-2 *Lett. sur les Superstitions du Pérou,* p. 111.

138-3 Schoolcraft, *Ind. Tribes,* iv. p. 224.

139-1 Chantico, according to Gama, means "Wolf's Head," though I cannot verify this from the vocabularies within my reach. He is sometimes called Cohuaxolotl Chantico, the snake-servant Chantico, considered by Gama as one, by Torquemada as two deities (see Gama, *Des. de las dos Piedras,* etc., i. p. 12; ii. p. 66). The English word *cantico* in the phrase, for instance, "to cut a cantico," though an Indian word, is not from this, but from the Algonkin Delaware *gentkehn,* to dance a sacred dance. The Dutch describe it as "a religious custom observed among them before death" (*Doc. Hist. of New York,* iv. p. 63). William Penn says of the Lenape, "their worship consists of two parts, sacrifice and cantico," the latter "performed by round dances, sometimes words, sometimes songs, then shouts; their postures very antic and differing." (*Letter to the Free Society of Traders,* 1683, sec. 21.)

139-2 Charlevoix, *Hist. Gén. de la Nouv. France,* i. p. 394: Paris, 1740. On the different species of dogs indigenous to America, see a note of Alex. von Humboldt, *Ansichten der Natur.,* i. p. 134. It may be noticed that Chichimec, properly Chichimecatl, the name of the Aztec tribe who succeeded the ancient Toltecs in Mexico, means literally "people of the dog," and was probably derived from some mythological fable connected with that animal.

140-1 *Narr. of the Captiv. of John Tanner,* p. 362. From the word for fire in many American tongues is formed the adjective *red.* Thus, Algonkin, *skoda,* fire, *miskoda,* red; Kolosch, *kan,* fire, *kan,* red; Ugalentz, *takak,* fire, *takak-uete,* red; Tahkali, *cūn,* fire, *tenil-cūn,* red; Quiche, *cak,* fire, *cak,* red, etc. From the adjective *red* comes often the word for *blood,* and in symbolism the color red may refer to either of these ideas. It was the royal color of the Incas, brothers of the sun, and a llama swathed in a red garment was the Peruvian sacrifice to fire (Garcia, *Or. de los Indios,* lib. iv. caps. 16, 19). On the other hand the war quipus, the war wampum, and the war paint were all of this hue, boding their sanguinary significance. The word for fire in the language of the Delawares, Nanticokes, and neighboring tribes puzzles me. It is *taenda* or *tinda.* This is the Swedish word *taenda,* from whose root comes our *tinder.* Yet it is found in vocabularies as early as 1650, and is universally current to-day. It has no resemblance to the word for fire in pure Algonkin. Was it adopted from the Swedes? Was it introduced by wandering Vikings in remote centuries? Or is it only a coincidence?

141-1 Compare D'Orbigny, *L'Homme Américain*, i. p. 243, Müller, *Amer. Urreligionen*, p. 51, and Squier, *Serpent Symbol in America*, p. 111. This is a striking instance of the confusion of ideas introduced by false systems of study, and also of the considerable misapprehension of American mythology which has hitherto prevailed.

142-1 La Hontan, *Voy. dans l'Amér. Sept.*, p. ii. 127; *Rel. Nouv. France*, 1637, p. 54.

142-2 Copway, *Trad. Hist. of the Ojibway Nation*, p. 165. *Kesuch* in Algonkin signifies both sky and sun (Duponceau, *Langues de l'Amér. du Nord*, p. 312). So apparently does *kin* in the Maya.

142-3 Payne's manuscripts quoted by Mr. Squier in his Serpent Symbol in America were compiled within this century, and from the extracts given can be of no great value.

143-1 The words for fire and sun in American languages are usually from distinct roots, but besides the example of the Natchez I may instance to the contrary the Kolosch of British America, in whose tongue fire is *kan*, sun, *kakan* (*gake*, great), and the Tezuque of New Mexico, who use *tah* for both sun and fire.

144-1 *Doc. Hist. of New York*, ii. p. 634.

144-2 Emory, *Milt'y Reconnoissance of New Mexico*, p. 30.

144-3 *Narrative of John Tanner*, p. 161.

144-4 Loskiel, *Ges. der Miss. der evang. Brüder*, p. 55.

144-5 *Nar. of John Tanner*, p. 351.

144-6 Sahagun, *Hist. Nueva España*, lib. vi. cap. 4.

145-1 *Letts. Edifiantes et Curieuses*, iv. p. 104, Oviedo; *Hist. du Nicaragua*, p. 49; Gumilla, *Hist. del Orinoco*, ii. cap. 2.

145-2 Oviedo, *Hist. Gen. de las Indias*, p. 16, in Barcia's *Hist. Prim.*

145-3 *Presdt's Message and Docs.* for 1851, pt. iii. p. 506.

146-1 Sahagun, *Hist. de la Nueva España*, i. cap. 13.

147-1 *Voyage Pittoresque dans le Yucatan*, p. 49.

147-2 Davila Padilla, *Hist. de la Prov. de Santiago de Mexico*, lib. ii. cap. 88 (Brusselas, 1625); Palacios, *Des. de Guatemala*, p. 40; Garcia, *Or. de los Indios*, p. 124. To such an extent did the priests of the Algonkin tribes who lived near Manhattan Island carry their austerity, such uncompromising celibates were they, that it is said on authority as old as 1624, that they never so much as partook of food prepared by a married woman. (*Doc. Hist. New York*, iv. p. 28.)

149-1 Martius, *Von dem Rechtzustande unter den Ureinwohnern Brasiliens*, p. 28, gives many references.

149-2 Id. *ibid.*, p. 61.

149-3 *Le Livre Sacré des Quichés*, Introd., pp. clxi., clxix.

149-4 *Travels in Yucatan*, i. p. 434.

150-1 Schoolcraft, *Ind. Tribes*, v. pp. 416, 417.

150-2 Mrs. Eastman, *Legends of the Sioux*, p. 161.

151-1 *Rel. de la Nouv. France*, 1634, p. 27; Schoolcraft, *Algic Researches*, ii. p. 116; *Ind. Tribes*, v. p. 420.

151-2 De Smet, *Western Missions*, p. 135; Schoolcraft, *Ind. Tribes*, i. p. 319.

151-3 Mrs. Eastman, *Legends of the Sioux*, p. 72. By another legend they claimed that their first ancestor obtained his fire from the sparks which a friendly panther struck from the rocks as he scampered up a stony hill (McCoy, *Hist. of Baptist Indian Missions*, p. 364).

152-1 Mrs. Eastman, ubi sup., p. 158; Schoolcraft, *Ind. Tribes*, iv. p. 645.

152-2 Waitz, *Anthropologie*, iii. p. 417; Müller, *Am. Urrelig.*, p. 271.

154-1 On the myth of Catequil see particularly the *Lettre sur les Superstitions du Pérou*, p. 95 sqq., and compare Montesinos, *Ancien Pérou*, chaps. ii., xx. The letters g and j do not exist in Quichua, therefore Ataguju should doubtless read *Ata-chuchu*, which means lord, or ruler of the twins, from *ati* root of *atini*, I am able, I control, and *chuchu*, twins. The change of the root *ati* to *ata*, though uncommon in Quichua, occurs also in *ata-hualpa*, cock, from *ati* and *hualpa*, fowl. Apo-Catequil, or as given by Arriaga, another old writer on Peruvian idolatry, Apocatequilla, I take to be properly *apu-ccatec-quilla*, which literally means *chief of the followers of the moon*. Acosta mentions that the native name for various constellations was *catachillay* or *catuchillay*, doubtless corruptions of *ccatec quilla*, literally "following the moon." Catequil, therefore, the dark spirit of the storm rack, was also appropriately enough, and perhaps primarily, lord of the night and stars. Piguerao, where the g appears again, is probably a compound of *piscu*, bird, and *uira*, white. Guachemines seems clearly the word *huachi*, a ray of light or an arrow, with the negative suffix *ymana*, thus meaning rayless, as in the text, or *ymana* may mean an excess as well as a want of anything beyond what is natural, which would give the signification "very bright shining." (Holguin, *Arte de la Lengua Quichua*, p. 106: Cuzco, 1607.) Is this sister of theirs the Dawn, who, as in the Rig Veda, brings forth at the cost of her own life the white and dark twins, the Day and the Night, the latter of whom drives from the heavens the far-shooting arrows of light, in order that he may restore his mother again to life? The answer may for the present be deferred. It is a coincidence perhaps worth mentioning that the Augustin monk who is our principal authority for this legend mentions two other twin deities, Yamo and Yama, whose names are almost identical with the twins Yama and Yami of the Veda.

155-1   *Hist. des Incas*, liv. ii. cap. 28, and corrected in Markham's *Quichua Grammar*.

155-2 The latter is a compound of *tici* or *ticcu*, a vase, and *ylla*, the root of *yllani*, to shine, *yllapantac*, it thunders and lightens. The former is from *tici* and *cun* or *con*, whence by reduplication *cun-un-un-an*, it thunders. From *cun* and *tura*, brother, is probably derived *cuntur*, the condor, the flying thunder-cloud being looked upon as a great bird also. Dr. Waitz has pointed out that the Araucanians call by the title *con*, the messenger who summons their chieftains to a general council.

156-1 *Le Livre Sacré*, p. 9. The name of the lightning in Quiché is *cak ul ha*, literally, "fire coming from water."

156-2 Morgan, *League of the Iroquois*, p. 158.

157-1 "El rayo, el relámpago, y el trueno." Gama, *Des. de las dos Piedras*, etc., ii. p. 76: Mexico, 1832.

157-2 Torquemada, *Monarquia Indiana*, lib. vi. cap. 23. Gama, ubi sup. ii. 76, 77.

158-1 Torquemada, ibid., lib. vi. cap. 41.

158-2 *Senate Report on the Indian Tribes*, p. 358: Washington, 1867.

158-3 Brasseur, *Hist du Mexique*, i. p. 201, and on the extent of his worship Waitz, *Anthropol.*, iv. p. 144.

158-4 Oviedo, *Hist. du Nicaragua*, p. 47.

CHAPTER VI
THE SUPREME GODS OF THE RED RACE

Analysis of American culture myths. — The Manibozho or Michabo of the Algonkins shown to be an impersonation of Light, a hero of the Dawn, and their highest deity. — The myths of Ioskeha of the Iroquois, Viracocha of the Peruvians, and Quetzalcoatl of the Toltecs essentially the same as that of Michabo. — Other examples. — Ante-Columbian prophecies of the advent of a white race from the east as conquerors. — Rise of later culture myths under similar forms.

THE philosopher Machiavelli, commenting on the books of Livy, lays it down as a general truth that every form and reform has been brought about by a single individual. Since a remorseless criticism has shorn so many heroes of their laurels, our faith in the maxim of the great Florentine wavers, and the suspicion is created that the popular fancy which personifies under one figure every social revolution is an illusion. It springs from that tendency to hero worship, ineradicable in the heart of the race, which leads every nation to have an ideal, the imagined author of its prosperity, the father of his country, and the focus of its legends. As has been hinted, history is not friendly to their renown, and dissipates them altogether into phantoms of the brain, or sadly dims the lustre of their fame. Arthur, bright star of chivalry, dwindles into a Welsh subaltern; the Cid Campeador, defender of the faith, sells his sword as often to Moslem as to Christian, and *sells* it ever; while Siegfried and Feridun vanish into nothings.

As elsewhere the world over, so in America many tribes had to tell of such a personage, some such august character, who taught them what they knew, the tillage of the soil, the properties of plants, the art of picture writing, the secrets of magic; who founded their institutions and established their religions, who governed them long with glory abroad and peace at home; and finally, did not die, but like Frederick Barbarossa, Charlemagne, King Arthur, and all great heroes, vanished mysteriously, and still lives somewhere, ready at the right moment to return to his beloved people and lead them to victory and happiness. Such to the Algonkins was Michabo or Manibozho, to the Iroquois Ioskeha, Wasi to the Cherokees, Tamoi to the Caribs; so the Mayas had Zamna, the Toltecs Quetzalcoatl, the Muyscas Nemqueteba; such among the Aymaras was Viracocha, among the Mandans Numock-muckenah, and among the natives of the Orinoko Amalivaca; and the catalogue could be extended indefinitely.

It is not always easy to pronounce upon these heroes, whether they belong to history or mythology, their nation's poetry or its prose. In arriving at a conclusion we must remember that a fiction built on an idea is infinitely more tenacious of life than a story founded on fact. Further, that if a striking similarity in the legends of two such heroes be discovered under circumstances which forbid the thought that one was derived from the other, then both are probably mythical. If this is the case in not two but in half a dozen instances, then the probability amounts to a certainty, and the only task remaining is to explain such narratives on consistent mythological principles. If after sifting out all foreign and later traits, it appears that when first known to Europeans, these heroes were assigned all the attributes of highest divinity, were the imagined creators and rulers of the world, and mightiest of spiritual powers, then their position must be set far higher than that of deified men. They must be accepted as the supreme gods of the red race, the analogues in the western continent of Jupiter, Osiris, and Odin in the eastern, and whatever opinions contrary to this may have been advanced by writers and travellers must be set down to the account of that prevailing ignorance of American mythology which has fathered so many other blunders. To solve these knotty points I shall choose for analysis the culture myths of the Algonkins, the Iroquois, the Toltecs of Mexico, and the Aymaras or Peruvians, guided in my choice by the fact that these four families are the best known, and, in many points of view, the most important on the continent.

From the remotest wilds of the northwest to the coast of the Atlantic, from the southern boundaries of Carolina to the cheerless swamps of Hudson's Bay, the Algonkins were never tired of gathering around the winter fire and repeating the story of Manibozho or Michabo, the Great Hare. With entire unanimity their various branches, the Powhatans of Virginia, the Lenni Lenape of the Delaware, the warlike hordes of New England, the Ottawas of the far north, and the western tribes perhaps without exception, spoke of "this chimerical beast," as one of the old missionaries calls it, as their common ancestor. The totem or clan which bore his name was looked up to with peculiar respect. In many of the tales which the whites have preserved of Michabo he seems half a wizzard , half a simpleton. He is full of pranks and wiles, but often at a loss for a meal of victuals; ever itching to try his arts magic on great beasts and often meeting ludicrous failures therein; envious of the powers of others, and constantly striving to outdo them in what they do best; in short, little more than a malicious buffoon delighting in practical jokes, and abusing his superhuman powers for selfish and ignoble ends. But this is a low, modern, and corrupt version of the character of Michabo, bearing no more resemblance to his real and ancient one than the language and acts of our Saviour and the apostles in the coarse Mystery Plays of the Middle Ages do to those recorded by the Evangelists.

What he really was we must seek in the accounts of older travellers, in the invocations of the jossakeeds or prophets, and in the part assigned to him in the solemn mysteries of religion. In these we find him portrayed as the patron and founder of the meda worship, 162-1 the inventor of picture writing, the father and guardian of their nation, the ruler of the winds, even the maker and preserver of the world and creator of the sun and moon. From a grain of sand brought from the bottom of the primeval ocean, he fashioned the habitable land and set it floating on the waters, till it grew to such a size that a strong young wolf, running constantly, died of old age ere he reached its limits. Under the name Michabo Ovisaketchak, the Great Hare who created the Earth, he was originally the highest divinity recognized by them, "powerful and beneficent beyond all others, maker of the heavens and the world." He was founder of the medicine hunt in which after appropriate ceremonies and incantations the Indian sleeps, and Michabo appears to him in a dream, and tells him where he may readily kill game. He himself was a mighty hunter of old; one of his footsteps measured eight leagues, the Great Lakes were the beaver dams he built, and when the cataracts impeded his progress he tore them away with his hands. Attentively watching the spider spread its web to trap unwary flies, he devised the art of knitting nets to catch fish, and the signs and charms he tested and handed down to his descendants are of marvellous efficacy in the chase. In the autumn, in "the moon of the falling leaf," ere he composes himself to his winter's sleep, he fills his great pipe and takes a god-like smoke. The balmy clouds float over the hills and woodlands, filling the air with the haze of the "Indian summer."

Sometimes he was said to dwell in the skies with his brother the snow, or, like many great spirits, to have built his wigwam in the far north on some floe of ice in the Arctic Ocean, while the Chipeways localized his birthplace and former home to the Island Michilimakinac at the outlet of Lake Superior. But in the oldest accounts of the missionaries he was alleged to reside toward the east, and in the holy formulæ of the meda craft, when the winds are invoked to the medicine lodge, the east is summoned in his name, the door opens in that direction, and there, at the edge of the earth, where the sun rises, on the shore of the infinite ocean that surrounds the land, he has his house and sends the luminaries forth on their daily journies. 164-1

It is passing strange that such an insignificant creature as the rabbit should have received this apotheosis. No explanation of it in the least satisfactory has ever been offered. Some have pointed it out as a senseless, meaningless brute worship. It leads to the suspicion that there may lurk here one of those confusions of words which have so often led to confusion of ideas in mythology. Manibozho, Nanibojou, Missibizi, Michabo, Messou, all variations of the same name in different dialects rendered according to different orthographies, scrutinize them closely as we may, they all seem compounded according to well ascertained laws of Algonkin euphony from the words corresponding to *great* and *hare* or *rabbit*, or the first two perhaps from *spirit* and *hare* (*michi*, great, *wabos*, hare, *manito wabos*, spirit hare, Chipeway dialect), and so they have invariably been translated even by the Indians themselves. But looking more narrowly at the second member of the word, it is clearly capable of another and very different interpretation, of an interpretation which discloses at once the origin and the secret meaning of the whole story of Michabo, in the light of which it appears no longer the incoherent fable of savages, but a true myth, instinct with nature, pregnant with matter, nowise inferior to those which fascinate in the chants of the Rig Veda, or the weird pages of the Edda.

On a previous page I have emphasized with what might have seemed superfluous force, how prominent in primitive mythology is the east, the source of the morning, the day-spring on high, the cardinal point which determines and controls all others. But I did not lay as much stress on it as others have. "The whole theogony and philosophy of the ancient world," says Max Müller, "centred in the Dawn, the mother of the bright gods, of the Sun in his various aspects, of the morn, the day, the spring; herself the brilliant image and visage of immortality." 165-1 Now it appears on attentively examining the Algonkin root *wab*, that it gives rise to words of very diverse meaning, that like many others in all languages while presenting but one form it represents ideas of wholly unlike origin and application, that in fact there are two distinct roots having this sound. One is the initial syllable of the word translated hare or rabbit, but the other means *white*, and from it is derived the words for the east, the dawn, the light, the day and the morning. 165-2 Beyond a doubt this is the compound in the names

Michabo and Manibozho which therefore mean the Great Light, the Spirit of Light, of the Dawn, or the East, and in the literal sense of the word the Great White One, as indeed he has sometimes been called.

In this sense all the ancient and authentic myths concerning him are plain and full of meaning. They divide themselves into two distinct cycles. In the one Michabo is the spirit of light who dispels the darkness; in the other as chief of the cardinal points he is lord of the winds, prince of the powers of the air, whose voice is the thunder, whose weapon the lightning, the supreme figure in the encounter of the air currents, in the unending conflict which the Dakotas described as waged by the waters and the winds.

In the first he is grandson of the moon, his father is the West Wind, and his mother, a maiden, dies in giving him birth at the moment of conception. For the moon is the goddess of night, the Dawn is her daughter, who brings forth the morning and perishes herself in the act, and the West, the spirit of darkness as the East is of light, precedes and as it were begets the latter as the evening does the morning. Straightway, however, continues the legend, the son sought the unnatural father to revenge the death of his mother, and then commenced a long and desperate struggle. "It began on the mountains. The West was forced to give ground. Manabozho drove him across rivers and over mountains and lakes, and at last he came to the brink of this world. 'Hold,' cried he, 'my son, you know my power and that it is impossible to kill me.'" 167-1 What is this but the diurnal combat of light and darkness, carried on from what time "the jocund morn stands tiptoe on the misty mountain tops," across the wide world to the sunset, the struggle that knows no end, for both the opponents are immortal?

In the second, and evidently to the native mind more important cycle of legends, he was represented as one of four brothers, the North, the South, the East, and the West, all born at a birth, whose mother died in ushering them into the world; 167-2 for hardly has the kindling orient served to fix the cardinal points than it is lost and dies in the advancing day. Yet it is clear that he was something more than a personification of the east or the east wind, for it is repeatedly said that it was he who assigned their duties to all the winds, to that of the east as well as the others. This is a blending of his two characters. Here too his life is a battle. No longer with his father, indeed, but with his brother Chakekenapok, the flint-stone, whom he broke in pieces and scattered over the land, and changed his entrails into fruitful vines. The conflict was long and terrible. The face of nature was desolated as by a tornado, and the gigantic boulders and loose rocks found on the prairies are the missiles hurled by the mighty combatants. Or else his foe was the glittering prince of serpents whose abode was the lake; or was the shining Manito whose home was guarded by fiery serpents and a deep sea; or was the great king of fishes; all symbols of the atmospheric waters, all figurative descriptions of the wars of the elements. In these affrays the thunder and lightning are at his command, and with them he destroys his enemies. For this reason the Chipeway pictography represents him brandishing a rattlesnake, the symbol of the electric flash, 168-1 and sometimes they called him the Northwest Wind, which in the region they inhabit usually brings the thunder-storms.

As ruler of the winds he was, like Quetzalcoatl, father and protector of all species of birds, their symbols. 168-2 He was patron of hunters, for their course is guided by the cardinal points. Therefore, when the medicine hunt had been successful, the prescribed sign of gratitude to him was to scatter a handful of the animal's blood toward each of these. 168-3 As daylight brings vision, and to see is to know, it was no fable that gave him as the author of their arts, their wisdom, and their institutions.

In effect, his story is a world-wide truth, veiled under a thin garb of fancy. It is but a variation of that narrative which every race has to tell, out of gratitude to that beneficent Father who everywhere has cared for His children. Michabo, giver of life and light, creator and preserver, is no apotheosis of a prudent chieftain, still less the fabrication of an idle fancy or a designing priestcraft, but in origin, deeds, and name the not unworthy personification of the purest conceptions they possessed concerning the Father of All. To Him at early dawn the Indian stretched forth his hands in prayer; and to the sky or the sun as his homes, he first pointed the pipe in his ceremonies, rites often misinterpreted by travellers as indicative of sun worship. As later observers tell us to this day the Algonkin prophet builds the medicine lodge to face the sunrise, and in the name of Michabo, who there has his home, summons the spirits of the four quarters of the world and Gizhigooke, the day maker, to come to his fire and disclose the hidden things of the distant and the future: so the earliest explorers relate that when they asked the native priests who it was they invoked, what demons or familiars, the invariable reply was, "the Kichigouai, the genii of light, those who make the day." 169-1

Our authorities on Iroquois traditions, though numerous enough, are not so satisfactory. The best, perhaps, is Father Brebeuf, a Jesuit missionary, who resided among the Hurons in 1626. Their culture myth, which he has recorded, is strikingly similar to that of the Algonkins. Two brothers appear in it, Ioskeha and Tawiscara, names which find their meaning in the Oneida dialect as the White one and the Dark one. 170-1 They are twins, born of a virgin mother, who died in giving them life. Their grandmother was the moon, called by the Hurons Ataensic, a word which signifies literally *she bathes herself,* and which, in the opinion of Father Bruyas, a most competent authority, is derived from the word for water. 170-2

The brothers quarrelled, and finally came to blows; the former using the horns of a stag, the latter the wild rose. He of the weaker weapon was very naturally discomfited and sorely wounded. Fleeing for life, the blood gushed from him at every step, and as it fell turned into flint-stones. The victor returned to his grandmother, and established his lodge in the far east, on the borders of the great ocean, whence the sun comes. In time he became the father of mankind, and special guardian of the Iroquois. The earth was at first arid and sterile, but he destroyed the gigantic frog which had swallowed all the waters, and guided the torrents into smooth streams and lakes. 171-1 The woods he stocked with game; and having learned from the great tortoise, who supports the world, how to make fire, taught his children, the Indians, this indispensable art. He it was who watched and watered their crops; and, indeed, without his aid, says the old missionary, quite out of patience with such puerilities, "they think they could not boil a pot." Sometimes they spoke of him as the sun, but this only figuratively. 171-2

From other writers of early date we learn that the essential outlines of this myth were received by the Tuscaroras and the Mohawks, and as the proper names of the two brothers are in the Oneida dialect, we cannot err in considering this the national legend of the Iroquois stock. There is strong likelihood that the Taronhiawagon, he who comes from the Sky, of the Onondagas, who was their supreme God, who spoke to them in dreams, and in whose honor the chief festival of their calendar was celebrated about the winter solstice, was, in fact, Ioskeha under another name. 172-1 As to the legend of the Good and Bad Minds given by Cusic, to which I have referred in a previous chapter, and the later and wholly spurious myth of Hiawatha, first made public by Mr. Clark in his History of Onondaga (1849), and which, in the graceful poem of Longfellow, is now familiar to the world, they are but pale and incorrect reflections of the early native traditions.

So strong is the resemblance Ioskeha bears to Michabo, that what has been said in explanation of the latter will be sufficient for both. Yet I do not imagine that the one was copied or borrowed from the other. We cannot be too cautious in adopting such a conclusion. The two nations were remote in everything but geographical position. I call to mind another similar myth. In it a mother is also said to have brought forth twins, or a pair of twins, and to have paid for them with her life. Again the one is described as the bright, the other as the dark twin; again it is said that they struggled one with the other for the mastery. Scholars, likewise, have interpreted the mother to mean the Dawn, the twins either Light and Darkness, or the Four Winds. Yet this is not Algonkin theology; nor is it at all related to that of the Iroquois. It is the story of Sarama in the Rig Veda, and was written in Sanscrit, under the shadow of the Himalayas, centuries before Homer.

Such uniformity points not to a common source in history, but in psychology. Man, chiefly cognizant of his soul through his senses, thought with an awful horror of the night which deprived him of the use of one and foreshadowed the loss of all. Therefore *light* and *life* were to him synonymous; therefore all religions promise to lead

"From night to light,
From night to heavenly light;"

therefore He who rescues is ever the Light of the World; therefore it is said "to the upright ariseth light in darkness;" therefore everywhere the kindling East, the pale Dawn, is the embodiment of his hopes and the centre of his reminiscences. Who shall say that his instinct led him here astray? For is not, in fact, all life dependent on light? Do not all those marvellous and subtle forces known to the older chemists as the imponderable elements, without which not even the inorganic crystal is possible, proceed from the rays of light? Let us beware of that shallow science so ready to shout Eureka, and reverently acknowledge a mysterious intuition here displayed which joins with the latest conquests of the human mind to repeat and emphasize that message which the Evangelist heard of the Spirit and declared unto men, that "God is Light." 173-1

Both these heroes, let it be observed, live in the uttermost east; both are the mythical fathers of the race. To the east, therefore, should these nations have pointed as their original dwelling place. This they did in spite of history. Cusic, who takes up the story of the Iroquois a thousand years before the Christian era, locates them first in the most eastern region they ever possessed. While the Algonkins with one voice called those of their tribes living nearest the rising sun *Abnakis*, our ancestors at the east, or at the dawn; literally our *white* ancestors. 174-1 I designedly emphasize this literal rendering. It reminds one of the white twin of Iroquois legend, and illustrates how the color white came to be intimately associated with the morning light and its beneficent effects. Moreover color has a specific effect on the mind; there is a music to the eye as well as to the ear; and white, which holds all hues in itself, disposes the soul to all pleasant and elevating emotions. 174-2 Not fashion alone bids the bride wreathe her brow with orange flowers, nor was it a mere figure of speech that led the inspired poet to call his love "fairest among women," and to prophecy a Messiah "fairer than the children of men," fulfilled in that day when He appeared "in garments so white as no fuller on earth could white them." No nation is free from the power of this law. "White," observes Adair of the southern

Indians, "is their fixed emblem of peace, friendship, happiness, prosperity, purity, and holiness." 175-1 Their priests dressed in white robes, as did those of Peru and Mexico; the kings of the various species of animals were all supposed to be white; 175-2 the cities of refuge established as asylums for alleged criminals by the Cherokees in the manner of the Israelites were called "white towns," and for sacrifices animals of this color were ever most highly esteemed. All these sentiments were linked to the dawn. Language itself is proof of it. Many Algonkin words for east, morning, dawn, day, light, as we have already seen, are derived from a radical signifying *white*. Or we can take a tongue nowise related, the Quiché, and find its words for east, dawn, morning, light, bright, glorious, happy, noble, all derived from *zak*, white. We read in their legends of the earliest men that they were "white children," "white sons," leading "a white life beyond the dawn," and the creation itself is attributed to the Dawn, the White One, the White Sacrificer of Blood. 175-3 But why insist upon the point when in European tongues we find the daybreak called *l'aube*, *alva*, from *albus*, white? Enough for the purpose if the error of those is manifest, who, in such expressions, would seek support for any theory of ancient European immigration; enough if it displays the true meaning of those traditions of the advent of benevolent visitors of fair complexion in ante-Columbian times, which both Algonkins and Iroquois 176-1 had in common with many other tribes of the western continent. Their explanation will not be found in the annals of Japan, the triads of the Cymric bards, nor the sagas of Icelandic skalds, but in the propensity of the human mind to attribute its own origin and culture to that white-shining orient where sun, moon, and stars, are daily born in renovated glory, to that fair mother, who, at the cost of her own life, gives light and joy to the world, to the brilliant womb of Aurora, the glowing bosom of the Dawn.

Even the complicated mythology of Peru yields to the judicious application of these principles of interpretation. Its peculiar obscurity arises from the policy of the Incas to blend the religions of conquered provinces with their own. Thus about 1350 the Inca Pachacutec subdued the country about Lima where the worship of Con and Pachacamà prevailed. 176-2 The local myth represented these as father and son, or brothers, children of the sun. They were without flesh or blood, impalpable, invisible, and incredibly swift of foot. Con first possessed the land, but Pachacamà attacked and drove him to the north. Irritated at his defeat he took with him the rain, and consequently to this day the sea-coast of Peru is largely an arid desert. Now when we are informed that the south wind, that in other words which blows to the north, is the actual cause of the aridity of the low-lands, 177-1 and consider the light and airy character of these antagonists, we cannot hesitate to accept this as a myth of the winds. The name of *Con tici*, the Thunder Vase, was indeed applied to Viracocha in later times, but they were never identical. Viracocha was the culture hero of the ancient Aymara-Quichua stock. He was more than that, for in their creed he was creator and possessor of all things. Lands and herds were assigned to other gods to support their temples, and offerings were heaped on their altars, but to him none. For, asked the Incas: "Shall the Lord and Master of the whole world need these things from us?" To him, says Acosta, "they did attribute the chief power and commandement over all things;" and elsewhere "in all this realm the chief idoll they did worship was Viracocha, and *after him* the Sunne." 178-1

Ere sun or moon was made, he rose from the bosom of Lake Titicaca, and presided over the erection of those wondrous cities whose ruins still dot its islands and western shores, and whose history is totally lost in the night of time. He himself constructed these luminaries and placed them in the sky, and then peopled the earth with its present inhabitants. From the lake he journeyed westward, not without adventures, for he was attacked with murderous intent by the beings whom he had created. When, however, scorning such unequal combat, he had manifested his power by hurling the lightning on the hill-sides and consuming the forests, they recognized their maker, and humbled themselves before him. He was reconciled, and taught them arts and agriculture, institutions and religion, meriting the title they gave him of *Pachayachachic*, teacher of all things. At last he disappeared in the western ocean. Four personages, companions or sons, were closely connected with him. They rose together with him from the lake, or else were his first creations. These are the four mythical civilizers of Peru, who another legend asserts emerged from the cave Pacarin tampu the Lodgings of the Dawn. 179-1 To these Viracocha gave the earth, to one the north, to another the south, to a third the east, to a fourth the west. Their names are very variously given, but as they have already been identified with the four winds, we can omit their consideration here. 179-2 Tradition, as has rightly been observed by the Inca Garcilasso de la Vega, 179-3 transferred a portion of the story of Viracocha to Manco Capac, first of the historical Incas. King Manco, however, was a real character, the Rudolph of Hapsburg of their reigning family, and flourished about the eleventh century.

There is a general resemblance between this story and that of Michabo. Both precede and create the sun, both journey to the west, overcoming opposition with the thunderbolt, both divide the world between the four winds, both were the fathers, gods, and teachers of their nations. Nor does it cease here. Michabo, I have shown, is the white spirit of the Dawn. Viracocha, all authorities translate "the fat or foam of the sea." The idea conveyed is of whiteness, foam being called fat from its color. 180-1 So true is this that to-day in Peru white men are called *viracochas*, and the early explorers constantly received the same epithet. 180-2 The name is a metaphor. The dawn rises above the horizon as the snowy foam on the surface of a lake. As the Algonkins spoke of the Abnakis, their white ancestors, as in Mexican legends the early Toltecs were of fair complexion, so the Aymaras sometimes called the first four brothers, *viracochas*, white men. 180-3 It is the ancient story how

> "Light
> Sprang from the deep, and from her native east
> To journey through the airy gloom began."

The central figure of Toltec mythology is Quetzalcoatl. Not an author on ancient Mexico but has something to say about the glorious days when he ruled over the land. No one denies him to have been a god, the god of the air, highest deity of the Toltecs, in whose honor was erected the pyramid of Cholula, grandest monument of their race. But many insist that he was at first a man, some deified king. There were in truth many Quetzalcoatls, for his high priest always bore his name, but he himself is a pure creation of the fancy, and all his alleged history is nothing but a myth.

His emblematic name, the Bird-Serpent, and his rebus and cross at Palenque, I have already explained. Others of his titles were, Ehecatl, the air; Yolcuat, the rattlesnake; Tohil, the rumbler; Huemac, the strong hand; Nani he hecatle, lord of the four winds. The same dualism reappears in him that has been noted in his analogues elsewhere; He is both lord of the eastern light and the winds.

As the former, he was born of a virgin in the land of Tula or Tlapallan, in the distant Orient, and was high priest of that happy realm. The morning star was his symbol, and the temple of Cholula was dedicated to him expressly as the author of light. 181-1 As by days we measure time, he was the alleged inventor of the calendar. Like all the dawn heroes, he too was represented as of white complexion, clothed in long white robes, and, as most of the Aztec gods, with a full and flowing beard. 181-2 When his earthly-work was done he too returned to the east, assigning as a reason that the sun, the ruler of Tlapallan, demanded his presence. But the real motive was that he had been overcome by Tezcatlipoca, otherwise called Yoalliehecatl, the wind or spirit of night, who had descended from heaven by a spider's web and presented his rival with a draught pretended to confer immortality, but, in fact, producing uncontrollable longing for home. For the wind and the light both depart when the gloaming draws near, or when the clouds spread their dark and shadowy webs along the mountains, and pour the vivifying rain upon the fields.

In his other character, he was begot of the breath of Tonacateotl, god of our flesh or subsistence, 182-1 or (according to Gomara) was the son of Iztac Mixcoatl, the white cloud serpent, the spirit of the tornado. Messenger of Tlaloc, god of rains, he was figuratively said to sweep the road for him, since in that country violent winds are the precursors of the wet seasons. Wherever he went all manner of singing birds bore him company, emblems of the whistling breezes. When he finally disappeared in the far east, he sent back four trusty youths who had ever shared his fortunes, "incomparably swift and light of foot," with directions to divide the earth between them and rule it till he should return and resume his power. When he would promulgate his decrees, his herald proclaimed them from Tzatzitepec, the hill of shouting, with such a mighty voice that it could be heard a hundred leagues around. The arrows which he shot transfixed great trees, the stones he threw levelled forests, and when he laid his hands on the rocks the mark was indelible. Yet as thus emblematic of the thunder-storm, he possessed in full measure its better attributes. By shaking his sandals he gave fire to men, and peace, plenty, and riches blessed his subjects. Tradition says he built many temples to Mictlanteuctli, the Aztec Pluto, and at the creation of the sun that he slew all the other gods, for the advancing dawn disperses the spectral shapes of night, and yet all its vivifying power does but result in increasing the number doomed to fell before the remorseless stroke of death. 183-1

His symbols were the bird, the serpent, the cross, and the flint, representing the clouds, the lightning, the four winds, and the thunderbolt. Perhaps, as Huemac, the Strong Hand, he was god of the earthquakes. The Zapotecs worshipped such a deity under the image of this member carved from a precious stone, 183-2 calling to mind the "Kab ul," the Working Hand, adored by the Mayas, 183-3 and said to be one of the images of Zamna, their hero god. The human hand, "that divine tool," as it has been called, might well be regarded by the reflective mind as the teacher of the arts and the amulet whose magic power has won for man what vantage he has gained in his long combat with nature and his fellows.

I might next discuss the culture myth of the Muyscas, whose hero Bochica or Nemqueteba bore the other name Sua, the White One, the Day, the East, an appellation they likewise gave the Europeans on their arrival. He had taught them in remotest times how to manufacture their clothing, build their houses, cultivate the soil, and reckon time. When he disappeared, he divided the land between four chiefs, and laid down many minute rules of government which ever after were religiously observed. 184-1 Or I might choose that of the Caribs, whose patron Tamu called Grandfather, and Old Man of the Sky, was a man of light complexion, who in the old times came from the east, instructed them in agriculture and arts, and disappeared in the same direction, promising them assistance in the future, and that at death he would receive their souls on the summit of the sacred tree, and transport them safely to his home in the sky. 184-2 Or from the more fragmentary mythology of ruder nations, proof might be brought of the well nigh universal reception of these fundamental views. As, for instance, when the Mandans of the Upper Missouri speak of their first ancestor as a son of the West, who preserved them at the flood, and whose garb was always of four milk-white wolf skins; 185-1 and when the Pimos, a people of the valley of the Rio Gila, relate that their birthplace was where the sun rises, that there for generations they led a joyous life, until their beneficent first parent disappeared in the heavens. From that time, say they, God lost sight of them, and they wandered west, and further west till they reached their present seats. 185-2 Or I might instance the Tupis of Brazil, who were named after the first of men, Tupa, he who alone survived the flood, who was one of four brothers, who is described as an old man of fair complexion, *un vieillard blanc*, 185-3 and who is now their highest divinity, ruler of the lightning and the storm, whose voice is the thunder, and who is the guardian of their nation. But is it not evident that these and all such legends are but variations of those already analyzed?

In thus removing one by one the wrappings of symbolism, and displaying at the centre and summit of these various creeds, He who is throned in the sky, who comes with the dawn, who manifests himself in the light and the storm, and whose ministers are the four winds, I set up no new god. The ancient Israelites prayed to him who was seated above the firmament, who commanded the morning and caused the day-spring to know its place, who answered out of the whirlwind, and whose envoys were the four winds, the four cherubim described with such wealth of imagery in the introduction to the book of Ezekiel. The Mahometan adores "the clement and merciful Lord of the Daybreak," whose star is in the east, who rides on the storm, and whose breath is the wind. The primitive man in the New World also associated these physical phenomena as products of an invisible power, conceived under human form, called by name, worshipped as one, and of whom all related the same myth differing but in unimportant passages. This was the primeval religion. It was not monotheism, for there were many other gods; it was not pantheism, for there was no blending of the cause with the effects; still less was it fetichism, an adoration of sensuous objects, for these were recognized as effects. It teaches us that the idea of God neither arose from the phenomenal world nor was sunk in it, as is the shallow theory of the day, but is as Kant long ago defined it, a conviction of a highest and first principle which binds all phenomena into one.

One point of these legends deserves closer attention for the influence it exerted on the historical fortunes of the race. The dawn heroes were conceived as of fair complexion, mighty in war, and though absent for a season, destined to return and claim their ancient power. Here was one of those unconscious prophecies, pointing to the advent of a white race from the east, that wrote the doom of the red man in letters of fire. Historians have marvelled at the instantaneous collapse of the empires of Mexico, Peru, the Mayas, and the Natchez, before a handful of Spanish filibusters. The fact was, wherever the whites appeared they were connected with these ancient predictions of the spirit of the dawn returning to claim his own. Obscure and ominous prophecies, "texts of bodeful song," rose in the memory of the natives, and paralyzed their arms.

"For a very long time," said Montezuma, at his first interview with Cortes, "has it been handed down that we are not the original possessors of this land, but came hither from a distant region under the guidance of a ruler who afterwards left us and returned. We have ever believed that some day his descendants would come and resume dominion over us. Inasmuch as you are from that direction, which is toward the rising of the sun, and serve so great a king as you describe, we believe that he is also our natural lord, and are ready to submit ourselves to him." 187-1

The gloomy words of Nezahualcoyotl, a former prince of Tezcuco, foretelling the arrival of white and bearded men from the east, who would wrest the power from the hands of the rightful rulers and destroy in a day the edifice of centuries, were ringing in his ears. But they were not so gloomy to the minds of his down-trodden subjects, for that day was to liberate them from the thralls of servitude. Therefore when they first beheld the fair complexioned Spaniards, they rushed into the water to embrace the prows of their vessels, and despatched messengers throughout the land to proclaim the return of Quetzalcoatl. 188-1

The noble Mexican was not alone in his presentiments. When Hernando de Soto on landing in Peru first met the Inca Huascar, the latter related an ancient prophecy which his father Huayna Capac had repeated on his dying bed, to the effect that in the reign of the thirteenth Inca, white men (*viracochas*) of surpassing strength and valor would come from their father the Sun and subject to their rule the nations of the world. "I command you," said the dying monarch, "to yield them homage and obedience, for they will be of a nature superior to ours." 188-2

The natives of Haiti told Columbus of similar predictions long anterior to his arrival. 188-3 And Father Lizana has preserved in the original Maya tongue several such foreboding chants. Doubtless he has adapted them somewhat to proselytizing purposes, but they seem very likely to be close copies of authentic aboriginal songs, referring to the return of Zamna or Kukulcan, lord of the dawn and the four winds, worshipped at Cozumel and Palenque under the sign of the cross. An extract will show their character: —

> "At the close of the thirteenth Age of the world,
> While the cities of Itza and Tancah still flourish,
> The sign of the Lord of the Sky will appear,
> The light of the dawn will illumine the land,
> And the cross will be seen by the nations of men.
> A father to you, will He be, Itzalanos,
> A brother to you, ye natives of Tancah;
> Receive well the bearded guests who are coming,
> Bringing the sign of the Lord from the daybreak,
> Of the Lord of the Sky, so clement yet powerful." 189-1

The older writers, Gomara, Cogolludo, Villagutierre, have taken pains to collect other instances of this presentiment of the arrival and domination of a white race. Later historians, fashionably incredulous of what they cannot explain, have passed them over in silence. That they existed there can be no doubt, and that they arose in the way I have stated, is almost proven by the fact that in Mexico, Bogota, and Peru, the whites were at once called from the proper names of the heroes of the Dawn, *Suas*, *Viracochas*, and *Quetzalcoatls*.

When the church of Rome had crushed remorselessly the religions of Mexico and Peru, all hope of the return of Quetzalcoatl and Viracocha perished with the institutions of which they were the mythical founders. But it was only to arise under new incarnations and later names. As well forbid the heart of youth to bud forth in tender love, as that of oppressed nationalities to cherish the faith that some ideal hero, some royal man, will yet arise, and break in fragments their fetters, and lead them to glory and honor.

When the name of Quetzalcoatl was no longer heard from the teocalli of Cholula, that of Montezuma took its place. From ocean to ocean, and from the river Gila to the Nicaraguan lake, nearly every aboriginal nation still cherishes the memory of Montezuma, not as the last unfortunate ruler of a vanished state, but as the prince of their golden era, their Saturnian age, lord of the winds and waters, and founder of their institutions. When, in the depth of the tropical forests, the antiquary disinters some statue of earnest mien, the natives whisper one to the other, "Montezuma! Montezuma!" 190-1 In the legends of New Mexico he is the founder of the pueblos, and intrusted to their guardianship the sacred fire. Departing, he planted a tree, and bade them watch it well, for when that tree should fall and the fire die out, then he would return from the far East, and lead his loyal people to victory and power. When the present generation saw their land glide, mile by mile, into the rapacious hands of the Yankees—when new and strange diseases desolated their homes—finally, when in 1846 the sacred tree was prostrated, and the guardian of the holy fire was found dead on its cold ashes, then they thought the hour of deliverance had come, and every morning at earliest dawn a watcher mounted to the house-tops, and gazed long and anxiously in the lightening east, hoping to descry the noble form of Montezuma advancing through the morning beams at the head of a conquering army. 191-1

Groaning under the iron rule of the Spaniards, the Peruvians would not believe that the last of the Incas had perished an outcast and a wanderer in the forests of the Cordilleras. For centuries they clung to the persuasion that he had but retired to another mighty kingdom beyond the mountains, and in due time would return and sweep the haughty Castilian back into the ocean. In 1781, a mestizo, Jose Gabriel Condorcanqui, of the province of Tinta, took advantage of this strong delusion, and binding around his forehead the scarlet fillet of the Incas, proclaimed himself the long lost Inca Tupac Amaru, and a true child of the sun. Thousands of Indians flocked to his standard, and at their head he took the field, vowing the extermination of every soul of the hated race. Seized at last by the Spaniards, and condemned to a public execution, so profound was the reverence with which he had inspired his followers, so full their faith in his claims, that, undeterred by the threats of the soldiery, they prostrated themselves on their faces before this last of the children of the sun, as he passed on to a felon's death. 191-2

These fancied reminiscences, these unfounded hopes, so vague, so child-like, let no one dismiss them as the babblings of ignorance. Contemplated in their broadest meaning as characteristics of the race of man, they have an interest higher than any history, beyond that of any poetry. They point to the recognized discrepancy between what man is, and what he feels he should be, must be; they are the indignant protests of the race against acquiescence in the world's evil as the world's law; they are the incoherent utterances of those yearnings for nobler conditions of existence, which no savagery, no ignorance, nothing but a false and lying enlightenment can wholly extinguish.

FOOTNOTE:

162-1 The *meda* worship is the ordinary religious ritual of the Algonkins. It consists chiefly in exhibitions of legerdemain, and in conjuring and exorcising demons. A *jossakeed* is an inspired prophet who derives his power directly from the higher spirits, and not as the *medawin*, by instruction and practice.

164-1 For these particulars see the *Rel. de la Nouv. France*, 1667, p. 12, 1670, p. 93; Charlevoix, *Journal Historique*, p. 344; Schoolcraft, *Indian Tribes*, v. pp. 420 sqq., and Alex. Henry, *Travs. in Canada and the Ind. Territories*, pp. 212 sqq. These are decidedly the best references of the many that could be furnished. Peter Jones' *History of the Ojibway Indians*, p. 35, may also be consulted.

165-1 *Science of Language*, Second Series, p. 518.

165-2 Dialectic forms in Algonkin for white,
are *wabi, wape, wompi, waubish, oppai*;
for morning, *wapan, wapaneh, opah*; for
east, *wapa, waubun, waubamo*; for dawn, *wapa, waubun*; for
day, *wompan, oppan*; for light, *oppung*; and many others
similar. In the Abnaki dialect, *wanbighen*, it is white, is
the customary idiom to express the breaking of the day
(Vetromile, *The Abnakis and their History*, p. 27: New
York, 1866). The loss in composition of the vowel sound
represented by the English w, and in the French writers
by the figure 8, is supported by frequent analogy.

167-1 Schoolcraft, *Algic Researches*, i. pp. 135-142.

167-2 The names of the four brothers, Wabun, Kabun, Kabibonokka, and Shawano, express in Algonkin both the cardinal points and the winds which blow from them. In another version of the legend, first reported by Father De Smet and quoted by Schoolcraft without acknowledgment, they are Nanaboojoo, Chipiapoos, Wabosso, and Chakekenapok. See for the support of the text, Schoolcraft, *Algic Res.*, ii. p. 214; De Smet, *Oregon Missions*, p. 347.

168-1 *Narrative of John Tanner*, p. 351.

168-2 Schoolcraft, *Algic Res.*, i. p. 216.

168-3 *Narrative of John Tanner*, p. 354.

]169-1 Compare the *Rel. de la Nouv. France*, 1634 p. 14, 1637, p. 46, with Schoolcraft, *Ind. Tribes*, v. p. 419. *Kichigouai* is the same word as *Gizhigooke*, according to a different orthography.

170-1 The names *I8skeha* and *Ta8iscara* I venture to identify with the Oneida *owisske* or *owiska*, white, and *tetiucalas* (*tyokaras, tewhgarlars*, Mohawk), dark or darkness. The prefix i to *owisske* is the impersonal third person singular; the suffix *ha* gives a future sense, so that *i-owisske-*

ha or *iouskeha* means "it is going to become white." Brebeuf gives a similar example of *gaon*, old; *a-gaon-ha*, *il va devenir vieux* (*Rel. Nouv. France*, 1636, p. 99). But "it is going to become white," meant to the Iroquois that the dawn was about to appear, just as *wanbighen*, it is white, did to the Abnakis (see note on page 166), and as the Eskimos say, *kau ma wok*, it is white, to express that it is daylight (Richardson's Vocab. of Labrador Eskimo in his *Arctic Expedition*). Therefore, that Ioskeha is an impersonation of the light of the dawn admits of no dispute.

170-2 The orthography of Brebeuf is *aataentsic*. This may be analyzed as follows: root *aouen*, water; prefix *at*, *il y a quelque chose là dedans*; *ataouen*, *se baigner*; from which comes the form *ataouensere*. (See Bruyas, *Rad. Verb. Iroquæor.*, pp. 30, 31.) Here again the mythological role of the moon as the goddess of water comes distinctly to light.

171-1 This offers an instance of the uniformity which prevailed in symbolism in the New World. The Aztecs adored the goddess of water under the figure of a frog carved from a single emerald; or of human form, but holding in her hand the leaf of a water lily ornamented with frogs. (Brasseur, *Hist. du Mexique*, i. p. 324.)

171-2 *Rel. de la Nouv. France*, 1636, p. 101.

172-1 *Rel. de la Nouv. France*, 1671, p. 17. Cusic spells it *Tarenyawagon*, and translates it Holder of the Heavens. But the name is evidently a compound of *garonhia*, sky, softened in the Onondaga dialect to *taronhia* (see Gallatin's Vocabs. under the word sky), and *wagin*, I come.

173-1 ☐ Θεος φως εστι, The First Epistle General of John, i. 5. In curious analogy to these myths is that of the Eskimos of Greenland. In the beginning, they relate, were two brothers, one of whom said: "There shall be night and there shall be day, and men shall die, one after another." But the second said, "There shall be no day, but only night all the time, and men shall live forever." They had a long struggle, but here once more he who loved darkness rather than light was worsted, and the day triumphed. (*Nachrichten von Grönland aus einem Tagebuche vom Bischof Paul Egede*, p. 157: Kopenhagen, 1790. The date of the entry is 1738.)

174-1 I accept without hesitation the derivation of this word, proposed and defended by that accomplished Algonkin scholar, the Rev. Eugene Vetromile, from *wanb*, white or east, and *naghi* ancestors (*The Abnakis and their History*, p. 29: New York, 1866).

174-2 White light, remarks Goethe, has in it something cheerful and ennobling; it possesses "eine heitere, muntere, sanft reizende Eigenschaft." *Farbenlehre*, sec's 766, 770.

175-1 *Hist. of the N. Am. Indians*, p. 159.

175-2 La Hontan, *Voy. dans l'Amér. Sept.*, ii. p. 42.

175-3 "Blanco pizote," Ximenes, p. 4, *Vocabulario Quiché*, s. v. *zak*. In the far north the Eskimo tongue presents the same analogy. Day, morning, bright, light, lightning, all are from the same root (*kau*), signifying white (Richardson, Vocab. of Labrador Eskimo).

176-1 Some fragments of them may be found in Campanius, *Acc. of New Sweden*, 1650, book iii. chap. 11, and in Byrd, *The Westover Manuscripts*, 1733, p. 82. They were in both instances alleged to have been white and bearded men, the latter probably a later trait in the legend.

176-2 *Con* or *Cun* I have already explained to mean thunder, *Con tici*, the mythical thunder vase. Pachacamà is doubtless, as M. Leonce Angrand has suggested, from *ppacha*, source, and *camà*, all, the Source of All things (Desjardins, *Le Pérou avant la Conq. Espagnole*, p. 23, note). But he and all other writers have been in error in considering this identical with *Pachacámac*, nor can the latter mean *creator of the world*, as it has constantly been translated. It is a participial adjective from *pacha*, place, especially the world, and *camac*, present participle of *camani*, I animate, from which also comes *camakenc*, the soul, and means *animating the world*. It was never used as a proper name. The following trochaic lines from the Quichua poem translated in the previous chapter, show its true meaning and correct accent: —

Păchă rūrăc,	World creating,
Păchă cāmăc,	World animating,
Viracocha,	Viracocha,
Camasunqui,	He animates thee.

The last word is the second transition, present tense, of *camani*, while *camac* is its present participle.

177-1 Ulloa, *Mémoires Philosophiques sur l'Amérique*, i. p. 105.

178-1 Acosta, *Hist. of the New World*, bk. v. chap. 4, bk. vi. chap. 19, Eng. trans., 1704.

179-1   The name is derived from *tampu*, corrupted by the Spaniards to *tambo*, an inn, and *paccari* morning, or *paccarin*, it dawns, which also has the figurative signification, it is born. It may therefore mean either Lodgings of the Dawn, or as the Spaniards usually translated it, House of Birth, or Production, *Casa de Producimiento*.

179-2   The names given by Balboa (*Hist. du Pérou*, p. 4) and Montesinos (*Ancien Pérou*, p. 5) are Manco, Cacha, Auca, Uchu. The meaning of Manco is unknown. The others signify, in their order, messenger, enemy or traitor, and the little one. The myth of Viracocha is given in its most antique form by Juan de Betanzos, in the *Historia de los Ingas*, compiled in the first years of the conquest from the original songs and legends. It is quoted in Garcia, *Origen de los Indios*, lib. v. cap. 7. Balboa, Montesinos, Acosta, and others have also furnished me some incidents. Whether Atachuchu mentioned in the last chapter was not another name of Viracocha may well be questioned. It is every way probable.

179-3   *Hist. des Incas*, liv. iii. chap. 25.

180-1   It is compounded of *vira*, fat, foam (which perhaps is akin to *yurac, white*), and *cocha*, a pond or lake.

180-2   See Desjardins, *Le Pérou avant la Conq. Espagnole*, p. 67.

180-3   Gomara, *Hist. de las Indias*, cap. 119, in Müller.

181-1   Brasseur, *Hist. du Mexique*, i. p. 302.

181-2   There is no reason to lay any stress upon this feature. Beard was nothing uncommon among the Aztecs and many other nations of the New World. It was held to add dignity to the appearance, and therefore Sahagun, in his description of the Mexican idols, repeatedly alludes to their beards, and Müller quotes various authorities to show that the priests wore them long and full (*Amer. Urreligionen*, p. 429). Not only was Quetzalcoatl himself reported to have been of fair complexion — white indeed — but the Creole historian Ixtlilxochitl says the old legends asserted that all the Toltecs, natives of Tollan, or Tula, as their name signifies, were so likewise. Still more, Aztlan, the traditional home of the Nahuas, or Aztecs proper, means literally the white land, according to one of our best authorities (Buschmann, *Ueber die Aztekischen Ortsnamen*, 612: Berlin, 1852).

182-1   Kingsborough, *Antiquities of Mexico*, v. p. 109.

183-1   The myth of Quetzalcoatl I have taken chiefly from Sahagun, *Hist. de la Nueva España*, lib. i. cap. 5; lib. iii. caps. 3, 13, 14; lib. x. cap. 29; and Torquemada, *Monarquia Indiana*, lib. vi. cap. 24. It must be remembered that the Quiché legends identify him positively with the Tohil of Central America (*Le Livre Sacré*, p. 247).

183-2 Padilla Davila, *Hist. de la Prov. de Santiago de Mexico*, lib. ii. cap. 89.

183-3 Cogolludo, *Hist. de Yucathan*, lib. iv. cap. 8.

184-1 He is also called Idacanzas and Nemterequetaba. Some have maintained a distinction between Bochica and Sua, which, however, has not been shown. The best authorities on the mythology of the Muyscas are Piedrahita, *Hist. de las Conq. del Nuevo Reyno de Granada*, 1668 (who is copied by Humboldt, *Vues des Cordillères*, pp. 246 sqq.), and Simon, *Noticias de Tierra Firme*, Parte ii., in Kingsborough's *Mexico*.

184-2 D'Orbigny, *L'Homme Américain*, ii. p. 319, and Rochefort, *Hist. des Isles Antilles*, p. 482 (Waitz). The name has various orthographies, Tamu, Tamöi, Tamou, Itamoulou, etc. Perhaps the Ama-livaca of the Orinoko Indians is another form. This personage corresponds even minutely in many points with the Tamu of the island Caribs.

185-1 Catlin, *Letters and Notes*, Letter 22.

185-2 Journal of Capt. Johnson, in Emory, *Reconnoissance of New Mexico*, p. 601.

185-3 M. De Charency, in the *Revue Américaine*, ii. p. 317. *Tupa* it may be observed means in Quichua, lord, or royal. Father Holguin gives as an example *â tupa Dios*, O Lord God (*Vocabulario Quichua*, p. 348: Ciudad de los Reyes, 1608). In the Quiché dialects *tepeu* is one of the common appellations of divinity and is also translated lord or ruler. We are not yet sufficiently advanced in the study of American philology to draw any inference from these resemblances, but they should not be overlooked.

187-1 Cortes, *Carta Primera*, pp. 113, 114.

188-1 Sahagun, *Hist. de la Nueva España*, lib. xii. caps. 2, 3.

188-2 La Vega, *Hist. des Incas*, lib. ix. cap. 15.

188-3 Peter Martyr, *De Reb. Oceanicis*, Dec. iii. lib. vii.

189-1 Lizana, *Hist. de Nuestra Señora de Itzamal*, lib. ii. cap. i. in Brasseur, *Hist. du Mexique*, ii. p. 605. The prophecies are of the priest who bore the title—not name—*chilan balam*, and whose offices were those of divination and astrology. The verse claims to date from about 1450, and was very well known throughout Yucatan, so it is said. The number thirteen which in many of these prophecies is the supposed limit of the present order of things, is doubtless derived from the observation that thirteen moons complete one solar year.

190-1 Squier, *Travels in Nicaragua*, ii. p. 35.

191-1 Whipple, *Report on the Ind. Tribes*, p. 36. Emory, *Recon. of New Mexico*, p. 64. The latter adds that among the Pueblo Indians, the Apaches, and Navajos, the name of Montezuma is "as familiar as Washington to us." This is the more curious, as neither the Pueblo Indians nor either of the other tribes are in any way related to the Aztec race by language, as has been shown by Dr. Buschman, *Die Voelker und Sprachen Neu Mexico's*, p. 262.

191-2 Humboldt, *Essay on New Spain*, bk. ii. chap. vi, Eng. trans.; *Ansichten der Natur*, ii. pp. 357, 386.

CHAPTER VII
THE MYTHS OF THE CREATION, THE DELUGE, THE EPOCHS OF NATURE, AND THE LAST DAY

Cosmogonies usually portray the action of the Spirit on the Waters. — Those of the Muscogees, Athapascas, Quichés, Mixtecs, Iroquois, Algonkins, and others. — The Flood-Myth an unconscious attempt to reconcile a creation in time with the eternity of matter. — Proof of this from American mythology. — Characteristics of American Flood-Myths. — The person saved usually the first man. — The number seven. — Their Ararats. — The rôle of birds. — The confusion of tongues. — The Aztec, Quiché, Algonkin, Tupi, and earliest Sanscrit flood-myths. — The belief in Epochs of Nature a further result of this attempt at reconciliation. — Its forms among Peruvians, Mayas, and Aztecs. — The expectation of the End of the World a corollary of this belief. — Views of various nations.

COULD the reason rest content with the belief that the universe always was as it now is, it would save much beating of brains. Such is the comfortable condition of the Eskimos, the Rootdiggers of California, the most brutish specimens of humanity everywhere. Vain to inquire their story of creation, for, like the knife-grinder of anti-Jacobin renown, they have no story to tell. It never occurred to them that the earth had a beginning, or underwent any greater changes than those of the seasons. 193-1 But no sooner does the mind begin to reflect, the intellect to employ itself on higher themes than the needs of the body, than the law of causality exerts its power, and the man, out of such materials as he has at hand, manufactures for himself a Theory of Things.

What these materials were has been shown in the last few chapters. A simple primitive substance, a divinity to mould it — these are the requirements of every cosmogony. Concerning the first no nation ever hesitated. All agree that before time began *water* held all else in solution, covered and concealed everything. The reasons for this assumed priority of water have been already touched upon. Did a tribe dwell near some great sea others can be imagined. The land is limited, peopled, stable; the ocean fluctuating, waste, boundless. It insatiably swallows all rains and rivers, quenches sun and moon in its dark chambers, and raves against its bounds as a beast of prey. Awe and fear are the sentiments it inspires; in Aryan tongues its synonyms are the *desert* and the *night*. 194-1 It produces an impression of immensity, infinity, formlessness, and barren changeableness, well suited to a notion of chaos. It is sterile, receiving all things, producing nothing. Hence the necessity of a creative power to act upon it, as it were to impregnate its barren germs. Some cosmogonies find this in one, some in another personification of divinity. Commonest of all is that of the wind, or its emblem the bird, types of the breath of life.

Thus the venerable record in Genesis, translated in the authorized version "and the Spirit of God moved on the face of the waters," may with equal correctness be rendered "and a mighty wind brooded on the surface of the waters," presenting the picture of a primeval ocean fecundated by the wind as a bird. 195-1 The eagle that in the Finnish epic of Kalewala floated over the waves and hatched the land, the egg that in Chinese legend swam hither and thither until it grew to a continent, the giant Ymir, the rustler (as wind in trees), from whose flesh, says the Edda, our globe was made and set to float like a speck in the vast sea between Muspel and Niflheim, all are the same tale repeated by different nations in different ages. But why take illustrations from the old world when they are so plenty in the new?

Before the creation, said the Muscogees, a great body of water was alone visible. Two pigeons flew to and fro over its waves, and at last spied a blade of grass rising above the surface. Dry land gradually followed, and the islands and continents took their present shapes. 195-2 Whether this is an authentic aboriginal myth, is not beyond question. No such doubt attaches to that of the Athapascas. With singular unanimity, most of the northwest branches of this stock trace their descent from a raven, "a mighty bird, whose eyes were fire, whose glances were lightning, and the clapping of whose wings was thunder. On his descent to the ocean, the earth instantly rose, and remained on the surface of the water. This omnipotent bird then called forth all the variety of animals." 196-1

Very similar, but with more of poetic finish, is the legend of the Quichés: —

"This is the first word and the first speech. There were neither men nor brutes; neither birds, fish, nor crabs, stick nor stone, valley nor mountain, stubble nor forest, nothing but the sky. The face of the land was hidden. There was naught but the silent sea and the sky. There was nothing joined, nor any sound, nor thing that stirred; neither any to do evil, nor to rumble in the heavens, nor a walker on foot; only the silent waters, only the pacified ocean, only it in its calm. Nothing was but stillness, and rest, and darkness, and the night; nothing but the Maker and Moulder, the Hurler, the Bird-Serpent. In the waters, in a limpid twilight, covered with green feathers, slept the mothers and the fathers." 196-2

Over this passed Hurakan, the mighty wind, and called out Earth! and straightway the solid land was there.

The picture writings of the Mixtecs preserved a similar cosmogony: "In the year and in the day of clouds, before ever were either years or days, the world lay in darkness; all things were orderless, and a water covered the slime and the ooze that the earth then was." By the efforts of two winds, called, from astrological associations, that of Nine Serpents and that of Nine Caverns, personified one as a bird and one as a winged serpent, the waters subsided and the land dried. 197-1

In the birds that here play such conspicuous parts, we cannot fail to recognize the winds and the clouds; but more especially the dark thunder cloud, soaring in space at the beginning of things, most forcible emblem of the aerial powers. They are the symbols of that divinity which acted on the passive and sterile waters, the fitting result being the production of a universe. Other symbols of the divine could also be employed, and the meaning remain the same. Or were the fancy too helpless to suggest any, they could be dispensed with, and purely natural agencies take their place. Thus the unimaginative Iroquois narrated that when their primitive female ancestor was kicked from the sky by her irate spouse, there was as yet no land to receive her, but that it "suddenly bubbled up under her feet, and waxed bigger, so that ere long a whole country was perceptible." 197-2 Or that certain amphibious animals, the beaver, the otter, and the muskrat, seeing her descent, hastened to dive and bring up sufficient mud to construct an island for her residence. 197-3 The muskrat is also the simple machinery in the cosmogony of the Takahlis of the northwest coast, the Osages and some Algonkin tribes.

These latter were, indeed, keen enough to perceive that there was really no *creation* in such an account. Dry land was wanting, but earth was there, though hidden by boundless waters. Consequently, they spoke distinctly of the action of the muskrat in bringing it to the surface as a formation only. Michabo directed him, and from the mud formed islands and main land. But when the subject of creation was pressed, they replied they knew nothing of that, or roundly answered the questioner that he was talking nonsense. 198-1 Their myth, almost identical with that of their neighbors, was recognized by them to be not of a construction, but a reconstruction only; a very judicious distinction, but one which has a most important corollary. A reconstruction supposes a previous existence. This they felt, and had something to say about an earth anterior to this of ours, but one without light or human inhabitants. A lake burst its bounds and submerged it wholly. This is obviously nothing but a mere and meagre fiction, invented to explain the origin of the primeval ocean. But mark it well, for this is the germ of those marvellous myths of the Epochs of Nature, the catastrophes of the universe, the deluges of water and of fire, which have laid such strong hold on the human fancy in every land and in every age.

The purpose for which this addition was made to the simpler legend is clear enough. It was to avoid the dilemma of a creation from nothing on the one hand, and the eternity of matter on the other. *Ex nihilo nihil* is an apothegm indorsed alike by the profoundest metaphysicians and the rudest savages. But the other horn was no easier. To escape accepting the theory that the world had ever been as it now is, was the only object of a legend of its formation. As either lemma conflicts with fundamental laws of thought, this escape was eagerly adopted, and in the suggestive words of Prescott, men "sought relief from the oppressive idea of eternity by breaking it up into distinct cycles or periods of time." 199-1 Vain but characteristic attempt of the ambitious mind of man! The Hindoo philosopher reconciles to his mind the suspension of the world in space by imagining it supported by an elephant, the elephant by a tortoise, and the tortoise by a serpent. We laugh at the Hindoo, and fancy we diminish the difficulty by explaining that it revolves around the sun, and the sun around some far-off star. Just so the general mind of humanity finds some satisfaction in supposing a world or a series of worlds anterior to the present, thus escaping the insoluble enigma of creation by removing it indefinitely in time.

The support lent to these views by the presence of marine shells on high lands, or by faint reminiscences of local geologic convulsions, I estimate very low. Savages are not inductive philosophers, and by nothing short of a miracle could they preserve the remembrance of even the most terrible catastrophe beyond a few generations. Nor has any such occurred within the ken of history of sufficient magnitude to make a very permanent or wide-spread impression. Not physics, but metaphysics, is the exciting cause of these beliefs in periodical convulsions of the globe. The idea of matter cannot be separated from that of time, and time and eternity are contradictory terms. Common words show this connection. World, for example, in the old language *waereld*, from the root to wear, by derivation means an age or cycle (Grimm).

In effect a myth of creation is nowhere found among primitive nations. It seems repugnant to their reason. Dry land and animate life had a beginning, but not matter. A series of constructions and demolitions may conveniently be supposed for these. The analogy of nature, as seen in the vernal flowers springing up after the desolation of winter, of the sapling sprouting from the fallen trunk, of life everywhere rising from death, suggests such a view. Hence arose the belief in Epochs of Nature, elaborated by ancient philosophers into the Cycles of the Stoics, the Great Days of Brahm, long periods of time rounded off by sweeping destructions, the Cataclysms and Ekpyrauses of the universe. Some thought in these all beings perished; others that a few survived. 200-1 This latter and more common view is the origin of the myth of the deluge. How familiar such speculations were to the aborigines of America there is abundant evidence to show.

The early Algonkin legends do not speak of an antediluvian race, nor of any family who escaped the waters. Michabo, the spirit of the dawn, their supreme deity, alone existed, and by his power formed and peopled it. Nor did their neighbors, the Dakotas, though firm in the belief that the globe had once been destroyed by the waters, suppose that any had escaped. 201-1 The same view was entertained by the Nicaraguans 201-2 and the Botocudos of Brazil. The latter attributed its destruction to the moon falling to the earth from time to time. 201-3

Much the most general opinion, however, was that some few escaped the desolating element by one of those means most familiar to the narrator, by ascending some mountain, on a raft or canoe, in a cave, or even by climbing a tree. No doubt some of these legends have been modified by Christian teachings; but many of them are so connected with local peculiarities and ancient religious ceremonies, that no unbiased student can assign them wholly to that source, as Professor Vater has done, even if the authorities for many of them were less trustworthy than they are. There are no more common heirlooms in the traditional lore of the red race. Nearly every old author quotes one or more of them. They present great uniformity of outline, and rather than engage in repetitions of little interest, they can be more profitably studied in the aggregate than in detail.

By far the greater number represent the last destruction of the world to have been by water. A few, however, the Takahlis of the North Pacific coast, the Yurucares of the Bolivian Cordilleras, and the Mbocobi of Paraguay, attribute it to a general conflagration which swept over the earth, consuming every living thing except a few who took refuge in a deep cave. 202-1 The more common opinion of a submersion gave rise to those traditions of a universal flood so frequently recorded by travellers, and supposed by many to be reminiscences of that of Noah.

There are, indeed, some points of striking similarity between the deluge myths of Asia and America. It has been called a peculiarity of the latter that in them the person saved is always the first man. This, though not without exception, is certainly the general rule. But these first men were usually the highest deities known to their nations, the only creators of the world, and the guardians of the race. 202-2

Moreover, in the oldest Sanscrit legend of the flood in the Zatapatha Brahmana, Manu is also the first man, and by his own efforts creates offspring. 202-3

A later Sanscrit work assigns to Manu the seven Richis or shining ones as companions. Seven was also the number of persons in the ark of Noah. Curiously enough one Mexican and one early Peruvian myth give out exactly seven individuals as saved in their floods. 203-1 This coincidence arises from the mystic powers attached to the number seven, derived from its frequent occurrence in astrology. Proof of this appears by comparing the later and the older versions of this myth, either in the book of Genesis, where the latter is distinguished by the use of the word Elohim for Jehovah, 203-2 or the Sanscrit account in the Zatapatha Brahmana with those in the later Puranas. 203-3 In both instances the number seven hardly or at all occurs in the oldest version, while it is constantly repeated in those of later dates.

As the mountain or rather mountain chain of Ararat was regarded with veneration wherever the Semitic accounts were known, so in America heights were pointed out with becoming reverence as those on which the few survivors of the dreadful scenes of the deluge were preserved. On the Red River near the village of the Caddoes was one of these, a small natural eminence, "to which all the Indian tribes for a great distance around pay devout homage," according to Dr. Sibley. 203-4 The Cerro Naztarny on the Rio Grande, the peak of Old Zuñi in New Mexico, that of Colhuacan on the Pacific Coast, Mount Apoala in Upper Mixteca, and Mount Neba in the province of Guaymi, are some of many elevations asserted by the neighboring nations to have been places of refuge for their ancestors when the fountains of the great deep broke forth.

One of the Mexican traditions related by Torquemada identified this with the mountain of Tlaloc in the terrestrial paradise, and added that one of the seven demigods who escaped commenced the pyramid of Cholula in its memory. He intended that its summit should reach the clouds, but the gods, angry at his presumption, drove away the builders with lightning. This has a suspicious resemblance to Bible stories. Equally fabulous was the retreat of the Araucanians. It was a three-peaked mountain which had the property of floating on water, called Theg-Theg, the Thunderer. This they believed would preserve them in the next as it did in the last cataclysm, and as its only inconvenience was that it approached too near the sun, they always kept on hand wooden bowls to use as parasols. 204-1

The intimate connection that once existed between the myths of the deluge and those of the creation is illustrated by the part assigned to birds in so many of them. They fly to and fro over the waves ere any land appears, though they lose in great measure the significance of bringing it forth, attached to them in the cosmogonies as emblems of the divine spirit. The dove in the Hebrew account appears in that of the Algonkins as a raven, which Michabo sent out to search for land before the muskrat brought it to him from the bottom. A raven also in the Athapascan myth saved their ancestors from the general flood, and in this instance it is distinctly identified with the mighty thunder bird, who at the beginning ordered the earth from the depths. Prometheus-like, it brought fire from heaven, and saved them from a second death by cold. 205-1 Precisely the same beneficent actions were attributed by the Natchez to the small red cardinal bird, 205-2 and by the Mandans and Cherokees an active participation in the event was assigned to wild pigeons. The Navajos and Aztecs thought that instead of being drowned by the waters the human race were transformed into birds and thus escaped. In all these and similar legends, the bird is a relic of the cosmogonal myth which explained the origin of the world from the action of the winds, under the image of the bird, on the primeval ocean.

The Mexican Codex Vaticanus No. 3738 represents after the picture of the deluge a bird perched on the summit of a tree, and at its foot men in the act of marching. This has been interpreted to mean that after the deluge men were dumb until a dove distributed to them the gift of speech. The New Mexican tribes related that all except the leader of those who escaped to the mountains lost the power of utterance by terror, 205-3 and the Quichés that the antediluvian race were "puppets, men of wood, without intelligence or language." These stories, so closely resembling that of the confusion of tongues at the tower of Babel or Borsippa, are of doubtful authenticity. The first is an entirely erroneous interpretation, as has been shown by Señor Ramirez, director of the Museum of Antiquities at Mexico. The name of the bird in the Aztec tongue was identical with the word *departure*, and this is its signification in the painting. 206-1

Stories of giants in the days of old, figures of mighty proportions looming up through the mist of ages, are common property to every nation. The Mexicans and Peruvians had them as well as others, but their connection with the legends of the flood and the creation is incidental and secondary. Were the case otherwise, it would offer no additional point of similarity to the Hebrew myth, for the word rendered *giants* in the phrase, "and there were giants in those days," has no such meaning in the original. It is a blunder which crept into the Septuagint, and has been cherished ever since, along with so many others in the received text.

A few specimens will serve as examples of all these American flood myths. The Abbé Brasseur has translated one from the Codex Chimalpopoca, a work in the Nahuatl language of Ancient Mexico, written about half a century after the conquest. It is as follows: —

"And this year was that of Ce-calli, and on the first day all was lost. The mountain itself was submerged in the water, and the water remained tranquil for fifty-two springs.

"Now towards the close of the year, Titlahuan had forewarned the man named Nata and his wife named Nena, saying, 'Make no more pulque, but straightway hollow out a large cypress, and enter it when in the month Tozoztli the water shall approach the sky.' They entered it, and when Titlacahuan had closed the door he said, 'Thou shalt eat but a single ear of maize, and thy wife but one also.'

"As soon as they had finished [eating], they went forth and the water was tranquil; for the log did not move any more; and opening it they saw many fish.

"Then they built a fire, rubbing together pieces of wood, and they roasted the fish. The gods Citlallinicue and Citlallatonac looking below exclaimed, 'Divine Lord, what means that fire below? Why do they thus smoke the heavens?'

"Straightway descended Titlacahuan Tezcatlipoca, and commenced to scold, saying, 'What is this fire doing here?' And seizing the fishes he moulded their hinder parts and changed their heads, and they were at once transformed into dogs." 207-1

That found in the oft quoted legends of the Quichés is to this effect: —

"Then by the will of the Heart of Heaven the waters were swollen and a great flood came upon the mannikins of wood. For they did not think nor speak of the Creator who had created them, and who had caused their birth. They were drowned, and a thick resin fell from heaven.

"The bird Xecotcovach tore out their eyes; the bird Camulatz cut off their heads; the bird Cotzbalam devoured their flesh; the bird Tecumbalam broke their bones and sinews, and ground them into powder." 207-2

"Because they had not thought of their Mother and Father, the Heart of Heaven, whose name is Hurakan, therefore the face of the earth grew dark and a pouring rain commenced, raining by day, raining by night.

"Then all sorts of beings, little and great, gathered together to abuse the men to their faces; and all spoke, their mill-stones, their plates, their cups, their dogs, their hens.

"Said the dogs and hens, 'Very badly have you treated us, and you have bitten us. Now we bite you in turn.'

"Said the mill-stones, 'Very much were we tormented by you, and daily, daily, night and day, it was *squeak, squeak, screech, screech,* for your sake. Now yourselves shall feel our strength, and we will grind your flesh, and make meal of your bodies,' said the mill-stones. 208-1

"And this is what the dogs said, 'Why did you not give us our food? No sooner did we come near than you drove us away, and the stick was always within reach when you were eating, because, forsooth, we were not able to talk. Now we will use our teeth and eat you,' said the dogs, tearing their faces.

"And the cups and dishes said, 'Pain and misery you gave us, smoking our tops and sides, cooking us over the fire, burning and hurting us as if we had no feeling. 209-1 Now it is your turn, and you shall burn,' said the cups insultingly.

"Then ran the men hither and thither in despair. They climbed to the roofs of the houses, but the houses crumbled under their feet; they tried to mount to the tops of the trees, but the trees hurled them far from them; they sought refuge in the caverns, but the caverns shut before them.

"Thus was accomplished the ruin of this race, destined to be destroyed and overthrown; thus were they given over to destruction and contempt. And it is said that their posterity are those little monkeys who live in the woods." 209-2

The Algonkin tradition has often been referred to. Many versions of it are extant, the oldest and most authentic of which is that translated from the Montagnais dialect by Father le Jeune, in 1634.

"One day as Messou was hunting, the wolves which he used as dogs entered a great lake and were detained there.

"Messou looking for them everywhere, a bird said to him, 'I see them in the middle of this lake.'

"He entered the lake to rescue them, but the lake overflowing its banks covered the land and destroyed the world.

"Messou, very much astonished at this, sent out the raven to find a piece of earth wherewith to rebuild the land, but the bird could find none; then he ordered the otter to dive for some, but the animal returned empty; at last he sent down the muskrat, who came back with ever so small a piece, which, however, was enough for Messou to form the land on which we are.

"The trees having lost their branches, he shot arrows at their naked trunks which became their limbs, revenged himself on those who had detained his wolves, and having married the muskrat, by it peopled the world."

Finally may be given the meagre legend of the Tupis of Brazil, as heard by Hans Staden, a prisoner among them about 1550, and Coreal, a later voyager. Their ancient songs relate that a long time ago a certain very powerful Mair, that is to say, a stranger, who bitterly hated their ancestors, compassed their destruction by a violent inundation. Only a very few succeeded in escaping—some by climbing trees, others in caves. When the waters subsided the remnant came together, and by gradual increase populated the world. 210-1

Or, it is given by an equally ancient authority as follows:—

"Monan, without beginning or end, author of all that is, seeing the ingratitude of men, and their contempt for him who had made them thus joyous, withdrew from them, and sent upon them *tata*, the divine fire, which burned all that was on the surface of the earth. He swept about the fire in such a way that in places he raised mountains, and in others dug valleys. Of all men one alone, Irin Monge, was saved, whom Monan carried into the heaven. He, seeing all things destroyed, spoke thus to Monan: 'Wilt thou also destroy the heavens and their garniture? Alas! henceforth where will be our home? Why should I live, since there is none other of my kind?' Then Monan was so filled with pity that he poured a deluging rain on the earth, which quenched the fire, and, flowing from all sides, formed the ocean, which we call *parana*, the bitter waters." 211-1

In these narratives I have not attempted to soften the asperities nor conceal the childishness which run through them. But there is no occasion to be astonished at these peculiarities, nor to found upon them any disadvantageous opinion of the mental powers of their authors and believers. We can go back to the cradle of our own race in Central Asia, and find traditions every whit as infantile. I cannot refrain from adding the earliest Aryan myth of the same great occurrence, as it is handed down to us in ancient Sanscrit literature. It will be seen that it is little, if at all, superior to those just rehearsed.

"Early in the morning they brought to Manu water to wash himself; when he had well washed, a fish came into his hands.

"It said to him these, words: 'Take care of me; I will save thee.' 'What wilt thou save me from?' 'A deluge will sweep away all creatures; I wish thee to escape.' 'But how shall I take care of thee?'

"The fish said: 'While we are small there is more than one danger of death, for one fish swallows another. Thou must, in the first place, put me in a vase. Then, when I shall exceed it in size, thou must dig a deep ditch, and place me in it. When I grow too large for it, throw me in the sea, for I shall then be beyond the danger of death.'

"Soon it became a great fish; it grew, in fact, astonishingly. Then it said to Manu, 'In such a year the Deluge will come. Thou must build a vessel, and then pay me homage. When the waters of the Deluge mount up, enter the vessel. I will save thee.'

"When Manu had thus taken care of the fish, he put it in the sea. The same year that the fish had said, in this very year, having built the vessel, he paid the fish homage. Then the Deluge mounting, he entered the vessel. The fish swam near him. To its horn Manu fastened the ship's rope, with which the fish passed the Mountain of the North.

"The fish said, 'See! I have saved thee. Fasten the vessel to a tree, so that the water does not float thee onward when thou art on the mountain top. As the water decreases, thou wilt descend little by little.' Thus Manu descended gradually. Therefore to the mountain of the north remains the name, Descent of Manu. The Deluge had destroyed all creatures; Manu survived alone." 213-1

Hitherto I have spoken only of the last convulsion which swept over the face of the globe, and of but one cycle which preceded the present. Most of the more savage tribes contented themselves with this, but it is instructive to observe how, as they advanced in culture, and the mind dwelt more intently on the great problems of Life and Time, they were impelled to remove further and further the dim and mysterious Beginning. The Peruvians imagined that *two* destructions had taken place, the first by a famine, the second by a flood—according to some a few only escaping—but, after the more widely accepted opinion, accompanied by the absolute extirpation of the race. Three eggs, which dropped from heaven, hatched out the present race; one of gold, from which came the priests; one of silver, which produced the warriors; and the last of copper, source of the common people. 213-2

The Mayas of Yucatan increased the previous worlds by one, making the present the *fourth*. Two cycles had terminated by devastating plagues. They were called "the sudden deaths," for it was said so swift and mortal was the pest, that the buzzards and other foul birds dwelt in the houses of the cities, and ate the bodies of their former owners. The third closed either by a hurricane, which blew from all four of the cardinal points at once, or else, as others said, by an inundation, which swept across the world, swallowing all things in its mountainous surges. 214-1

As might be expected, the vigorous intellects of the Aztecs impressed upon this myth a fixity of outline nowhere else met with on the continent, and wove it intimately into their astrological reveries and religious theories. Unaware of its prevalence under more rudimentary forms throughout the continent, Alexander von Humboldt observed that, "of all the traits of analogy which can be pointed out between the monuments, manners, and traditions of Asia and America, the most striking is that offered by the Mexican mythology in the cosmogonical fiction of the periodical destructions and regenerations of the universe." 215-1 Yet it is but the same fiction that existed elsewhere, somewhat more definitely outlined. There exists great discrepancy between the different authorities, both as to the number of Aztec ages or Suns, as they were called, their durations, their terminations, and their names. The preponderance of testimony is in favor of *four* antecedent cycles, the present being the *fifth*. The interval from the first creation to the commencement of the present epoch, owing to the equivocal meaning of the numeral signs expressing it in the picture writings, may have been either 15228, 2316, or 1404 solar years. Why these numbers should have been chosen, no one has guessed. It has been looked for in combinations of numbers connected with the calendar, but so far in vain.

While most authorities agree as to the character of the destructions which terminated the suns, they vary much as to their sequence. Water, winds, fire, and hunger, are the agencies, and in one Codex (Vaticanus) occur in this order. Gama gives the sequence, hunger, winds, fire, and water; Humboldt hunger, fire, winds, and water; Boturini water, hunger, winds, fire. As the cycle ending by a famine, is called the Age of Earth, Ternaux-Compans, the distinguished French *Américaniste*, has imagined that the four Suns correspond mystically to the domination exercised in turn over the world by its four constituent elements. But proof is wanting that Aztec philosophers knew the theory on which this explanation reposes.

Baron Humboldt suggested that the suns were "fictions of mythological astronomy, modified either by obscure reminiscences of some great revolution suffered by our planet, or by physical hypotheses, suggested by the sight of marine petrifactions and fossil remains," 216-1 while the Abbé Brasseur, in his late works on ancient Mexico, interprets them as exaggerated references to historical events. As no solution can be accepted not equally applicable to the same myth as it appears in Yucatan, Peru, and the hunting tribes, and to the exactly parallel teachings of the Edda, 216-2 the Stoics, the Celts, and the Brahmans, both of these must be rejected. And although the Hindoo legend is so close to the Aztec, that it, too, defines four ages, each terminating by a general catastrophe, and each catastrophe exactly the same in both, 216-3 yet this is not at all indicative of a derivation from one original, but simply an illustration how the human mind, under the stimulus of the same intellectual cravings, produces like results. What these cravings are has already been shown.

The reason for adopting four ages, thus making the present the fifth, probably arose from the sacredness of that number in general; but directly, because this was the number of secular days in the Mexican week. A parallel is offered by the Hebrew narrative. In it six epochs or days precede the seventh or present cycle, in which the creative power rests. This latter corresponded to the Jewish Sabbath, the day of repose; and in the Mexican calendar each fifth day was also a day of repose, employed in marketing and pleasure.

Doubtless the theory of the Ages of the world was long in vogue among the Aztecs before it received the definite form in which we now have it; and as this was acquired long after the calendar was fixed, it is every way probable that the latter was used as a guide to the former. Echevarria, a good authority on such matters, says the number of the Suns was agreed upon at a congress of astrologists, within the memory of tradition. 217-1 Now in the calendar, these signs occur in the order, earth, air, water, fire, corresponding to the days distinguished by the symbols house, rabbit, reed, and flint. This sequence, commencing with Tochtli (rabbit, air), is that given as that of the Suns in the Codex Chimalpopoca, translated by Brasseur, though it seems a taint of European teaching, when it is added that on the *seventh* day of the creation man was formed. 217-2

Neither Jews nor Aztecs, nor indeed any American nation, appear to have supposed, with some of the old philosophers, that the present was an exact repetition of previous cycles, 218-1 but rather that each was an improvement on the preceding, a step in endless progress. Nor did either connect these beliefs with astronomical reveries of a great year, defined by the return of the heavenly bodies to one relative position in the heavens. The latter seems characteristic of the realism of Europe, the former of the idealism of the Orient; both inconsistent with the meagre astronomy and more scanty metaphysics of the red race.

The expectation of the end of the world is a natural complement to the belief in periodical destructions of our globe. As at certain times past the equipoise of nature was lost, and the elements breaking the chain of laws that bound them ran riot over the universe, involving all life in one mad havoc and desolation, so in the future we have to expect that day of doom, when the ocean tides shall obey no shore, but overwhelm the continents with their mountainous billows, or the fire, now chafing in volcanic craters and smoking springs, will leap forth on the forests and grassy meadows, wrapping all things in a winding sheet of flame, and melting the very elements with fervid heat. Then, in the language of the Norse prophetess, "shall the sun grow dark, the land sink in the waters, the bright stars be quenched, and high flames climb heaven itself." 218-2 These fearful foreboding shave cast their dark shadow on every literature. The seeress of the north does but paint in wilder colors the terrible pictures of Seneca, 219-1 and the sibyl of the capitol only re-echoes the inspired predictions of Malachi. Well has the Christian poet said: —

Dies iræ, dies illa,
Solvet sæclum in favillâ,
Testis David cum Sibylâ.

Savage races, isolated in the impenetrable forests of another continent, could not escape this fearful looking for of destruction to come. It oppressed their souls like a weight of lead. On the last night of each cycle of fifty-two years, the Aztecs extinguished every fire, and proceeded, in solemn procession, to some sacred spot. Then the priests, with awe and trembling, sought to kindle a new fire by friction. Momentous was the endeavor, for did it fail, their fathers had taught them on the morrow no sun would rise, and darkness, death, and the waters would descend forever on this beautiful world.

The same terror inspired the Peruvians at every eclipse, for some day, taught the Amautas, the shadow will veil the sun forever, and land, moon, and stars will be wrapt in the vortex of a devouring conflagration to know no regeneration; or a drought will wither every herb of the field, suck up the waters, and leave the race to perish to the last creature; or the moon will fall from her place in the heavens and involve all things in her own ruin, a figure of speech meaning that the waters would submerge the land. 220-1 In that dreadful day, thought the Algonkins, when in anger Michabo will send a mortal pestilence to destroy the nations, or, stamping his foot on the ground, flames will burst forth to consume the habitable land, only a pair, or only, at most, those who have maintained inviolate the institutions he ordained, will he protect and preserve to inhabit the new world he will then fabricate. Therefore they do not speak of this catastrophe as the end of the world, but use one of those nice grammatical distinctions so frequent in American aboriginal languages and which can only be imitated, not interpreted, in ours, signifying "when it will be near its end," "when it will no longer be available for man." 220-2

An ancient prophecy handed down from their ancestors warns the Winnebagoes that their nation shall be annihilated at the close of the thirteenth generation. Ten have already passed, and that now living has appointed ceremonies to propitiate the powers of heaven, and mitigate its stern decree. 220-3 Well may they be about it, for there is a gloomy probability that the warning came from no false prophet. Few tribes were destitute of such presentiments. The Chikasaw, the Mandans of the Missouri, the Pueblo Indians of New Mexico, the Muyscas of Bogota, the Botocudos of Brazil, the Araucanians of Chili, have been asserted on testimony that leaves no room for scepticism, to have entertained such forebodings from immemorial time. Enough for the purpose if the list is closed with the prediction of a Maya priest, cherished by the inhabitants of Yucatan long before the Spaniard desolated their stately cities. It is one of those preserved by Father Lizana, curé of Itzamal, and of which he gives the original. Other witnesses inform us that this nation "had a tradition that the world would end," 221-1 and probably, like the Greeks and Aztecs, they supposed the gods would perish with it.

"At the close of the ages, it hath been decreed,
Shall perish and vanish each weak god of men,
And the world shall be purged with a ravening fire.
Happy the man in that terrible day,
Who bewails with contrition the sins of his life, 221-2
And meets without flinching the fiery ordeal."

FOOTNOTE:

193-1 So far as this applies to the Eskimos, it might be questioned on the authority of Paul Egede, whose valuable *Nachrichten von Grönland* contains several flood-myths, &c. But these Eskimos had had for generations intercourse with European missionaries and sailors, and as the other tribes of their stock were singularly devoid of corresponding traditions, it is likely that in Greenland they were of foreign origin.

194-1 Pictet, *Origines Indo-Européennes* in Michelet, *La Mer*. The latter has many eloquent and striking remarks on the impressions left by the great ocean.

195-1 "Spiritus Dei incubuit superficei aquarum" is the translation of one writer. The word for spirit in Hebrew, as in Latin, originally meant wind, as I have before remarked.

195-2 Schoolcraft, *Ind. Tribes*, i. p. 266.

196-1 Mackenzie, *Hist. of the Fur Trade*, p. 83; Richardson, *Arctic Expedition*, p. 239.

196-2 Ximenes, *Or. de los Ind. de Guat.*, pp. 5-7. I translate freely, following Ximenes rather than Brasseur.

197-1 Garcia, *Or. de los Indios*, lib. v. cap. 4.

197-2 *Doc. Hist. of New York*, iv. p. 130 (circ. 1650).

197-3 *Rel. de la Nouv. France*, An 1636, p. 101.

198-1 *Rel. de la Nouv. France*, An 1634, p. 13.

199-1 *Conquest of Mexico,* i. p. 61.

200-1 For instance, Epictetus favors the opinion that at the solstices of the great year not only all human beings, but even the gods, are annihilated; and speculates whether at such times Jove feels lonely (*Discourses,* bk. iii. chap. 13). Macrobius, so far from coinciding with him, explains the great antiquity of Egyptian civilization by the hypothesis that that country is so happily situated between the pole and equator, as to escape both the deluge and conflagration of the great cycle (*Somnium Scipionis,* lib. ii. cap. 10).

201-1 Schoolcraft, *Ind. Tribes,* iii. p. 263, iv. p. 230.

201-2 Oviedo, *Hist. du Nicaragua,* pp. 22, 27.

201-3 Müller, *Amer. Urrelig.,* p. 254, from Max and Denis.

202-1 Morse, *Rep. on the Ind. Tribes,* App. p. 346; D'Orbigny, *Frag. d'un Voyage dans l'Amér. Mérid.,* p. 512.

202-2 When, as in the case of one of the Mexican Noahs, Coxcox, this does not seem to hold good, it is probably owing to a loss of the real form of the myth. Coxcox is also known by the name of Cipactli, Fish-god, and Huehue tonaca cipactli, Old Fish-god of Our Flesh.

202-3 My knowledge of the Sanscrit form of the flood-myth is drawn principally from the dissertation of Professor Felix Nève, entitled *La Tradition Indienne du Deluge dans sa Forme la plus ancienne,* Paris, 1851. There is in the oldest versions no distinct reference to an antediluvian race, and in India Manu is by common consent the Adam as well as the Noah of their legends.

203-1 Prescott, *Conquest of Peru,* i. p. 88; *Codex Vaticanus,* No. 3776, in Kingsborough.

203-2 And also various peculiarities of style and language lost in translation. The two accounts of the Deluge are given side by side in Dr. Smith's *Dictionary of the Bible* under the word Pentateuch.

203-3 See the dissertation of Prof. Nève referred to above.

203-4 *American State Papers,* Indian Affairs, i. p. 729. Date of legend, 1801.

204-1 Molina, *Hist. of Chili,* ii. p. 82.

205-1 Richardson, *Arctic Expedition,* p. 239.

205-2 Dumont, *Mems. Hist. sur la Louisiane,* i. p. 163.

205-3 Schoolcraft, *Ind. Tribes,* v. p. 686.

206-1 Desjardins, *Le Pérou avant la Conq. Espagn.,* p. 27.

207-1 Cod. Chimalpopoca, in Brasseur, *Hist. du Mexique,* Pièces Justificatives.

207-2 These four birds, whose names have lost their signification, represent doubtless the four winds, or the four rivers, which, as in so many legends, are the active agents in overwhelming the world in its great crises.

208-1 The word rendered mill-stone, in the original means those large hollowed stones on which the women were accustomed to bruise the maize. The imitative sounds for which I have substituted others in English, are in Quiché, *holi, holi, huqui, huqui.*

209-1 Brasseur translates "quoique nous ne sentissions rien," but Ximenes, "nos quemasteis, y sentimos el dolor." As far as I can make out the original, it is the negative conditional as I have given it in the text.

209-2 *Le Livre Sacré,* p. 27; Ximenes, *Or. de los Indios,* p. 13.

210-1 The American nations among whom a distinct and well-authenticated myth of the deluge was found are as follows: Athapascas, Algonkins, Iroquois, Cherokees, Chikasaws, Caddos, Natchez, Dakotas, Apaches, Navajos, Mandans, Pueblo Indians, Aztecs, Mixtecs, Zapotecs, Tlascalans, Mechoacans, Toltecs, Nahuas, Mayas, Quiches, Haitians, natives of Darien and Popoyan, Muyscas, Quichuas, Tuppinambas, Achaguas, Araucanians, and doubtless others. The article by M. de Charency in the *Revue Américaine, Le Deluge, d'après les Traditions Indiennes de l'Amérique du Nord,* contains some valuable extracts, but is marred by a lack of criticism of sources, and makes no attempt at analysis, nor offers for their existence a rational explanation.

211-1 *Une Fête Brésilienne célébré à Rouen en 1550, par M. Ferdinand Denis,* p. 82 (quoted in the *Revue Américaine,* ii. p. 317). The native words in this account guarantee its authenticity. In the Tupi language, *tata* means fire; *parana,* ocean; Monan, perhaps from *monáne,* to mingle, to temper, as the potter the clay (*Dias, Diccionario da Lingua Tupy*: Lipsia, 1858). Irin monge may be an old form from *mongat-iron,* to set in order, to restore, to improve (*Martius, Beiträge zur Ethnographie und Sprachenkunde Amerika's,* ii. p. 70).

213-1 Professor Nève, *ubi supra,* from the Zatapatha Brahmana.

213-2 Avendano, *Sermones,* Lima, 1648, in Rivero and Tschudi, *Peruv. Antiqs.,* p. 114. In the year 1600, Oñate found on the coast of California a tribe whose idol held in one hand a shell containing three eggs, in the other an ear of maize, while before it was placed a cup of water. Vizcaino, who visited the same people a few years afterwards, mentions that they kept in their temples tame ravens, and looked upon them as sacred birds (Torquemada, *Mon. Ind.*, lib. v. cap. 40 in Waitz). Thus, in all parts of the continent do we find the bird, as a symbol of the clouds, associated with the rains and the harvests.

214-1   The deluge was called *hun yecil*, which, according to Cogolludo, means *the inundation of the trees*, for all the forests were swept away (*Hist. de Yucathan*, lib. iv. cap. 5). Bishop Landa adds, to substantiate the legend, that all the woods of the peninsula appear as if they had been planted at one time, and that to look at them one would say they had been trimmed with scissors (*Rel. de las Cosas de Yucatan*, 58, 60).

215-1   *Vues des Cordillères*, p. 202.

216-1   Ubi sup., p. 207.

216-2   The Scandinavians believed the universe had been destroyed nine times: —

Ni Verdener yeg husker, Og ni Himle,

says the Voluspa (i. 2, in Klee, *Le Deluge*, p. 220). I observe some English writers have supposed from these lines that the Northmen believed in the existence of nine abodes for the blessed. Such is not the sense of the original.

216-3   At least this is the doctrine of one of the Shastas. The race, it teaches, has been destroyed four times; first by water, secondly by winds, thirdly the earth swallowed them, and lastly fire consumed them (Sepp., *Heidenthum und Christenthum*, i. p. 191).

217-1   Echevarria y Veitia, *Hist. de la Nueva España*, lib. i. cap. 4, in Waitz.

217-2   Brasseur, *Hist. du Mexique*, iii. p. 495.

218-1   The contrary has indeed been inferred from such expressions of the writer of the book of Ecclesiastes as, "that which hath been, is now, and that which is to be, hath already been" (chap. iii. 15), and the like, but they are susceptible of an application entirely subjective.

218-2   Voluspa, xiv. 51, in Klee, *Le Deluge*.

219-1   *Natur. Quæstiones*, iii. cap. 27.

220-1   Velasco, *Hist. du Royaume du Quito*, p. 105; Navarrete, *Viages*, iii. p. 444.

220-2 *Rel. de la Nouv. France*, An 1637, p. 54; Schoolcraft, *Ind. Tribes*, i. p. 319, iv. p. 420.

220-3 Schoolcraft, ibid., iv. p. 240.

221-1 Cogolludo, *Hist. de Yucathan*, lib. iv. cap. 7.

221-2 The Spanish of Lizana is—

> "En la ultima edad, segun esta determinado,
> Avra fin el culto de dioses vanos;
> Y el mundo sera purificado con fuego.
> El que esto viere sera llamado dichoso
> Si con dolor lloraré sus pecados."

(*Hist. de Nuestra Señora de Itzamal*, in Brasseur, *Hist. du Mexique*, ii. p. 603). I have attempted to obtain a more literal rendering from the original Maya, but have not been successful.

CHAPTER VIII
THE ORIGIN OF MAN

Usually man is the Earth-born, both in language and myths. — Illustrations from the legends of the Caribs, Apalachians, Iroquois, Quichuas, Aztecs, and others. — The underworld. — Man the product of one of the primal creative powers, the Spirit, or the Water, in the myths of the Athapascas, Eskimos, Moxos, and others. — Never literally derived from an inferior species.

NO man can escape the importunate question, whence am I? The first replies framed to meet it possess an interest to the thoughtful mind, beyond that of mere fables. They illustrate the position in creation claimed by our race, and the early workings of self-consciousness. Often the oldest terms for man are synopses of these replies, and merit a more than passing contemplation.

The seed is hidden in the earth. Warmed by the sun, watered by the rain, presently it bursts its dark prison-house, unfolds its delicate leaves, blossoms, and matures its fruit. Its work done, the earth draws it to itself again, resolves the various structures into their original mould, and the unending round recommences.

This is the marvellous process that struck the primitive mind. Out of the Earth rises life, to it it returns. She it is who guards all germs, nourishes all beings. The Aztecs painted her as a woman with countless breasts, the Peruvians called her Mama Allpa, *mother* Earth. *Homo, Adam, chamaigenēs,* what do all these words mean but the earth-born, the son of the soil, repeated in the poetic language of Attica in *anthropos,* he who springs up as a flower?

The word that corresponds to the Latin *homo* in American languages has such singular uniformity in so many of them, that we might be tempted to regard it as a fragment of some ancient and common tongue, their parent stem. In the Eskimo it is *inuk, innuk,* plural *innuit;* in Athapasca it is *dinni, tenné;* in Algonkin, *inini, lenni, inwi;* in Iroquois, *onwi, eniha;* in the Otomi of Mexico *n-aniehe;* in the Maya, *inic, winic, winak;* all in North America, and the number might be extended. Of these only the last mentioned can plausibly be traced to a radical (unless the Iroquois *onwi* is from *onnha* life, *onnhe* to live). This Father Ximenes derives from *win*, meaning to grow, to gain, to increase, 223-1 in which the analogy to vegetable life is not far off, an analogy strengthened by the myth of that stock, which relates that the first of men were formed of the flour of maize. 223-2

In many other instances religious legend carries out this idea. The mythical ancestor of the Caribs created his offspring by sowing the soil with stones or with the fruit of the Mauritius palm, which sprouted forth into men and women, 224-1 while the Yurucares, much of whose mythology was perhaps borrowed from the Peruvians, clothed this crude tenet in a somewhat more poetic form, fabling that at the beginning the first of men were pegged, Ariel-like, in the knotty entrails of an enormous hole, until the god Tiri—a second Prospero—released them by cleaving it in twain. 224-2

As in oriental legends the origin of man from the earth was veiled under the story that he was the progeny of some mountain fecundated by the embrace of Mithras or Jupiter, so the Indians often pointed to some height or some cavern, as the spot whence the first of men issued, adult and armed, from the womb of the All-mother Earth. The oldest name of the Alleghany Mountains is Paemotinck or Pemolnick, an Algonkin word, the meaning of which is said to be "the origin of the Indians." 224-3

The Witchitas, who dwelt on the Red River among the mountains named after them, have a tradition that their progenitors issued from the rocks about their homes, 225-1 and many other tribes the Tahkalis, Navajos, Coyoteras, and the Haitians, for instance, set up this claim to be autochthones. Most writers have interpreted this simply to mean that they knew nothing at all about their origin, or that they coined these fables merely to strengthen the title to the territory they inhabited when they saw the whites eagerly snatching it away on every pretext. No doubt there is some truth in this, but if they be carefully sifted, there is sometimes a deep historical significance in these myths, which has hitherto escaped the observation of students. An instance presents itself in our own country.

All those tribes, the Creeks, Seminoles, Choctaws, Chicasaws, and Natchez, who, according to tradition, were in remote times banded into one common confederacy under the headship of the last mentioned, unanimously located their earliest ancestry near an artificial eminence in the valley of the Big Black River, in the Natchez country, whence they pretended to have emerged. Fortunately we have a description, though a brief one, of this interesting monument from the pen of an intelligent traveller. It is described as "an elevation of earth about half a mile square and fifteen or twenty feet high. From its northeast corner a wall of equal height extends for near half a mile to the high land." This was the Nunne Chaha or Nunne Hamgeh, the High Hill, or the Bending Hill, famous in Choctaw stories, and which

Captain Gregg found they have not yet forgotten in their western home. The legend was that in its centre was a cave, the house of the Master of Breath. Here he made the first men from the clay around him, and as at that time the waters covered the earth, he raised the wall to dry them on. When the soft mud had hardened into elastic flesh and firm bone, he banished the waters to their channels and beds, and gave the dry land to his creatures. 226-1 When in 1826 Albert Gallatin obtained from some Natchez chiefs a vocabulary of their language, they gave to him as their word for *hill* precisely the same word that a century and a quarter before the French had found among them as their highest term for God; 226-2 reversing the example of the ancient Greeks who came in time to speak of Olympus, at first the proper name of a peak in Thessaly, as synonymous with heaven and Jove.

A parallel to this southern legend occurs among the Six Nations of the north. They with one consent, if we may credit the account of Cusic, looked to a mountain near the falls of the Oswego River in the State of New York, as the locality where their forefathers first saw the light of day, and that they had some such legend the name Oneida, people of the Stone, would seem to testify.

The cave of Pacari Tampu, the Lodgings of the Dawn, was five leagues distant from Cuzco, surrounded by a sacred grove and inclosed with temples of great antiquity. From its hallowed recesses the mythical civilizers of Peru, the first of men, emerged, and in it during the time of the flood, the remnants of the race escaped the fury of the waves. 227-1 Viracocha himself is said to have dwelt there, though it hardly needed this evidence to render it certain that this consecrated cavern is but a localization of the general myth of the dawn rising from the deep. It refers us for its prototype to the Aymara allegory of the morning light flinging its beams like snow-white foam athwart the waves of Lake Titicaca.

An ancient legend of the Aztecs derived their nation from a place called Chicomoztoc, the Seven Caverns, located north of Mexico. Antiquaries have indulged in all sorts of speculations as to what this means. Sahagun explains it as a valley so named; Clavigero supposes it to have been a city; Hamilton Smith, and after him Schoolcraft, construed caverns to be a figure of speech for the *boats* in which the early Americans paddled across from Asia(!); the Abbé Brasseur confounds it with Aztlan, and very many have discovered in it a distinct reference to the fabulous "seven cities of Cibola" and the Casas Grandes, ruins of large buildings of unburnt brick in the valley of the River Gila. From this story arose the supposed sevenfold division of the Nahuas, a division which never existed except in the imagination of Europeans. When Torquemada adds that *seven* hero gods ruled in Chicomoztoc and were the progenitors of all its inhabitants, when one of them turns out to be Xelhua, the giant who with six others escaped the flood by ascending the mountain of Tlaloc in the terrestrial paradise and afterwards built the pyramid of Cholula, and when we remember that in one of the flood-myths *seven* persons were said to have escaped the waters, the whole narrative acquires a fabulous aspect that shuts it out from history, and brands it as one of those fictions of the origin of man from the earth so common to the race. Fictions yet truths; for caverns and hollow trees were in fact the houses and temples of our first parents, and from them they went forth to conquer and adorn the world; and from the inorganic constituents of the soil acted on by Light, touched by Divine Force, vivified by the Spirit, did in reality the first of men proceed.

This cavern, which thus dimly lingered in the memories of nations, occasionally expanded to a nether world, imagined to underlie this of ours, and still inhabited by beings of our kind, who have never been lucky enough to discover its exit. The Mandans and Minnetarees on the Missouri River supposed this exit was near a certain hill in their territory, and as it had been, as it were, the womb of the earth, the same power was attributed to it that in ancient times endowed certain shrines with such charms; and thither the barren wives of their nation made frequent pilgrimages when they would become mothers. 229-1 The Mandans added the somewhat puerile fable that the means of ascent had been a grapevine, by which many ascended and descended, until one day an immoderately fat old lady, anxious to get a look at the upper earth, broke it with her weight, and prevented any further communication.

Such tales of an under-world are very frequent among the Indians, and are a very natural outgrowth of the literal belief that the race is earth-born.

Man is indeed like the grass that springs up and soon withers away; but he is also more than this. The quintessence of dust, he is a son of the gods as well as a son of the soil. He is the direct product of the great creative power; therefore all the Athapascan tribes west of the Rocky Mountains—the Kenai, the Kolushes, and the Atnai—claim descent from a raven—from that same mighty cloud-bird, who in the beginning of things seized the elements and brought the world from the abyss of the primitive ocean. Those of the same stock situate more eastwardly, the Dogribs, the Chepewyans, the Hare Indians, and also the west coast Eskimos, and the natives of the Aleutian Isles, all believe that they have sprung from a dog. 229-2 The latter animal, we have already seen, both in the old and new world was the fixed symbol of the water goddess. Therefore in these myths, which are found over so many thousand square leagues, we cannot be in error in perceiving a reflex of their cosmogonical traditions already discussed, in which from the winds and the waters, represented here under their emblems of the bird and the dog, all animate life proceeded.

Without this symbolic coloring, a tribe to the south of them, a band of the Minnetarees, had the crude tradition that their first progenitor emerged from the waters, bearing in his hand an ear of maize, 230-1 very much as Viracocha and his companions rose from the sacred waves of Lake Titicaca, or as the Moxos imagined that they were descended from the lakes and rivers on whose banks their villages were situated.

These myths, and many others, hint of general conceptions of life and the world, wide-spread theories of ancient date, such as we are not accustomed to expect among savage nations, such as may very excusably excite a doubt as to their native origin, but a doubt infallibly dispelled by a careful comparison of the best authorities. Is it that hitherto, in the pride of intellectual culture, we have never done justice to the thinking faculty of those whom we call barbarians? Or shall we accept the only other alternative, that these are the unappreciated heirlooms bequeathed a rude race by a period of higher civilization, long since extinguished by constant wars and ceaseless fear? We are not yet ready to answer these questions. With almost unanimous consent the latter has been accepted as the true solution, but rather from the preconceived theory of a state of primitive civilization from which man fell, than from ascertained facts.

It would, perhaps, be pushing symbolism too far to explain as an emblem of the primitive waters the coyote, which, according to the Root-Diggers of California, brought their ancestors into the world; or the wolf, which the Lenni Lenape pretended released mankind from the dark bowels of the earth by scratching away the soil. They should rather be interpreted by the curious custom of the Toukaways, a wild people in Texas, of predatory and unruly disposition. They celebrate their origin by a grand annual dance. One of them, naked as he was born, is buried in the earth. The others, clothed in wolf-skins, walk over him, snuff around him, howl in lupine style, and finally dig him up with their nails. The leading wolf then solemnly places a bow and arrow in his hands, and to his inquiry as to what he must do for a living, paternally advises him "to do as the wolves do — rob, kill, and murder, rove from place to place, and never cultivate the soil." 231-1 Most wise and fatherly counsel! But what is there new under the sun? Three thousand years ago the Hirpini, or Wolves, an ancient Sabine tribe, were wont to collect on Mount Soracte, and there go through certain rites in memory of an oracle which predicted their extinction when they ceased to gain their living as wolves by violence and plunder. Therefore they dressed in wolf-skins, ran with barks and howls over burning coals, and gnawed wolfishly whatever they could seize. 231-2

Though hasty writers have often said that the Indian tribes claim literal descent from different wild beasts, probably in all other instances, as in these, this will prove, on examination, to be an error resting on a misapprehension arising from the habit of the natives of adopting as their totem or clan-mark the figure and name of some animal, or else, in an ignorance of the animate symbols employed with such marked preference by the red race to express abstract ideas. In some cases, doubtless, the natives themselves came, in time, to confound the symbol with the idea, by that familiar process of personification and consequent debasement exemplified in the history of every religion; but I do not believe that a single example could be found where an Indian tribe had a tradition whose real purport was that man came by natural process of descent from an ancestor, a brute.

The reflecting mind will not be offended at the contradictions in these different myths, for a myth is, in one sense, a theory of natural phenomena expressed in the form of a narrative. Often several explanations seem equally satisfactory for the same fact, and the mind hesitates to choose, and rather accepts them all than rejects any. Then, again, an expression current as a metaphor by-and-by crystallizes into a dogma, and becomes the nucleus of a new mythological growth. These are familiar processes to one versed in such studies, and involve no logical contradiction, because they are never required to be reconciled.

FOOTNOTE:

223-1 *Vocabulario Quiche*, s. v., ed. Brasseur, Paris, 1862.

223-2 The Eskimo *innuk*, man, means also a possessor or owner; the yelk of an egg; and the pus of an abscess (Egede, *Nachrichten von Grönland*, p. 106). From it is derived *innuwok*, to live, life. Probably *innuk* also means the *semen masculinum*, and in its identification with pus, may not there be the solution of that strange riddle which in so many myths of the West Indies and Central America makes the first of men to be "the purulent one?" (See ante, p. 135.)

224-1 Müller, *Amer. Urrelig.*, pp. 109, 229.

224-2 D'Orbigny, *Frag. d'une Voy. dans l'Amér. Mérid.*, p. 512. It is still a mooted point whence Shakspeare drew the plot of The Tempest. The coincidence mentioned in the text between some parts of it and South American mythology does not stand alone. Caliban, the savage and brutish native of the island, is undoubtedly the word Carib, often spelt Caribani, and Calibani in older writers; and his "dam's god Setebos" was the supreme divinity of the Patagonians when first visited by Magellan. (Pigafetta, *Viaggio intorno al Globo*, Germ. Trans.: Gotha, 1801, p. 247.)

224-3 Both Lederer and John Bartram assign it this meaning. Gallatin gives in the Powhatan dialect the word for mountain as *pomottinke,* doubtless another form of the same.

225-1 Marcy, *Exploration of the Red River,* p. 69.

226-1 Compare Romans, *Hist. of Florida,* pp. 58, 71; Adair, *Hist. of the North Am. Indians,* p. 195; and Gregg, *Commerce of the Prairies,* ii. p. 235. The description of the mound is by Major Heart, in the *Trans. of the Am. Philos. Soc.,* iii. p. 216. (1st series.)

226-2 The French writers give for Great Spirit *coyocopchill;* Gallatin for hill, *kweya koopsel.* The blending of these two ideas, at first sight so remote, is easily enough explained when we remember that on "the hill of heaven" in all religions is placed the throne of the mightiest of existences. The Natchez word can be analyzed as follows: *sel, sil,* or *chill,* great; *cop,* a termination very frequent in their language, apparently signifying existence; *kweya, coyo,* for *kue ya,* from the Maya *kue,* god; the great living God. The Tarahumara language of Sonora offers an almost parallel instance. In it *regui,* is *above,* up, over, *reguiki,* heaven, *reguiguiki,* a hill or mountain (Buschmann, *Spuren der Aztek. Sprache im nörd. Mexico,* p. 244). In the Quiché dialects *tepeu* is lord, ruler, and is often applied to the Supreme Being. With some probability Brasseur derives it from the Aztec *tepetl,* mountain (*Hist. du Mexique,* i. p. 106).

227-1 Balboa, *Hist. du Pérou,* p. 4.

229-1 Long's *Expedition to the Rocky Mountains,* i. p. 274; Catlin's *Letters,* i. p. 178.

229-2 Richardson, *Arctic Expedition,* pp. 239, 247; Klemm, *Culturgeschichte der Menschheit,* ii. p. 316.

230-1 Long, *Exped. to the Rocky Mountains,* i. p. 326.

231-1 Schoolcraft, *Ind. Tribes,* v. p. 683.

231-2 Schwarz, *Ursprung der Mythologie,* p. 121.

CHAPTER IX
THE SOUL AND ITS DESTINY

Universality of the belief in a soul and a future state shown by the aboriginal tongues, by expressed opinions, and by sepulchral rites. — The future world never a place of rewards and punishments. — The house of the Sun the heaven of the red man. — The terrestrial paradise and the underworld. — Çupay. — Xibalba. — Mictlan. — Metempsychosis? — Belief in a resurrection of the dead almost universal.

THE missionary Charlevoix wrote several excellent works on America toward the beginning of the last century, and he is often quoted by later authors; but probably no one of his sayings has been thus honored more frequently than this: "The belief the best established among our Americans is that of the immortality of the soul." 233-1 The tremendous stake that every one of us has on the truth of this dogma makes it quite a satisfaction to be persuaded that no man is willing to live wholly without it. Certainly exceptions are very rare, and most of those which materialistic philosophers have taken such pains to collect, rest on misunderstandings or superficial observation.

In the new world I know of only one well authenticated instance where all notion of a future state appears to have been entirely wanting, and this in quite a small clan, the Lower Pend d'Oreilles, of Oregon. This people had no burial ceremonies, no notion of a life hereafter, no word for soul, spiritual existence, or vital principle. They thought that when they died, that was the last of them. The Catholic missionaries who undertook the unpromising task of converting them to Christianity, were at first obliged to depend upon the imperfect translations of half-breed interpreters. These "made the idea of soul intelligible to their hearers by telling them they had a gut which never rotted, and that this was their living principle!" Yet even they were not destitute of religious notions. No tribe was more addicted to the observance of charms, omens, dreams, and guardian spirits, and they believed that illness and bad luck generally were the effects of the anger of a fabulous old woman. 234-1 The aborigines of the Californian peninsula were as near beasts as men ever become. The missionaries likened them to "herds of swine, who neither worshipped the true and only God, nor adored false deities." Yet they must have had some vague notion of an after.world, for the writer who paints the darkest picture of their condition remarks, "I saw them frequently putting shoes on the feet of the dead, which seems to indicate that they entertain the idea of a journey after death." 234-2

Proof of Charlevoix's opinion may be derived from three independent sources. The aboriginal languages may be examined for terms corresponding to the word soul, the opinions of the Indians themselves may be quoted, and the significance of sepulchral rites as indicative of a belief in life after death may be determined.

The most satisfactory is the first of these. *We* call the soul a ghost or spirit, and often a shade. In these words, the *breath* and the *shadow* are the sensuous perceptions transferred to represent the immaterial object of our thought. Why the former was chosen, I have already explained; and for the latter, that it is man's intangible image, his constant companion, and is of a nature akin to darkness, earth, and night, are sufficiently obvious reasons.

These same tropes recur in American languages in the same connection. The New England tribes called the soul *chemung*, the shadow, and in Quiché *natub*, in Eskimo *tarnak*, express both these ideas. In Mohawk *atonritz*, the soul, is from *atonrion*, to breathe, and other examples to the same purpose have already been given. 235-1

Of course no one need demand that a strict immateriality be attached to these words. Such a colorless negative abstraction never existed for them, neither does it for us, though we delude ourselves into believing that it does. The soul was to them the invisible man, material as ever, but lost to the appreciation of the senses.

Nor let any one be astonished if its unity was doubted, and several supposed to reside in one body. This is nothing more than a somewhat gross form of a doctrine upheld by most creeds and most philosophies. It seems the readiest solution of certain psychological enigmas, and may, for aught we know, be an instinct of fact. The Rabbis taught a threefold division—*nephesh*, the animal, *ruah*, the human, and *neshamah*, the divine soul, which corresponds to that of Plato into *thumos, epithumia*, and *nous*. And even Saint Paul seems to have recognized such inherent plurality when he distinguishes between the bodily soul, the intellectual soul, and the spiritual gift, in his Epistle to the Romans. No such refinements of course as these are to be expected among the red men; but it may be looked upon either as the rudiments of these teachings, or as a gradual debasement of them to gross and material expression, that an old and wide-spread notion was found among both Iroquois and Algonkins, that man has two souls, one of a vegetative character, which gives bodily life, and remains with the corpse after death, until it is called to enter another body; another of more ethereal texture, which in life can depart from the body in sleep or trance, and wander over the world, and at death goes directly to the land of Spirits. 236-1

The Sioux extended it to Plato's number, and are said to have looked forward to one going to a cold place, another to a warm and comfortable country, while the third was to watch the body. Certainly a most impartial distribution of rewards and punishments. 237-1 Some other Dakota tribes shared their views on this point, but more commonly, doubtless owing to the sacredness of the number, imagined *four* souls, with separate destinies, one to wander about the world, one to watch the body, the third to hover around the village, and the highest to go to the spirit land. 237-2 Even this number is multiplied by certain Oregon tribes, who imagine one in every member; and by the Caribs of Martinique, who, wherever they could detect a pulsation, located a spirit, all subordinate, however, to a supreme one throned in the heart, which alone would be transported to the skies at death. 237-3 For the heart that so constantly sympathizes with our emotions and actions, is, in most languages and most nations, regarded as the seat of life; and when the priests of bloody religions tore out the heart of the victim and offered it to the idol, it was an emblem of the life that was thus torn from the field of this world and consecrated to the rulers of the next.

Various motives impel the living to treat with respect the body from which life has departed. Lowest of them is a superstitious dread of death and the dead. The stoicism of the Indian, especially the northern tribes, in the face of death, has often been the topic of poets, and has often been interpreted to be a fearlessness of that event. This is by no means true. Savages have an awful horror of death; it is to them the worst of ills; and for this very reason was it that they thought to meet it without flinching was the highest proof of courage. Everything connected with the deceased was, in many tribes, shunned with superstitious terror. His name was not mentioned, his property left untouched, all reference to him was sedulously avoided. A Tupi tribe used to hurry the body at once to the nearest water, and toss it in; the Akanzas left it in the lodge and burned over it the dwelling and contents; and the Algonkins carried it forth by a hole cut opposite the door, and beat the walls with sticks to fright away the lingering ghost. Burying places were always avoided, and every means taken to prevent the departed spirits exercising a malicious influence on those remaining behind.

These craven fears do but reveal the natural repugnance of the animal to a cessation of existence, and arise from the instinct of self-preservation essential to organic life. Other rites, undertaken avowedly for the behoof of the soul, prove and illustrate a simple but unshaken faith in its continued existence after the decay of the body.

None of these is more common or more natural than that which attributes to the emancipated spirit the same wants that it felt while on earth, and with loving foresight provides for their satisfaction. Clothing and utensils of war and the chase were, in ancient times, uniformly placed by the body, under the impression that they would be of service to the departed in his new home. Some few tribes in the far west still retain the custom, but most were soon ridiculed into its neglect, or were forced to omit it by the violation of tombs practised by depraved whites in hope of gain. To these harmless offerings the northern tribes often added a dog slain on the grave; and doubtless the skeletons of these animals in so many tombs in Mexico and Peru point to similar customs there. It had no deeper meaning than to give a companion to the spirit in its long and lonesome journey to the far off land of shades. The peculiar appropriateness of the dog arose not only from the guardianship it exerts during life, but further from the symbolic signification it so often had as representative of the goddess of night and the grave.

Where a despotic form of government reduced the subject almost to the level of a slave and elevated the ruler almost to that of a superior being, not animals only, but men, women, and children were frequently immolated at the tomb of the cacique. The territory embraced in our own country was not without examples of this horrid custom. On the lower Mississippi, the Natchez Indians brought it with them from Central America in all its ghastliness. When a sun or chief died, one or several of his wives and his highest officers were knocked on the head and buried with him, and at such times the barbarous privilege was allowed to any of the lowest caste to at once gain admittance to the highest by the deliberate murder of their own children on the funeral pyre—a privilege which respectable writers tell us human beings were found base enough to take advantage of. 239-1

Oviedo relates that in the province of Guataro, in Guatemala, an actual rivalry prevailed among the people to be slain at the death of their cacique, for they had been taught that only such as went with him would ever find their way to the paradise of the departed. 240-1 Theirs was therefore somewhat of a selfish motive, and only in certain parts of Peru, where polygamy prevailed, and the rule was that only one wife was to be sacrificed, does the deportment of husbands seem to have been so creditable that their widows actually disputed one with another for the pleasure of being buried alive with the dead body, and bearing their spouse company to the other world. 240-2 Wives who have found few parallels since the famous matron of Ephesus!

The fire built nightly on the grave was to light the spirit on his journey. By a coincidence to be explained by the universal sacredness of the number, both Algonkins and Mexicans maintained it for *four* nights consecutively. The former related the tradition that one of their ancestors returned from the spirit land and informed their nation that the journey thither consumed just *four* days, and that collecting fuel every night added much to the toil and fatigue the soul encountered, all of which could be spared it by the relatives kindling nightly a fire on the grave. Or as Longfellow has told it:—

"Four days is the spirit's journey
To the land of ghosts and shadows,
Four its lonely night encampments.
Therefore when the dead are buried,
Let a fire as night approaches
Four times on the grave be kindled,
That the soul upon its journey
May not grope about in darkness."

The same length of time, say the Navajos, does the departed soul wander over a gloomy marsh ere it can discover the ladder leading to the world below, where are the homes of the setting and the rising sun, a land of luxuriant plenty, stocked with game and covered with corn. To that land, say they, sink all lost seeds and germs which fall on the earth and do not sprout. There below they take root, bud, and ripen their fruit. 241-1

After four days, once more, in the superstitions of the Greenland Eskimos, does the soul, for that term after death confined in the body, at last break from its prison-house and either rise in the sky to dance in the aurora borealis or descend into the pleasant land beneath the earth, according to the manner of death. 241-2

That there are logical contradictions in this belief and these ceremonies, that the fire is always in the same spot, that the weapons and utensils are not carried away by the departed, and that the food placed for his sustenance remains untouched, is very true. But those who would therefore argue that they were not intended for the benefit of the soul, and seek some more recondite meaning in them as "unconscious emblems of struggling faith or expressions of inward emotions," 242-1 are led astray by the very simplicity of their real intention. Where is the faith, where the science, that does not involve logical contradictions just as gross as these? They are tolerable to us merely because we are used to them. What value has the evidence of the senses anywhere against a religious faith? None whatever. A stumbling block though this be to the materialist, it is the universal truth, and as such it is well to accept it as an experimental fact.

The preconceived opinions that saw in the meteorological myths of the Indian, a conflict between the Spirit of Good and the Spirit of Evil, have with like unconscious error falsified his doctrine of a future life, and almost without an exception drawn it more or less in the likeness of the Christian heaven, hell, and purgatory. Very faint traces of any such belief except where derived from the missionaries are visible in the New World. Nowhere was any well-defined doctrine that moral turpitude was judged and punished in the next-world. No contrast is discoverable between a place of torments and a realm of joy; at the worst but a negative castigation awaited the liar, the coward, or the niggard. The typical belief of the tribes of the United States was well expressed in the reply of Esau Hajo, great medal chief and speaker for the Creek nation in the National Council, to the question, Do the red people believe in a future state of rewards and punishments? "We have an opinion that those who have behaved well are taken under the care of Esaugetuh Emissee, and assisted; and that those who have behaved ill are left to shift for themselves; and that there is no other punishment." 243-1

Neither the delights of a heaven on the one hand, nor the terrors of a hell on the other, were ever held out by priests or sages as an incentive to well-doing, or a warning to the evil-disposed. Different fates, indeed, awaited the departed souls, but these rarely, if ever, were decided by their conduct while in the flesh, but by the manner of death, the punctuality with which certain sepulchral rites were fulfilled by relatives, or other similar arbitrary circumstance beyond the power of the individual to control. This view, which I am well aware is directly at variance with that of all previous writers, may be shown to be that natural to the uncultivated intellect everywhere, and the real interpretation of the creeds of America. Whether these arbitrary circumstances were not construed to signify the decision of the Divine Mind on the life of the man, is a deeper question, which there is no means at hand to solve.

Those who have complained of the hopeless confusion of American religions have but proven the insufficiency of their own means of analyzing them. The uniformity which they display in so many points is nowhere more fully illustrated than in the unanimity with which they all point to the *sun* as the land of the happy souls, the realm of the blessed, the scene of the joyous hunting-grounds of the hereafter. Its perennial glory, its comfortable warmth, its daily analogy to the life of man, marked its abode as the pleasantest spot in the universe. It matters not whether the eastern Algonkins pointed to the south, others of their nation, with the Iroquois and Creeks, to the west, or many tribes to the east, as the direction taken by the spirit; all these myths but mean that its bourn is the home of the sun, which is perhaps in the Orient whence he comes forth, in the Occident where he makes his bed, or in the South whither he retires in the chilling winter. Where the sun lives, they informed the earliest foreign visitors, were the villages of the deceased, and the milky way which nightly spans the arch of heaven, was, in their opinion, the road that led thither, and was called the path of the souls (le chemin des âmes). 244-1 To hueyu ku, the mansion of the sun, said the Caribs, the soul passes when death overtakes the body. 244-2 Our knowledge is scanty of the doctrines taught by the Incas concerning the soul, but this much we do know, that they looked to the sun, their recognized lord and protector, as he who would care for them at death, and admit them to his palaces. There—not, indeed, exquisite joys—but a life of unruffled placidity, void of labor, vacant of strong emotions, a sort of material Nirvana, awaited them. 244-3 For these reasons, they, with most other American nations, interred the corpse lying east and west, and not as the traveller Meyen has suggested, 244-4 from the reminiscences of some ancient migration. Beyond the Cordilleras, quite to the coast of Brazil, the innumerable hordes who wandered through the sombre tropical forests of that immense territory, also pointed to the west, to the region beyond the mountains, as the land where the souls of their ancestors lived in undisturbed serenity; or, in the more brilliant imaginations of the later generations, in a state of perennial inebriety, surrounded by infinite casks of rum, and with no white man to dole it out to them. 245-1 The natives of the extreme south, of the Pampas and Patagonia, suppose the stars are the souls of the departed. At night they wander about the sky, but the moment the sun rises they hasten to the cheerful light, and are seen no more until it disappears in the west. So the Eskimo of the distant north, in the long winter nights when the aurora bridges the sky with its changing hues and arrowy shafts of light, believes he sees the spirits of his ancestors clothed in celestial raiment, disporting themselves in the absence of the sun, and calls the phenomenon the dance of the dead.

The home of the sun was the heaven of the red man; but to this joyous abode not every one without distinction, no miscellaneous crowd, could gain admittance. The conditions were as various as the national temperaments. As the fierce gods of the Northmen would admit no soul to the banquets of Walhalla but such as had met the "spear-death" in the bloody play of war, and shut out pitilessly all those who feebly breathed their last in the "straw death" on the couch of sickness, so the warlike Aztec race in Nicaragua held that the shades of those who died in their beds went downward and to naught; but of those who fell in battle for their country to the east, "to the place whence comes the sun." 246-1 In ancient Mexico not only the warriors who were thus sacrificed on the altar of their country, but with a delicate and poetical sense of justice that speaks well for the refinement of the race, also those women who perished in child-birth, were admitted to the home of the sun. For are not they also heroines in the battle of life? Are they not also its victims? And do they not lay down their lives for country and kindred? Every morning, it was imagined, the heroes came forth in battle array, and with shout and song and the ring of weapons, accompanied the sun to the zenith, where at every noon the souls of the mothers, the Cihuapipilti, received him with dances, music, and flowers, and bore him company to his western couch. 246-2 Except these, none—without, it may be, the victims sacrificed to the gods, and this is doubtful—were deemed worthy of the highest heaven.

A mild and unwarlike tribe of Guatemala, on the other hand, were persuaded that to die by any other than a natural death was to forfeit all hope of life hereafter, and therefore left the bodies of the slain to the beasts and vultures.

The Mexicans had another place of happiness for departed souls, not promising perpetual life as the home of the sun, but unalloyed pleasure for a certain term of years. This was Tlalocan, the realm of the god of rains and waters, the terrestrial paradise, whence flowed all the rivers of the earth, and all the nourishment of the race. The diseases of which persons died marked this destination. Such as were drowned, or struck by lightning, or succumbed to humoral complaints, as dropsies and leprosy, were by these tokens known to be chosen as the subjects of Tlaloc. To such, said the natives, "death is the commencement of another life, it is as waking from a dream, and the soul is no more human but divine (*teot*)." Therefore they addressed their dying in terms like these: "Sir, or lady, awake, awake; already does the dawn appear; even now is the light approaching; already do the birds of yellow plumage begin their songs to greet thee; already are the gayly-tinted butterflies flitting around thee." 247-1

Before proceeding to the more gloomy portion of the subject, to the destiny of those souls who were not chosen for the better part, I must advert to a curious coincidence in the religious reveries of many nations which finds its explanation in the belief that the house of the sun is the home of the blessed, and proves that this was the first conception of most natural religions. It is seen in the events and obstacles of the journey to the happy land. We everywhere hear of a water which the soul must cross, and an opponent, either a dog or an evil spirit, which it has to contend with. We are all familiar with the dog Cerberus (called by Homer simply "the dog"), which disputed the passage of the river Styx over which the souls must cross; and with the custom of the vikings, to be buried in a boat so that they might cross the waters of Ginunga-gap to the inviting strands of Godheim. Relics of this belief are found in the Koran which describes the bridge *el*

Sirat, thin as a hair and sharp as a scimetar, stretched in a single span from heaven to earth; in the Persian legend, where the rainbow arch Chinevad is flung across the gloomy depths between this world and the home of the happy; and even in the current Christian allegory which represents the waters of the mythical Jordan rolling between us and the Celestial City.

How strange at first sight does it seem that the Hurons and Iroquois should have told the earliest missionaries that after death the soul must cross a deep and swift river on a bridge formed by a single slender tree most lightly supported, where it had to defend itself against the attacks of a dog? 248-1 If only they had expressed this belief, it might have passed for a coincidence merely. But the Athapascas (Chepewyans) also told of a great water, which the soul must cross in a stone canoe; the Algonkins and Dakotas, of a stream bridged by an enormous snake, or a narrow and precipitous rock, and the Araucanians of Chili of a sea in the west, in crossing which the soul was required to pay toll to a malicious old woman. Were it unluckily impecunious, she deprived it of an eye. 248-2 With the Aztecs this water was called Chicunoapa, the Nine Rivers. It was guarded by a dog and a green dragon, to conciliate which the dead were furnished with slips of paper by way of toll. The Greenland Eskimos thought that the waters roared through an unfathomable abyss over which there was no other bridge than a wheel slippery with ice, forever revolving with fearful rapidity, or a path narrow as a cord with nothing to hold on by. On the other side sits a horrid old woman gnashing her teeth and tearing her hair with rage. As each soul approaches she burns a feather under its nose; if it faints she seizes it for her prisoner, but if the soul's guardian spirit can overcome her, it passes through in safety. 249-1

The similarity to the passage of the soul across the Styx, and the toll of the obolus to Charon is in the Aztec legend still more striking, when we remember that the Styx was the ninth head of Oceanus (omitting the Cocytus, often a branch of the Styx). The Nine Rivers probably refer to the nine Lords of the Night, ancient Aztec deities guarding the nocturnal hours, and introduced into their calendar. The Tupis and Caribs, the Mayas and Creeks, entertained very similar expectations.

We are to seek the explanation of these wide-spread theories of the soul's journey in the equally prevalent tenet that the sun is its destination, and that that luminary has his abode beyond the ocean stream, which in all primitive geographies rolls its waves around the habitable land. This ocean stream is the water which all have to attempt to pass, and woe to him whom the spirit of the waters, represented either as the old woman, the dragon, or the dog of Hecate, seizes and overcomes. In the lush fancy of the Orient, the spirit of the waters becomes the spirit of evil, the ocean stream the abyss of hell, and those who fail in the passage the damned, who are foredoomed to evil deeds and endless torture.

No such ethical bearing as this was ever assigned the myth by the red race before they were taught by Europeans. Father Brebeuf could only find that the souls of suicides and those killed in war were supposed to live apart from the others; "but as to the souls of scoundrels," he adds, "so far from being shut out, they are the welcome guests, though for that matter if it were not so, their paradise would be a total desert, as Huron and scoundrel (*Huron et larron*) are one and the same." 250-1 When the Minnetarees told Major Long and the Mannicicas of the La Plata the Jesuits, 250-2 that the souls of the bad fell into the waters and were swept away, these are, beyond doubt, attributable either to a false interpretation, or to Christian instruction. No such distinction is probable among savages. The Brazilian natives divided the dead into classes, supposing that the drowned, those killed by violence, and those yielding to disease, lived in separate regions; but no ethical reason whatever seems to have been connected with this. 250-3 If the conception of a place of moral retribution was known at all to the race, it should be found easily recognizable in Mexico, Yucatan, or Peru. But the so-called "hells" of their religions have no such significance, and the spirits of evil, who were identified by early writers with Satan, no more deserve the name than does the Greek Pluto.

Çupay or Supay, the Shadow, in Peru was supposed to rule the land of shades in the centre of the earth. To him went all souls not destined to be the companions of the Sun. This is all we know of his attributes; and the assertion of Garcilasso de la Vega, that he was the analogue of the Christian Devil, and that his name was never pronounced without spitting and muttering a curse on his head, may be invalidated by the testimony of an earlier and better authority on the religion of Peru, who calls him the god of rains, and adds that the famous Inca, Huayna Capac, was his high priest. 251-1

"The devil," says Cogolludo of the Mayas, "is called by them Xibilha, which means he who disappears or vanishes." 251-2 In the legends of the Quichés, the name Xibalba is given as that of the under-world ruled by the grim lords One Death and Seven Deaths. The derivation of the name is from a root meaning to fear, from which comes the term in Maya dialects for a ghost or phantom. 251-3 Under the influence of a century of Christian catechizing, the Quiché legends portray this really as a place of torment, and its rulers as malignant and powerful; but as I have before pointed out, they do so, protesting that such was not the ancient belief, and they let fall no word that shows that it was regarded as the destination of the morally bad. The original meaning of the name given by Cogolludo points unmistakably to the simple fact of disappearance from among men, and corresponds in harmlessness to the true sense of those words of fear, Scheol, Hades, Hell, all signifying hidden from sight, and only endowed with more grim associations by the imaginations of later generations. 252-1

Mictlanteuctli, Lord of Mictlan, from a word meaning to die, was the Mexican Pluto. Like Çupay, he dwelt in the subterranean regions, and his palace was named Tlalxicco, the navel of the earth. Yet he was also located in the far north, and that point of the compass and the north wind were named after him. Those who descended to him were oppressed by the darkness of his abode, but were subjected to no other trials; nor were they sent thither as a punishment, but merely from having died of diseases unfitting them for Tlalocan. Mictlanteuctli was said to be the most powerful of the gods. For who is stronger than Death? And who dare defy the Grave? As the skald lets Odin say to Bragi: "Our lot is uncertain; even on the hosts of the gods gazes the gray Fenris wolf." 252-2

These various abodes to which the incorporeal man took flight were not always his everlasting home. It will be remembered that where a plurality of souls was believed, one of these, soon after death, entered another body to recommence life on earth. Acting under this persuasion, the Algonkin women who desired to become mothers, flocked to the couch of those about to die, in hope that the vital principle, as it passed from the body, would enter theirs, and fertilize their sterile wombs; and when, among the Seminoles of Florida, a mother died in childbirth, the infant was held over her face to receive her parting spirit, and thus acquire strength and knowledge for its future use. 253-1 So among the Tahkalis, the priest is accustomed to lay his hand on the head of the nearest relative of the deceased, and to blow into him the soul of the departed, which is supposed to come to life in his next child. 253-2 Probably, with a reference to the current tradition that ascribes the origin of man to the earth, and likens his life to that of the plant, the Mexicans were accustomed to say that at one time all men have been stones, and that at last they would all return to stones; 253-3 and, acting literally on this conviction, they interred with the bones of the dead a small green stone, which was called the principle of life.

Whether any nations accepted the doctrine of metempsychosis, and thought that "the souls of their grandams might haply inhabit a partridge," we are without the means of knowing. La Hontan denies it positively of the Algonkins; but the natives of Popoyan refused to kill doves, says Coreal, 254-1 because they believe them inspired by the souls of the departed. And Father Ignatius Chomé relates that he heard a woman of the Chiriquanes in Buenos Ayres say of a fox: "May that not be the spirit of my dead daughter?" 254-2 But before accepting such testimony as decisive, we must first inquire whether these tribes believed in a multiplicity of souls, whether these animals had a symbolical value, and if not, whether the soul was not simply presumed to put on this shape in its journey to the land of the hereafter: inquiries which are unanswered. Leaving, therefore, the question open, whether the sage of Samos had any disciples in the new world, another and more fruitful topic is presented by their well-ascertained notions of the resurrection of the dead.

This seemingly extraordinary doctrine, which some have asserted was entirely unknown and impossible to the American Indians, 254-3 was in fact one of their most deeply-rooted and wide-spread convictions, especially among the tribes of the eastern United States. It is indissolubly connected with their highest theories of a future life, their burial ceremonies, and their modes of expression. The Moravian Brethren give the grounds of this belief with great clearness: "That they hold the soul to be immortal, and perhaps think the body will rise again, they give not unclearly to understand when they say, 'We Indians shall not for ever die; even the grains of corn we put under the earth, grow up and become living things.' They conceive that when the soul has been a while with God, it can, if it chooses, return to earth and be born again." 255-1 This is the highest and typical creed of the aborigines. But instead of simply being born again in the ordinary sense of the word, they thought the soul would return to the bones, that these would clothe themselves with flesh, and that the man would rejoin his tribe. That this was the real, though often doubtless the dimly understood reason of the custom of preserving the bones of the deceased, can be shown by various arguments.

This practice was almost universal. East of the Mississippi nearly every nation was accustomed, at stated periods—usually once in eight or ten years—to collect and clean the osseous remains of those of its number who had died in the intervening time, and inter them in one common sepulchre, lined with choice furs, and marked with a mound of wood, stone, and earth. Such is the origin of those immense tumuli filled with the mortal remains of nations and generations which the antiquary, with irreverent curiosity, so frequently chances upon in all portions of our territory. Throughout Central America the same usage obtained in various localities, as early writers and existing monuments abundantly testify. Instead of interring the bones, were they those of some distinguished chieftain, they were deposited in the temples or the council-houses, usually in small chests of canes or splints. Such were the charnel-houses which the historians of De Soto's expedition so often mention, and these are the "arks" which Adair and other authors, who have sought to trace the descent of the Indians from the Jews, have likened to that which the ancient Israelites bore with them on their migrations. A widow among the Tahkalis was obliged to carry the bones of her deceased husband wherever she went for four years, preserving them in such a casket handsomely decorated with feathers. 256-1 The Caribs of the mainland adopted the custom for all without exception. About a year after death the bones were cleaned, bleached, painted, wrapped in odorous balsams, placed in a wicker basket, and kept suspended from the door of their dwellings. 256-2 When the quantity of these heirlooms became burdensome, they were removed to some inaccessible cavern, and stowed away with reverential care. Such was the cave Ataruipe, a visit to which has been so eloquently described by Alexander von Humboldt in his "Views of Nature."

So great was the filial respect for these remains by the Indians, that on the Mississippi, in Peru, and elsewhere, no tyranny, no cruelty, so embittered the indigenes against the white explorers as the sacrilegious search for treasures perpetrated among the sepulchres of past generations. Unable to understand the meaning of such deep feeling, so foreign to the European who, without a second thought, turns a cemetery into a public square, or seeds it down in wheat, the Jesuit missionaries in Paraguay accuse the natives of worshipping the skeletons of their forefathers, 257-1 and the English in Virginia repeated it of the Powhatans.

The question has been debated and variously answered, whether the art of mummification was known and practised in America. Without entering into the discussion, it is certain that preservation of the corpse by a long and thorough process of exsiccation over a slow fire was nothing unusual, not only in Peru, Popoyan, the Carib countries, and Nicaragua, but among many of the tribes north of the Gulf of Mexico, as I have elsewhere shown. 257-2 The object was essentially the same as when the bones alone were preserved; and in the case of rulers, the same homage was often paid to their corpses as had been the just due of their living bodies.

The opinion underlying all these customs was, that a part of the soul, or one of the souls, dwelt in the bones; that these were the seeds which, planted in the earth, or preserved unbroken in safe places, would, in time, put on once again a garb of flesh, and germinate into living human beings. Language illustrates this not unusual theory. The Iroquois word for bone is *esken* — for soul, *atisken*, literally that which is within the bone. 257-3 In an Athapascan dialect bone is *yani*, soul *i-yune*. 257-4 The Hebrew Rabbis taught that in the bone *lutz*, the coccyx, remained at death the germ of a second life, which, at the proper time, would develop into the purified body, as the plant from the seed.

But mythology and supersitions add more decisive testimony. One of the Aztec legends of the origin of man was, that after one of the destructions of the world the gods took counsel together how to renew the species. It was decided that one of their number, Xolotl, should descend to Mictlan, the realm of the dead, and bring thence a bone of the perished race. The fragments of this they sprinkled with blood, and on the fourth day it grew into a youth, the father of the present race. 258-1 The profound mystical significance of this legend is reflected in one told by the Quichés, in which the hero gods Hunahpu and Xblanque succumb to the rulers of Xibalba, the darksome powers of death. Their bodies are burned, but their bones are ground in a mill and thrown in the waters, lest they should come to life. Even this precaution is insufficient—"for these ashes did not go far; they sank to the bottom of the stream, where, in the twinkling of an eye, they were changed into handsome youths, and their very same features appeared anew. On the fifth day they displayed themselves anew, and were seen in the water by the people," 258-2 whence they emerged to overcome and destroy the powers of death and hell (Xibalba).

The strongest analogies to these myths are offered by the superstitious rites of distant tribes. Some of the Tupis of Brazil were wont on the death of a relative to dry and pulverize his bones and then mix them with their food, a nauseous practice they defended by asserting that the soul of the dead remained in the bones and lived again in the living. 259-1 Even the lower animals were supposed to follow the same law. Hardly any of the hunting tribes, before their original manners were vitiated by foreign influence, permitted the bones of game slain in the chase to be broken, or left carelessly about the encampment. They were collected in heaps, or thrown into the water. Mrs. Eastman observes that even yet the Dakotas deem it an omen of ill luck in the hunt, if the dogs gnaw the bones or a woman inadvertently steps over them; and the Chipeway interpreter, John Tanner, speaks of the same fear among that tribe. The Yurucares of Bolivia carried it to such an inconvenient extent, that they carefully put by even small fish bones, saying that unless this was done the fish and game would disappear from the country. 259-2 The traveller on our western prairies often notices the buffalo skulls, countless numbers of which bleach on those vast plains, arranged in circles and symmetrical piles by the careful hands of the native hunters. The explanation they offer for this custom gives the key to the whole theory and practice of preserving the osseous relics of the dead, as well human as brute. They say that, "the bones contain the spirits of the slain animals, and that some time in the future they will rise from the earth, re-clothe themselves with flesh, and stock the prairies anew." 259-3 This explanation, which comes to us from indisputable authority, sets forth in its true light the belief of the red race in a resurrection. It is not possible to trace it out in the subtleties with which theologians have surrounded it as a dogma. The very attempt would be absurd. They never occurred to the Indian. He thought that the soul now enjoying the delights of the happy hunting grounds would some time return to the bones, take on flesh, and live again. Such is precisely the much discussed statement that Garcilasso de la Vega says he often heard from the native Peruvians. He adds that so careful were they lest any of the body should be lost that they preserved even the parings of their nails and clippings of the hair. 260-1 In contradiction to this the writer Acosta has been quoted, who says that the Peruvians embalmed their dead because they "had no knowledge that the bodies should rise with the soul." 260-2 But, rightly understood, this is a confirmation of La Vega's account. Acosta means that the Christian doctrine of the body rising from the dust being unknown to the Peruvians (which is perfectly true), they preserved the body just as it was, so that the soul when it returned to earth, as all expected, might not be at a loss for a house of flesh.

The notions thus entertained by the red race on the resurrection are peculiar to it, and stand apart from those of any other. They did not look for the second life to be either better or worse than the present one; they regarded it neither as a reward nor a punishment to be sent back to the world of the living; nor is there satisfactory evidence that it was ever distinctly connected with a moral or physical theory of the destiny of the universe, or even with their prevalent expectation of recurrent epochs in the course of nature. It is true that a writer whose personal veracity is above all doubt, Mr. Adam Hodgson, relates an ancient tradition of the Choctaws, to the effect that the present world will be consumed by a general conflagration, after which it will be reformed pleasanter than it now is, and that then the spirits of the dead will return to the bones in the bone mounds, flesh will knit together their loose joints, and they shall again inhabit their ancient territory. 261-1

There was also a similar belief among the Eskimos. They said that in the course of time the waters would overwhelm the land, purify it of the blood of the dead, melt the icebergs, and wash away the steep rocks. A wind would then drive off the waters, and the new land would be peopled by reindeers and young seals. Then would He above blow once on the bones of the men and twice on those of the women, whereupon they would at once start into life, and lead thereafter a joyous existence. 261-2

But though there is nothing in these narratives alien to the course of thought in the native mind, yet as the date of the first is recent (1820), as they are not supported (so far as I know) by similar traditions elsewhere, and as they may have arisen from Christian doctrines of a millennium, I leave them for future investigation.

What strikes us the most in this analysis of the opinions entertained by the red race on a future life is the clear and positive hope of a hereafter, in such strong contrast to the feeble and vague notions of the ancient Israelites, Greeks, and Romans, and yet the entire inertness of this hope in leading them to a purer moral life. It offers another proof that the fulfilment of duty is in its nature nowise connected with or derived from a consideration of ultimate personal consequences. It is another evidence that the religious is wholly distinct from the moral sentiment, and that the origin of ethics is not to be sought in connection with the ideas of divinity and responsibility.

FOOTNOTE:

233-1 *Journal Historique*, p. 351: Paris, 1740.

234-1 *Rep. of the Commissioner of Ind. Affairs*, 1854, pp. 211, 212. The old woman is once more a personification of the water and the moon.

234-2 Bægert, *Acc. of the Aborig. Tribes of the Californian Peninsula*, translated by Chas. Rau, in Ann. Rep. Smithson. Inst., 1866, p. 387.

235-1 Of the Nicaraguans Oviedo says: "Ce n'est pas leur cœur qui va en haut, mais ce qui les faisait vivre; c'est-à-dire, le souffle qui leur sort par la bouche, et que l'on nomme *Julio*" (*Hist. du Nicaragua*, p. 36). The word should be *yulia*, kindred with *yoli*, to live. (Buschmann, *Uber die Aztekischen Ortsnamen*, p. 765.) In the Aztec and cognate languages we have already seen that *ehecatl* means both *wind, soul,* and *shadow* (Buschmann, *Spuren der Aztek. Spr. in Nördlichen Mexico*, p. 74).

236-1 *Rel. de la Nouv. France*, An 1636, p. 104; "Keating's *Narrative*," i. pp. 232, 410.

237-1 French, *Hist. Colls. of Louisiana*, iii. p. 26.

237-2 Mrs. Eastman, *Legends of the Sioux*, p. 129.

237-3 *Voy. à la Louisiane fait en 1720*, p. 155: Paris, 1768.

239-1 Dupratz, *Hist. of Louisiana*, ii. p. 219; Dumont, *Mems. Hist. sur la Louisiane*, i. chap. 26.

240-1 *Rel. de la Prov. de Cueba*, p. 140.

240-2 Coreal, *Voiages aux Indes Occidentales*, ii. p. 94: Amsterdam, 1722.

241-1 *Senate Rep. on the Ind. Tribes*, p. 358: Wash. 1867.

241-2 Egede, *Nachrichten von Grönland*, p. 145.

242-1 Alger, *Hist. of the Doctrine of a Future Life*, p. 76.

243-1 Hawkins, *Sketch of the Creek Country*, p. 80.

244-1 *Rel. de la Nouv. France*, 1634, pp. 17, 18.

244-2 Müller, *Amer. Urreligionen*, p. 229.

244-3 La Vega, *Hist. des Incas.*, lib. ii. cap. 7.

244-4 *Ueber die Ureinwohner von Peru*, p. 41.

245-1 Coreal, *Voy. aux Indes Occident.*, i. p. 224; Müller, *Amer. Urrelig.*, p. 289.

246-1 Oviedo, *Hist. du Nicaragua*, p. 22.

246-2 Torquemada, *Monarquia Indiana*, lib. vi. cap. 27.

247-1 Sahagun, *Hist. de la Nueva España*, lib. x. cap. 29.

248-1 *Rel. de la Nouv. France*, 1636, p. 105.

248-2 Molina, *Hist. of Chili*, ii. p. 81, and others in Waitz, *Anthropologie*, iii. p. 197.

249-1 *Nachrichten von Grönland aus dem Tagebuche vom Bischof Paul Egede*, p. 104: Kopenhagen, 1790.

250-1 *Rel. de la Nouv. France*, 1636, p. 105.

250-2 Long's *Expedition*, i. p. 280; Waitz, *Anthropologie*, iii. p. 531.

250-3 Müller, *Amer. Urreligionen*, p. 287.

251-1 Compare Garcilasso de la Vega, *Hist. des Incas.*, liv. ii. chap. ii., with *Lett. sur les Superstitions du Pérou*, p. 104. Çupay is undoubtedly a personal form from *Çupan*, a shadow. (See Holguin, *Vocab. de la Lengua Quichua*, p. 80: Cuzco, 1608.)

251-2 "El que desparece ô desvanece," *Hist. de Yucathan*, lib. iv. cap. 7.

251-3 Ximenes, *Vocab. Quiché*, p. 224. The attempt of the Abbé Brasseur to make of Xibalba an ancient kingdom of renown with Palenque as its capital, is so utterly unsupported and wildly hypothetical, as to justify the humorous flings which have so often been cast at antiquaries.

252-1 Scheol is from a Hebrew word, signifying to dig, to hide in the earth. Hades signifies the *unseen* world. Hell Jacob Grimm derives from *hilan*, to conceal in the earth, and it is cognate with *hole* and *hollow*.

252-2 Pennock, *Religion of the Northmen*, p. 148.

253-1 La Hontan, *Voy. dans l'Am. Sept.*, i. p. 232; *Narrative of Oceola Nikkanoche*, p. 75.

253-2 Morse, *Rep. on the Ind. Tribes*, App. p. 345.

253-3 Garcia, *Or. de los Indios*, lib. iv. cap. 26, p. 310.

254-1 *Voiages aux Indes Oc.*, ii. p. 132.

254-2 *Lettres Edif. et Cur.*, v. p. 203.

254-3 Alger, *Hist. of the Doctrine of a Future Life*, p. 72.

255-1 Loskiel, *Ges. der Miss. der evang. Brüder*, p. 49.

256-1 Richardson, *Arctic Expedition*, p. 260.

256-2 Gumilla, *Hist. del Orinoco*, i. pp. 199, 202, 204.

257-1 Ruis, *Conquista Espiritual del Paraguay*, p. 48, in Lafitau.

257-2 *Notes on the Floridian Peninsula*, pp. 191 sqq.

257-3 Bruyas, *Rad. Verborum Iroquæorum*.

257-4 Buschmann, *Athapask. Sprachstamm*, pp. 182, 188.

258-1 Torquemada, *Monarquia Indiana*, lib. vi. cap. 41.

258-2 *Le Livre Sacré des Quichés*, pp. 175-177.

259-1 Müller, *Amer. Urrelig.*, p. 290, after Spix.

259-2 D'Orbigny, *Annuaire des Voyages*, 1845, p. 77.

259-3 Long's *Expedition*, i. p. 278.

260-1 *Hist. des Incas*, lib. iii. chap. 7.

260-2 *Hist. of the New World*, bk. v. chap. 7.

261-1 *Travels in North America*, p. 280.

261-2 Egede, *Nachrichten von Grönland*, p. 156.

CHAPTER X
THE NATIVE PRIESTHOOD

Their titles. — Practitioners of the healing art by supernatural means. — Their power derived from natural magic and the exercise of the clairvoyant and mesmeric faculties. — Examples. — Epidemic hysteria. — Their social position. — Their duties as religious functionaries. — Terms of admission to the Priesthood. — Inner organization in various nations. — Their esoteric languages and secret societies.

THUS picking painfully amid the ruins of a race gone to wreck centuries ago, thus rejecting much foreign rubbish and scrutinizing each stone that lies around, if we still are unable to rebuild the edifice in its pristine symmetry and beauty, yet we can at least discern and trace the ground plan and outlines of the fane it raised to God. Before leaving the field to the richer returns of more fortunate workmen, it will not be inappropriate to add a sketch of the ministers of these religions, the servants in this temple.

Shamans, conjurers, sorcerers, medicine men, wizards, and many another hard name have been given them, but I shall call them *priests*, for in their poor way, as well as any other priesthood, they set up to be the agents of the gods, and the interpreters of divinity. No tribe was so devoid of religious sentiment as to be without them. Their power was terrible, and their use of it unscrupulous. Neither men nor gods, death nor life, the winds nor the waves, were beyond their control. Like Old Men of the Sea, they have clung to the neck of their nations, throttling all attempts at progress, binding them to the thraldom of superstition and profligacy, dragging them down to wretchedness and death. Christianity and civilization meet in them their most determined, most implacable foes. But what is this but the story of priestcraft and intolerance everywhere, which Old Spain can repeat as well as New Spain, the white race as well as the red? Blind leaders of the blind, dupers and duped fall into the ditch.

In their own languages they are variously called; by the Algonkins and Dakotas, "those knowing divine things" and "dreamers of the gods" (*manitousiou, wakanwacipi*); in Mexico, "masters or guardians of the divine things" (*teopixqui, teotecuhtli*); in Cherokee, their title means, "possessed of the divine fire" (*atsilung kelawhi*); in Iroquois, "keepers of the faith" (*honundeunt*); in Quichua, "the learned" (*amauta*); in Maya, "the listeners" (*cocome*). The popular term in French and English of "medicine men" is not such a misnomer as might be supposed. The noble science of medicine is connected with divinity not only by the rudest savage but the profoundest philosopher, as has been already adverted to. When sickness is looked upon as the effect of the anger of a god, or as the malicious infliction of a sorcerer, it is natural to seek help from those who assume to control the unseen world, and influence the fiats of the Almighty. The recovery from disease is the kindliest exhibition of divine power. Therefore the earliest canons of medicine in India and Egypt are attributed to no less distinguished authors than the gods Brahma and Thoth; 265-1 therefore the earliest practitioners of the healing art are universally the ministers of religion.

But, however creditable this origin is to medicine, its partnership with theology was no particular advantage to it. These mystical doctors shared the contempt still so prevalent among ourselves for a treatment based on experiment and reason, and regarded the administration of emetics and purgatives, baths and diuretics, with a contempt quite equal to that of the disciples of Hahnemann. The practitioners of the rational school formed a separate class among the Indians, and had nothing to do with amulets, powwows, or spirits. 265-2 They were of different name and standing, and though held in less estimation, such valuable additions to the pharmacopœia as guaiacum, cinchona, and ipecacuanha, were learned from them. The priesthood scorned such ignoble means. Were they summoned to a patient, they drowned his groans in a barbarous clangor of instruments in order to fright away the demon that possessed him; they sucked and blew upon the diseased organ, they sprinkled him with water, and catching it again threw it on the ground, thus drowning out the disease; they rubbed the part with their hands, and exhibiting a bone or splinter asserted that they drew it from the body, and that it had been the cause of the malady, they manufactured a little image to represent the spirit of sickness, and spitefully knocked it to pieces, thus vicariously destroying its prototype; they sang doleful and monotonous chants at the top of their voices, screwed their countenances into hideous grimaces, twisted their bodies into unheard of contortions, and by all accounts did their utmost to merit the honorarium they demanded for their services. A double motive spurred them to spare no pains. For if they failed, not only was their reputation gone, but the next expert called in was likely enough to hint, with that urbanity so traditional in the profession, that the illness was in fact caused or much increased by the antagonistic nature of the remedies previously employed, whereupon the chances were that the doctor's life fell into greater jeopardy than that of his quondam patient.

Considering the probable result of this treatment, we may be allowed to doubt whether it redounded on the whole very much to the honor of the fraternity. Their strong points are rather to be looked for in the real knowledge gained by a solitary and reflective life, by an earnest study of the appearances of nature, and of those hints and forest signs which are wholly lost on the white man and beyond the ordinary insight of a native. Travellers often tell of changes of the weather predicted by them with astonishing foresight, and of information of singular accuracy and extent gleaned from most meagre materials. There is nothing in this to shock our sense of probability — much to elevate our opinion of the native sagacity. They were also adepts in tricks of sleight of hand, and had no mean acquaintance with what is called natural magic. They would allow themselves to be tied hand and foot with knots innumerable, and at a sign would shake them loose as so many wisps of straw; they would spit fire and swallow hot coals, pick glowing stones from the flames, walk naked through a fire, and plunge their arms to the shoulder in kettles of boiling water with apparent impunity. 267-1 Nor was this all. With a skill not inferior to that of the jugglers of India, they could plunge knives into vital parts, vomit blood, or kill one another out and out to all appearances, and yet in a few minutes be as well as ever; they could set fire to articles of clothing and even houses, and by a touch of their magic restore them instantly as perfect as before. 267-2 If it were not within our power to see most of these miracles performed any night in one of our great cities by a well dressed professional, we would at once deny their possibility. As it is, they astonish us only too little.

One of the most peculiar and characteristic exhibitions of their power, was to summon a spirit to answer inquiries concerning the future and the absent. A great similarity marked this proceeding in all northern tribes from the Eskimos to the Mexicans. A circular or conical lodge of stout poles four or eight in number planted firmly in the ground, was covered with skins or mats, a small aperture only being left for the seer to enter. Once in, he carefully closed the hole and commenced his incantations. Soon the lodge trembles, the strong poles shake and bend as with the united strength of a dozen men, and strange, unearthly sounds, now far aloft in the air, now deep in the ground, anon approaching near and nearer, reach the ears of the spectators. At length the priest announces that the spirit is present, and is prepared to answer questions. An indispensable preliminary to any inquiry is to insert a handful of tobacco, or a string of beads, or some such douceur under the skins, ostensibly for the behoof of the celestial visitor, who would seem not to be above earthly wants and vanities. The replies received, though occasionally singularly clear and correct, are usually of that profoundly ambiguous purport which leaves the anxious inquirer little wiser than he was before. For all this, ventriloquism, trickery, and shrewd knavery are sufficient explanations. Nor does it materially interfere with this view, that converted Indians, on whose veracity we can implicitly rely, have repeatedly averred that in performing this rite they themselves did not move the medicine lodge; for nothing is easier than in the state of nervous excitement they were then in to be self-deceived, as the now familiar phenomenon of table-turning illustrates.

But there is something more than these vulgar arts now and then to be perceived. There are statements supported by unquestionable testimony, which ought not to be passed over in silence, and yet I cannot but approach them with hesitation. They are so revolting to the laws of exact science, so alien, I had almost said, to the experience of our lives. Yet is this true, or are such experiences only ignored and put aside without serious consideration? Are there not in the history of each of us passages which strike our retrospective thought with awe, almost with terror? Are there not in nearly every community individuals who possess a mysterious power, concerning whose origin, mode of action, and limits, we and they are alike in the dark? I refer to such organic forces as are popularly summed up under the words clairvoyance, mesmerism, rhabdomancy, animal magnetism, physical spiritualism. Civilized thousands stake their faith and hope here and hereafter, on the truths of these manifestations; rational medicine recognizes their existence, and while it attributes them to morbid and exceptional influences, confesses its want of more exact knowledge, and refrains from barren theorizing. Let us follow her example, and hold it enough to show that such powers, whatever they are, were known to the native priesthood as well as the modern spiritualists, and the miracle mongers of the Middle Ages.

Their highest development is what our ancestors called "second sight." That under certain conditions knowledge can pass from one mind to another otherwise than through the ordinary channels of the senses, is familiarly shown by the examples of persons *en rapport*. The limit to this we do not know, but it is not unlikely that clairvoyance or second sight is based upon it. In his autobiography, the celebrated Sac chief Black Hawk, relates that his great grandfather "was inspired by a belief that at the end of four years, he should see a white man, who would be to him a father." Under the direction of this vision he travelled eastward to a certain spot, and there, as he was forewarned, met a Frenchman, through whom the nation was brought into alliance with France. 269-1 No one at all versed in the Indian character will doubt the implicit faith with which this legend was told and heard. But we may be pardoned our scepticism, seeing there are so many chances of error. It is not so with an anecdote related by Captain Jonathan Carver, a cool-headed English trader, whose little book of travels is an unquestioned authority. In 1767, he was among the Killistenoes at a time when they were in great straits for food, and depending upon the arrival of the traders to rescue them from starvation. They persuaded the chief priest to consult the divinities as to when the relief would arrive. After the usual preliminaries, this magnate announced that next day, precisely when the sun reached the zenith, a canoe would arrive with further tidings. At the appointed hour the whole village, together with the incredulous Englishman, was on the beach, and sure enough, at the minute specified, a canoe swung round a distant point of land, and rapidly approaching the shore brought the expected news. 270-1

Charlevoix is nearly as trustworthy a writer as Carver. Yet he deliberately relates an equally singular instance. 270-2

But these examples are surpassed by one described in the *Atlantic Monthly* of July, 1866, the author of which, John Mason Brown, Esq., has assured me of its accuracy in every particular. Some years since, at the head of a party of voyageurs, he set forth in search of a band of Indians somewhere on the vast plains along the tributaries of the Copper-mine and Mackenzie rivers. Danger, disappointment, and the fatigues of the road, induced one after another to turn back, until of the original ten only three remained. They also were on the point of giving up the apparently hopeless quest, when they were met by some warriors of the very band they were seeking. These had been sent out by one of their medicine men to find three whites, whose horses, arms, attire, and personal appearance he minutely described, which description was repeated to Mr. Brown by the warriors before they saw his two companions. When afterwards, the priest, a frank and simple-minded man, was asked to explain this extraordinary occurrence, he could offer no other explanation than that "he saw them coming, and heard them talk on their journey." 271-1

Many tales such as these have been recorded by travellers, and however much they may shock our sense of probability, as well-authenticated exhibitions of a power which sways the Indian mind, and which has ever prejudiced it so unchangeably against Christianity and civilization, they cannot be disregarded. Whether they too are but specimens of refined knavery, whether they are instigations of the Devil, or whether they must be classed with other facts as illustrating certain obscure and curious mental faculties, each may decide as the bent of his mind inclines him, for science makes no decision.

Those nervous conditions associated with the name of Mesmer were nothing new to the Indian magicians. Rubbing and stroking the sick, and the laying on of hands, were very common parts of their clinical procedures, and at the initiations to their societies they were frequently exhibited. Observers have related that among the Nez Percés of Oregon, the novice was put to sleep by songs, incantations, and "certain passes of the hand," and that with the Dakotas he would be struck lightly on the breast at a preconcerted moment, and instantly "would drop prostrate on his face, his muscles rigid and quivering in every fibre." 272-1

There is no occasion to suppose deceit in this. It finds its parallel in every race and every age, and rests on a characteristic trait of certain epochs and certain men, which leads them to seek the divine, not in thoughtful contemplation on the laws of the universe and the facts of self-consciousness, but in an entire immolation of the latter, a sinking of their own individuality in that of the spirits whose alliance they seek. This is an outgrowth of that ignoring of the universality of Law, which belongs to the lower stages of enlightenment. 273-1   And as this is never done with impunity, but with iron certainty brings its punishment with it, the study of the mental conditions thus evoked, and the results which follow them, offers a salutary subject of reflection to the theologian as well as the physician. For these examples of nervous pathology are identical in kind, and alike in consequences, whether witnessed in the primitive forests of the New World, among the convulsionists of St. Medard, or in the excited scenes of a religious revival in one of our own churches.

Sleeplessness and abstemiousness, carried to the utmost verge of human endurance — seclusion, and the pertinacious fixing of the mind on one subject — obstinate gloating on some morbid fancy, rarely failed to bring about hallucinations with all the garb of reality. Physicians are well aware that the more frequently these diseased conditions of the mind are sought, the more readily they are found. Then, again, they were often induced by intoxicating and narcotic herbs. Tobacco, the maguey, coca; in California the chucuaco; among the Mexicans the snake plant, ollinhiqui or coaxihuitl; and among the southern tribes of our own country the cassine yupon and iris versicolor, 273-2 were used; and, it is even said, were cultivated for this purpose. The seer must work himself up to a prophetic fury, or speechless lie in apparent death before the mind of the gods would be opened to him. Trance and ecstasy were the two avenues he knew to divinity; fasting and seclusion the means employed to discover them. His ideal was of a prophet who dwelt far from men, without need of food, in constant communion with divinity. Such an one, in the legends of the Tupis, resided on a mountain glittering with gold and silver, near the river Uaupe, his only companion a dog, his only occupation dreaming of the gods. When, however, an eclipse was near, his dog would bark; and then, taking the form of a bird, he would fly over the villages, and learn the changes that had taken place. 274-1

But man cannot trample with impunity on the laws of his physical life, and the consequences of these deprivations and morbid excitements of the brain show themselves in terrible pictures. Not unfrequently they were carried to the pitch of raving mania, reminding one of the worst forms of the Berserker fury of the Scandinavians, or the Bacchic rage of Greece. The enthusiast, maddened with the fancies of a disordered intellect, would start forth from his seclusion in an access of demoniac frenzy. Then woe to the dog, the child, the slave, or the woman who crossed his path; for nothing but blood could satisfy his inappeasable craving, and they fell instant victims to his madness. But were it a strong man, he bared his arm, and let the frenzied hermit bury his teeth in the quivering flesh. Such is a scene at this day not uncommon on the northwest coast, and few of the natives around Milbank Sound are without the scars the result of this horrid custom. 275-1

This frenzy, terrible enough in individuals, had its most disastrous effects when with that peculiar facility of contagion which marks hysterical maladies, it swept through whole villages, transforming them into bedlams filled with unrestrained madmen. Those who have studied the strange and terrible mental epidemics that visited Europe in the middle ages, such as the tarantula dance of Apulia, the chorea Germanorum, and the great St. Vitus' dance, will be prepared to appreciate the nature of a scene at a Huron village, described by Father le Jeune in 1639. A festival of three days and three nights had been in progress to relieve a woman who, from the description, seems to have been suffering from some obscure nervous complaint. Toward the close of this vigil, which throughout was marked by all sorts of debaucheries and excesses, all the participants seemed suddenly seized by ten thousand devils. They ran howling and shrieking through the town, breaking everything destructible in the cabins, killing dogs, beating the women and children, tearing their garments, and scattering the fires in every direction with bare hands and feet. Some of them dropped senseless, to remain long or permanently insane, but the others continued until worn out with exhaustion. The Father learned that during these orgies not unfrequently whole villages were consumed, and the total extirpation of some families had resulted. No wonder that he saw in them the diabolical workings of the prince of evil, but the physician is rather inclined to class them with those cases of epidemic hysteria, the common products of violent and ill-directed mental stimuli. 276-1

These various considerations prove beyond a doubt that the power of the priesthood did by no means rest exclusively on deception. They indorse and explain the assertions of converted natives, that their power as prophets was something real, and entirely inexplicable to themselves. And they make it easily understood how those missionaries failed who attempted to persuade them that all this boasted power was false. More correct views than these ought to have been suggested by the facts themselves, for it is indisputable that these magicians did not hesitate at times to test their strength on each other. In these strange duels à l'outrance, one would be seated opposite his antagonist, surrounded with the mysterious emblems of his craft, and call upon his gods one after another to strike his enemy dead. Sometimes one, "gathering his medicine," as it was termed, feeling within himself that hidden force of will which makes itself acknowledged even without words, would rise in his might, and in a loud and severe voice command his opponent to die! Straightway the latter would drop dead, or yielding in craven fear to a superior volition, forsake the implements of his art, and with an awful terror at his heart, creep to his lodge, refuse all nourishment, and presently perish. Still more terrible was the tyranny they exerted on the superstitious minds of the masses. Let an Indian once be possessed of the idea that he is bewitched, and he will probably reject all food, and sink under the phantoms of his own fancy.

How deep the superstitious veneration of these men has struck its roots in the soul of the Indian, it is difficult for civilized minds to conceive. Their power is currently supposed to be without any bounds, "extending to the raising of the dead and the control of all laws of nature." 277-1 The grave offers no escape from their omnipotent arms. The Sacs and Foxes, Algonkin tribes, think that the soul cannot leave the corpse until set free by the medicine men at their great annual feast; 277-2 and the Puelches of Buenos Ayres guard a profound silence as they pass by the tomb of some redoubted necromancer, lest they should disturb his repose, and suffer from his malignant skill. 278-1

While thus investigating their real and supposed power over the physical and mental world, their strictly priestly functions, as performers of the rites of religion, have not been touched upon. Among the ruder tribes these, indeed, were of the most rudimentary character. Sacrifices, chiefly in the form of feasts, where every one crammed to his utmost, dances, often winding up with the wildest scenes of licentiousness, the repetition of long and monotonous chants, the making of the new fire, these are the ceremonies that satisfy the religious wants of savages. The priest finds a further sphere for his activity in manufacturing and consecrating amulets to keep off ill luck, in interpreting dreams, and especially in lifting the veil of the future. In Peru, for example, they were divided into classes, who made the various means of divination specialties. Some caused the idols to speak, others derived their foreknowledge from words spoken by the dead, others predicted by leaves of tobacco or the grains and juice of cocoa, while to still other classes, the shapes of grains of maize taken at random, the appearance of animal excrement, the forms assumed by the smoke rising from burning victims, the entrails and viscera of animals, the course taken by a certain species of spider, the visions seen in drunkeness, the flights of birds, and the directions in which fruits would fall, all offered so many separate fields of prognostication, the professors of which were distinguished by different ranks and titles. 279-1

As the intellectual force of the nation was chiefly centred in this class, they became the acknowledged depositaries of its sacred legends, the instructors in the art of preserving thought; and from their duty to regulate festivals, sprang the observation of the motions of the heavenly bodies, the adjustment of the calendars, and the pseudo-science of judicial astrology. The latter was carried to as subtle a pitch of refinement in Mexico as in the old world; and large portions of the ancient writers are taken up with explaining the method adopted by the native astrologers to cast the horoscope, and reckon the nativity of the newly-born infant.

How was this superior power obtained? What were the terms of admission to this privileged class? In the ruder communities the power was strictly personal. It was revealed to its possessor by the character of the visions he perceived at the ordeal he passed through on arriving at puberty; and by the northern nations was said to be the manifestation of a more potent personal spirit than ordinary. It was not a faculty, but an inspiration; not an inborn strength, but a spiritual gift. The curious theory of the Dakotas, as recorded by the Rev. Mr. Pond, was that the necromant first wakes to consciousness as a winged seed, wafted hither and thither by the intelligent action of the Four Winds. In this form he visits the homes of the different classes of divinities, and learns the chants, feasts, and dances, which it is proper for the human race to observe, the art of omnipresence or clairvoyance, the means of inflicting and healing diseases, and the occult secrets of nature, man, and divinity. This is called "dreaming of the gods." When this instruction is completed, the seed enters one about to become a mother, assumes human form, and in due time manifests his powers. *Four* such incarnations await it, each of increasing might, and then the spirit returns to its original nothingness. The same necessity of death and resurrection was entertained by the Eskimos. To become of the highest order of priests, it was supposed requisite, says Bishop Egede, that one of the lower order should be drowned and eaten by sea monsters. Then, when his bones, one after another, were all washed ashore, his spirit, which meanwhile had been learning the secrets of the invisible world, would return to them, and, clothed in flesh, he would go back to his tribe. At other times a vague and indescribable longing seizes a young person, a morbid appetite possesses them, or they fall a prey to an inappeasable and aimless restlessness, or a causeless melancholy. These signs the old priests recognize as the expression of a personal spirit of the higher order. They take charge of the youth, and educate him to the mysteries of their craft. For months or years he is condemned to entire seclusion, receiving no visits but from the brethren of his order. At length he is initiated with ceremonies of more or less pomp into the brotherhood, and from that time assumes that gravity of demeanor, sententious style of expression, and general air of mystery and importance, everywhere deemed so eminently becoming in a doctor and a priest. A peculiarity of the Moxos was, that they thought none designated for the office but such as had escaped from the claws of the South American tiger, which, indeed, it is said they worshipped as a god. 281-1

Occasionally, in very uncultivated tribes, some family or totem claimed a monopoly of the priesthood. Thus, among the Nez Percès of Oregon, it was transmitted in one family from father to son and daughter, but always with the proviso that the children at the proper age reported dreams of a satisfactory character. 281-2 Perhaps alone of the Algonkin tribes the Shawnees confined it to one totem, but it is remarkable that the greatest of their prophets, Elskataway, brother of Tecumseh, was not a member of this clan. From the most remote times, the Cherokees have had one family set apart for the priestly office. This was when first known to the whites that of the Nicotani, but its members, puffed up with pride and insolence, abused their birthright so shamefully, and prostituted it so flagrantly to their own advantage, that with savage justice they were massacred to the last man. Another was appointed in their place who to this day officiates in all religious rites. They have, however, the superstition, possibly borrowed from Europeans, that the *seventh* son is a natural born prophet, with the gift of healing by touch. 281-3 Adair states that their former neighbors, the Choctaws, permitted the office of high priest, or Great Beloved Man, to remain in one family, passing from father to eldest son, and the very influential *piaches* of the Carib tribes very generally transmitted their rank and position to their children.

In ancient Anahuac the prelacy was as systematic and its rules as well defined, as in the Church of Rome. Except those in the service of Huitzilopochtli, and perhaps a few other gods, none obtained the priestly office by right of descent, but were dedicated to it from early childhood.

Their education was completed at the *Calmecac*, a sort of ecclesiastical college, where instruction was given in all the wisdom of the ancients, and the esoteric lore of their craft. The art of mixing colors and tracing designs, the ideographic writing and phonetic hieroglyphs, the songs and prayers used in public worship, the national traditions and the principles of astrology, the hidden meaning of symbols and the use of musical instruments, all formed parts of the really extensive course of instruction they there received. When they manifested a satisfactory acquaintance with this curriculum, they were appointed by their superiors to such positions as their natural talents and the use they had made of them qualified them for, some to instruct children, others to the service of the temples, and others again to take charge of what we may call country parishes. Implicit subordination of all to the high priest of Huitzilopochtli, hereditary *pontifex maximus*, chastity, or at least temperate indulgence in pleasure, gravity of carriage, and strict attention to duty, were laws laid upon all.

The state religion of Peru was conducted under the supervision of a high priest of the Inca family, and its ministers, as in Mexico, could be of either sex, and hold office either by inheritance, education, or election. For political reasons, the most important posts were usually enjoyed by relatives of the ruler, but this was usage, not law. It is stated by Garcilasso de la Vega 283-1 that they served in the temples by turns, each being on duty the fourth of a lunar month at a time. Were this substantiated it would offer the only example of the regulation of public life by a week of seven days to be found in the New World.

In every country there is perceptible a desire in this class of men to surround themselves with mystery, and to concentrate and increase their power by forming an intimate alliance among themselves. They affected singularity in dress and a professional costume. Bartram describes the junior priests of the Creeks as dressed in white robes and carrying on their head or arm "a great owlskin, stuffed very ingeniously, as an insignia of wisdom and divination. These bachelors are also distinguishable from the other people by their taciturnity, grave and solemn countenance, dignified step, and singing to themselves songs or hymns, in a low sweet voice, as they stroll about the towns." 283-2 The priests of the civilized nations adopted various modes of dress to typify the divinity which they served, and their appearance was often in the highest degree unprepossessing.

To add to their self-importance they pretended to converse in a tongue different from that used in ordinary life, and the chants containing the prayers and legends were often in this esoteric dialect. Fragments of one or two of these have floated down to us from the Aztec priesthood. The travellers Balboa and Coreal, mention that the temple services of Peru were conducted in a language not understood by the masses, 284-1 and the incantations of the priests of Powhatan were not in ordinary Algonkin, but some obscure jargon. 284-2 The same peculiarity has been observed among the Dakotas and Eskimos, and in these nations, fortunately, it fell under the notice of competent linguistic scholars, who have submitted it to a searching examination. The results of their labors prove that certainly in these two instances the supposed foreign tongues were nothing more than the ordinary dialects of the country modified by an affected accentuation, by the introduction of a few cabalistic terms, and by the use of descriptive circumlocutions and figurative words in place of ordinary expressions, a slang, in short, such as rascals and pedants invariably coin whenever they associate. 285-1

All these stratagems were intended to shroud with impenetrable secrecy the mysteries of the brotherhood. With the same motive, the priests formed societies of different grades of illumination, only to be entered by those willing to undergo trying ordeals, whose secrets were not to be revealed under the severest penalties. The Algonkins had three such grades, the *waubeno*, the *meda*, and the *jossakeed*, the last being the highest. To this no white man was ever admitted. All tribes appear to have been controlled by these secret societies. Alexander von Humboldt mentions one, called that of the Botuto or Holy Trumpet, among the Indians of the Orinoko, whose members must vow celibacy and submit to severe scourgings and fasts. The Collahuayas of Peru were a guild of itinerant quacks and magicians, who never remained permanently in one spot.

Withal, there was no class of persons who so widely and deeply influenced the culture and shaped the destiny of the Indian tribes, as their priests. In attempting to gain a true conception of the race's capacities and history, there is no one element of their social life which demands closer attention than the power of these teachers. Hitherto, they have been spoken of with a contempt which I hope this chapter shows is unjustifiable. However much we may deplore the use they made of their skill, we must estimate it fairly, and grant it its due weight in measuring the influence of the religious sentiment on the history of man.

FOOTNOTE:

265-1 Haeser, *Geschichte der Medicin*, pp. 4, 7: Jena, 1845.

265-2 Schoolcraft, *Ind. Tribes*, v. p. 440.

267-1   Carver, *Travels in North America*, p. 73: Boston, 1802; *Narrative of John Tanner*, p. 135.

267-2 Sahagun, *Hist. de la Nueva España*, lib. x. cap. 20; *Le Livre Sacré des Quichés*, p. 177; *Lett. sur les Superstit. du Pérou*, pp. 89, 91.

269-1 *Life of Black Hawk*, p. 13.

270-1 *Travs. in North America*, p. 74.

270-2 *Journal Historique*, p. 362.

271-1   Sometimes facts like this can be explained by the quickness of perception acquired by constant exposure to danger. The mind takes cognizance unconsciously of trifling incidents, the sum of which leads it to a conviction which the individual regards almost as an inspiration. This is the explanation of *presentiments*. But this does not apply to cases like that of Swedenborg, who described a conflagration going on at Stockholm, when he was at Gottenberg, three hundred miles away. Psychologists who scorn any method of studying the mind but through physiology, are at a loss in such cases, and take refuge in refusing them credence. Theologians call them inspirations either of devils or angels, as they happen to agree or disagree in religious views with the person experiencing them. True science reserves its opinion until further observation enlightens it.

272-1 Schoolcraft, *Indian Tribes*, iii. p. 287; v. p. 652.

273-1   "The progress from deepest ignorance to highest enlightenment," remarks Herbert Spencer in his *Social Statics*, "is a progress from entire unconsciousness of law, to the conviction that law is universal and inevitable."

273-2 The Creeks had, according to Hawkins, not less than seven sacred plants; chief of them were the cassine yupon, called by botanists *Ilex vomitoria*, or *Ilex cassina*, of the natural order Aquifoliaceæ; and the blue flag, *Iris versicolor*, natural order Iridaceæ. The former is a powerful diuretic and mild emetic, and grows only near the sea. The latter is an active emeto-cathartic, and is abundant on swampy grounds throughout the Southern

States. From it was formed the celebrated "black drink," with which they opened their councils, and which served them in place of spirits.

274-1 Martius, *Von dem Rechtzustande unter den Ureinwohnern Brasiliens*, p. 32.

275-1 Mr. Anderson, in the *Am. Hist. Mag.*, vii. p. 79.

276-1 Such spectacles were nothing uncommon. They are frequently mentioned in the Jesuit Relations, and they were the chief obstacles to missionary labor. In the debauches and excesses that excited these temporary manias, in the recklessness of life and property they fostered, and in their disastrous effects on mind and body, are depicted more than in any other one trait the thorough depravity of the race and its tendency to ruin. In the quaint words of one of the Catholic fathers, "If the old proverb is true that every man has a grain of madness in his composition, it must be confessed that this is a people where each has at least half an ounce" (De Quen, *Rel. de la Nouv. France*, 1656, p. 27). For the instance in the text see *Rel. de la Nouv. France*, An 1639, pp. 88-94.

277-1 Schoolcraft, *Indian Tribes*, v. p. 423.

277-2 J. M. Stanley, in the *Smithsonian Miscellaneous Contributions*, ii. p. 38.

278-1 D'Orbigny, *L'Homme Américain*, ii. p. 81.

279-1 See Balboa, *Hist. du Pérou*, pp. 28-30.

281-1 D'Orbigny, *L'Homme Américain*, ii. p. 235.

281-2 Schoolcraft, *Ind. Tribes*, v. p. 652.

281-3 Dr. Mac Gowan, in the *Amer. Hist. Mag.*, x. p. 139; Whipple, *Rep. on the Ind. Tribes*, p. 35.

283-1 *Hist. des Incas*, lib. iii. ch. 22.

283-2 *Travels in the Carolinas*, p. 504.

284-1 *Hist. du Pérou*, p. 128; *Voiages aux Indes Occidentales*, ii. p. 97.

284-2 Beverly, *Hist. de la Virginie*, p. 266. The dialect he specifies is "celle d'Occaniches," and on page 252 he says, "On dit que la langue universelle des Indiens de ces Quartiers est celle des *Occaniches*, quoiqu'ils ne soient qu'une petite Nation, depuis que les Anglois connoissent ce Pais; mais je ne sais pas la difference qui'l y a entre cette langue et celle des Algonkins."

(French trans., Orleans, 1707.) This is undoubtedly the same people that Johannes Lederer, a German traveller, visited in 1670, and calls *Akenatzi*. They dwelt on an island, in a branch of the Chowan River, the Sapona, or Deep River (Lederer's *Discovery of North America*, in Harris, Voyages, p. 20). Thirty years later the English surveyor, Lawson, found them in the same spot, and speaks of them as the *Acanechos* (see *Am. Hist. Mag.*, i. p. 163). Their totem was that of the serpent, and their name is not altogether unlike the Tuscarora name of this animal *usquauhne*. As the serpent was so widely a sacred animal, this gives Beverly's remarks an unusual significance. It by no means follows from this name that they were of Iroquois descent. Lederer travelled with a Tuscarora (Iroquois) interpreter, who gave them their name in his own tongue. On the contrary, it is extremely probable that they were an Algonkin totem, which had the exclusive right to the priesthood.

285-1 Riggs, *Gram. and Dict. of the Dakota*, p. ix; Kane, *Second Grinnell Expedition*, ii. p. 127. Paul Egede gives a number of words and expressions in the dialect of the sorcerers, *Nachrichten von Grönland*, p. 122.

CHAPTER XI
THE INFLUENCE OF THE NATIVE RELIGIONS ON THE MORAL AND SOCIAL LIFE OF THE RACE

Natural religions hitherto considered of Evil rather than of Good. — Distinctions to be drawn. — Morality not derived from religion. — The positive side of natural religions in incarnations of divinity. — Examples. — Prayers as indices of religious progress. — Religion and social advancement. — Conclusion.

DRAWING toward the conclusion of my essay, I I am sensible that the vast field of American mythology remains for most part untouched — that I have but proved that it is not an absolute wilderness, pathless as the tropical jungles which now conceal the temples of the race; but that, go where we will, certain landmarks and guide-posts are visible, revealing uniformity of design and purpose, and refuting, by their presence, the oft-repeated charge of entire incoherence and aimlessness. It remains to examine the subjective power of the native religions, their influence on those who held them, and the place they deserve in the history of the race. What are their merits, if merits they have? what their demerits? Did they purify the life and enlighten the mind, or the contrary? Are they in short of evil or of good? The problem is complex — its solution most difficult. The author who of late years has studied most profoundly the savage races of the globe, expresses the discouraging conviction: "Their religions have not acted as levers to raise them to civilization; they have rather worked, and that powerfully, to impede every step in advance, in the first place by ascribing everything unintelligible in nature to spiritual agency, and then by making the fate of man dependent on mysterious and capricious forces, not on his own skill and foresight." 288-1

It would ill accord with the theory of mythology which I have all along maintained if this verdict were final. But in fact these false doctrines brought with them their own antidotes, at least to some extent, and while we give full weight to their evil, let us also acknowledge their good. By substituting direct divine interference for law, belief for knowledge, a dogma for a fact, the highest stimulus to mental endeavor was taken away. Nature, to the heathen, is no harmonious whole swayed by eternal principles, but a chaos of causeless effects, the meaningless play of capricious ghosts. He investigates not, because he doubts not. All events are to him miracles. Therefore his faith knows no bounds, and those who teach that doubt is sinful must contemplate him with admiration. The damsels of Nicaragua destined to be thrown into the seething craters of volcanoes, went to their fate, says Pascual de Andagoya, "happy as if they were going to be saved," 288-2 and doubtless believing so. The subjects of a Central American chieftain, remarks Oviedo, "look upon it as the crown of favors to be permitted to die with their cacique, and thus to acquire immortality." 288-3 The terrible power exerted by the priests rested, as they themselves often saw, largely on the implicit and literal acceptance of their dicta.

In some respects the contrast here offered to enlightened nations is not always in favor of the latter. Borrowing the pointed antithesis of the poet, the mind is often tempted to exclaim—

"This is all
The gain we reap from all the wisdom sown
Through ages: Nothing doubted those first sons
Of Time, while we, the schooled of centuries,
Nothing believe."

But the complaint is unfounded. Faith is dearly bought at the cost of knowledge; nor in a better sense has it yet gone from among us. Far more sublime than any known to the barbarian is the faith of the astronomer, who spends the nights in marking the seemingly wayward motions of the stars, or of the anatomist, who studies with unwearied zeal the minute fibres of the organism, each upheld by the unshaken conviction that from least to greatest throughout this universe, purpose and order everywhere prevail.

Natural religions rarely offer more than this negative opposition to reason. They are tolerant to a degree. The savage, void of any clear conception of a supreme deity, sets up no claim that his is the only true church. If he is conquered in battle, he imagines that it is owing to the inferiority of his own gods to those of his victor, and he rarely therefore requires any other reasons to make him a convert. Acting on this principle, the Incas, when they overcame a strange province, sent its most venerated idol for a time to the temple of the Sun at Cuzco, thus proving its inferiority to their own divinity, but took no more violent steps to propagate their creeds. 290-1 So in the city of Mexico there was a temple appropriated to the idols of conquered nations in which they were shut up, both to prove their weakness and prevent them from doing mischief. A nation, like an individual, was not inclined to patronize a deity who had manifested his incompetence by allowing his charge to be gradually worn away by constant disaster. As far as can now be seen, in matters intellectual, the religions of ancient Mexico and Peru were far more liberal than that introduced by the Spanish conquerors, which, claiming the monopoly of truth, sought to enforce its claim by inquisitions and censorships.

In this view of the relative powers of deities lay a potent corrective to the doctrine that the fate of man was dependent on the caprices of the gods. For no belief was more universal than that which assigned to each individual a guardian spirit. This invisible monitor was an ever present help in trouble. He suggested expedients, gave advice and warning in dreams, protected in danger, and stood ready to foil the machinations of enemies, divine or human. With unlimited faith in this protector, attributing to him the devices suggested by his own quick wits and the fortunate chances of life, the savage escaped the oppressive thought that he was the slave of demoniac forces, and dared the dangers of the forest and the war path without anxiety.

By far the darkest side of such a religion is that which it presents to morality. The religious sense is by no means the voice of conscience. The Takahli Indian when sick makes a full and free confession of sins, but a murder, however unnatural and unprovoked, he does not mention, not counting it crime. 291-1 Scenes of brutal licentiousness were approved and sustained throughout the continent as acts of worship; maidenhood was in many parts freely offered up or claimed by the priests as a right; in Central America twins were slain for religious motives; human sacrifice was common throughout the tropics, and was not unusual in higher latitudes; cannibalism was often enjoined; and in Peru, Florida, and Central America it was not uncommon for parents to slay their own children at the behest of a priest. 291-2 The philosophical moralist, contemplating such spectacles, has thought to recognize in them one consoling trait. All history, it has been said, shows man living under an irritated God, and seeking to appease him by sacrifice of blood; the essence of all religion, it has been added, lies in that of which sacrifice is the symbol, namely, in the offering up of self, in the rendering up of our will to the will of God. 291-3 But sacrifice, when not a token of gratitude, cannot be thus explained. It is not a rendering up, but a *substitution* of our will for God's will. A deity is angered by neglect of his dues; he will revenge, certainly, terribly, we know not how or when. But as punishment is all he desires, if we punish ourselves he will be satisfied; and far better is such self-inflicted torture than a fearful looking for of judgment to come. Craven fear, not without some dim sense of the implacability of nature's laws, is at its root. Looking only at this side of religion, the ancient philosopher averred that the gods existed solely in the apprehensions of their votaries, and the moderns have asserted that "fear is the father of religion, love her late-born daughter;" 292-1 that "the first form of religious belief is nothing else but a horror of the unknown," and that "no natural religion appears to have been able to develop from a germ within itself anything whatever of real advantage to civilization." 292-2

Far be it from me to excuse the enormities thus committed under the garb of religion, or to ignore their disastrous consequences on human progress. Yet this question is a fair one—If the natural religious belief has in it no germ of anything better, whence comes the manifest and undeniable improvement occasionally witnessed—as, for example, among the Toltecs, the Peruvians, and the Mayas? The reply is, by the influence of great men, who cultivated within themselves a purer faith, lived it in their lives, preached it successfully to their fellows, and, at their death, still survived in the memory of their nation, unforgotten models of noble qualities. 293-1 Where, in America, is any record of such men? We are pointed, in answer, to Quetzalcoatl, Viracocha, Zamna, and their congeners. But these august figures I have shown to be wholly mythical, creations of the religious fancy, parts and parcels of the earliest religion itself. The entire theory falls to nothing, therefore, and we discover a positive side to natural religions—one that conceals a germ of endless progress, which vindicates their lofty origin, and proves that He "is not far from every one of us."

I have already analyzed these figures under their physical aspect. Let it be observed in what antithesis they stand to most other mythological creations. Let it be remembered that they primarily correspond to the stable, the regular, the cosmical phenomena, that they are always conceived under human form, not as giants, fairies, or strange beasts; that they were said at one time to have been visible leaders of their nations, that they did not suffer death, and that, though absent, they are ever present, favoring those who remain mindful of their precepts. I touched but incidentally on their moral aspects. This was likewise in contrast to the majority of inferior deities. The worship of the latter was a tribute extorted by fear. The Indian deposits tobacco on the rocks of a rapid, that the spirit of the swift waters may not swallow his canoe; in a storm he throws overboard a dog to appease the siren of the angry waves. He used to tear the hearts from his captives to gain the favor of the god of war. He provides himself with talismans to bind hostile deities. He fees the conjurer to exorcise the demon of disease. He loves none of them, he respects none of them; he only fears their wayward tempers. They are to him mysterious, invisible, capricious goblins. But, in his highest divinity, he recognized a Father and a Preserver, a benign Intelligence, who provided for him the comforts of life—man, like himself, yet a god—God of

All. "Go and do good," was the parting injunction of his father to Michabo in Algonkin legend; 294-1 and in their ancient and uncorrupted stories such is ever his object. "The worship of Tamu," the culture hero of the Guaranis, says the traveller D'Orbigny, "is one of reverence, not of fear." 294-2 They were ideals, summing up in themselves the best traits, the most approved virtues of whole nations, and were adored in a very different spirit from other divinities.

None of them has more humane and elevated traits than Quetzalcoatl. He was represented of majestic stature and dignified demeanor. In his train came skilled artificers and men of learning. He was chaste and temperate in life, wise in council, generous of gifts, conquering rather by arts of peace than of war; delighting in music, flowers, and brilliant colors, and so averse to human sacrifices that he shut his ears with both hands when they were even mentioned. 295-1 Such was the ideal man and supreme god of a people who even a Spanish monk of the sixteenth century felt constrained to confess were "a good people, attached to virtue, urbane and simple in social intercourse, shunning lies, skilful in arts, pious toward their gods." 295-2 Is it likely, is it possible, that with such a model as this before their minds, they received no benefit from it? Was not this a lever, and a mighty one, lifting the race toward civilization and a purer faith?

Transfer the field of observation to Yucatan, and we find in Zamna, to New Granada and in Nemqueteba, to Peru and in Viracocha, or his reflex Manco Capac, the lineaments of Quetzalcoatl — modified, indeed, by difference of blood and temperament, but each combining in himself all the qualities most esteemed by their several nations. Were one or all of these proved to be historical personages, still the fact remains that the primitive religious sentiment, investing them with the best attributes of humanity, dwelling on them as its models, worshipping them as gods, contained a kernel of truth potent to encourage moral excellence. But if they were mythical, then this truth was of spontaneous growth, self-developed by the growing distinctness of the idea of God, a living witness that the religious sense, like every other faculty, has within itself a power of endless evolution.

If we inquire the secret of the happier influence of this element in natural worship, it is all contained in one word — its *humanity*. "The Ideal of Morality," says the contemplative Novalis, "has no more dangerous rival than the Ideal of the Greatest Strength, of the most vigorous life, the Brute Ideal" (*das Thier-Ideal*). 296-1 Culture advances in proportion as man recognizes what faculties are peculiar to him *as man*, and devotes himself to their education. The moral value of religions can be very precisely estimated by the human or the brutal character of their gods. The worship of Quetzalcoatl in the city of Mexico was subordinate to that of lower conceptions, and consequently the more sanguinary and immoral were the rites there practised. The Algonkins, who knew no other meaning for Michabo than the Great Hare, had lost, by a false etymology, the best part of their religion.

Looking around for other standards wherewith to measure the progress of the knowledge of divinity in the New World, *prayer* suggests itself as one of the least deceptive. "Prayer," to quote again the words of Novalis, 296-2 "is in religion what thought is in philosophy. The religious sense prays, as the reason thinks." Guizot, carrying the analysis farther, thinks that it is prompted by a painful conviction of the inability of our will to conform to the dictates of reason. 296-3 Originally it was connected with the belief that divine caprice, not divine law, governs the universe, and that material benefits rather than spiritual gifts are to be desired. The gradual recognition of its limitations and proper objects marks religious advancement. The Lord's Prayer contains seven petitions, only one of which is for a temporal advantage, and it the least that can be asked for. What immeasurable interval between it and the prayer of the Nootka Indian on preparing for war! —

"Great Quahootze, let me live, not be sick, find the enemy, not fear him, find him asleep, and kill a great many of him." 297-1

Or again, between it and the petition of a Huron to a local god, heard by Father Brebeuf: —

"Oki, thou who livest in this spot, I offer thee tobacco. Help us, save us from shipwreck, defend us from our enemies, give us a good trade, and bring us back safe and sound to our villages." 297-2

This is a fair specimen of the supplications of the lowest religion. Another equally authentic is given by Father Allouez. 297-3 In 1670 he penetrated to an outlying Algonkin village, never before visited by a white man. The inhabitants, startled by his pale face and long black gown, took him for a divinity. They invited him to the council lodge, a circle of old men gathered around him, and one of them, approaching him with a double handful of tobacco, thus addressed him, the others grunting approval: —

"This, indeed, is well, Blackrobe, that thou dost visit us. Have mercy upon us. Thou art a Manito. We give thee to smoke.

"The Naudowessies and Iroquois are devouring us. Have mercy upon us.

"We are often sick; our children die; we are hungry. Have mercy upon us. Hear me, O Manito, I give thee to smoke.

"Let the earth yield us corn; the rivers give us fish; sickness not slay us; nor hunger so torment us. Hear us, O Manito, we give thee to smoke."

In this rude but touching petition, wrung from the heart of a miserable people, nothing but their wretchedness is visible. Not the faintest trace of an aspiration for spiritual enlightenment cheers the eye of the philanthropist, not the remotest conception that through suffering we are purified can be detected.

By the side of these examples we may place the prayers of Peru and Mexico, forms composed by the priests, written out, committed to memory, and repeated at certain seasons. They are not less authentic, having been collected and translated in the first generation after the conquest. One to Viracocha Pachacamac, was as follows: —

"O Pachacamac, thou who hast existed from the beginning and shalt exist unto the end, powerful and pitiful; who createdst man by saying, let man be; who defendest us from evil and preservest our life and health; art thou in the sky or in the earth, in the clouds or in the depths? Hear the voice of him who implores thee, and grant him his petitions. Give us life everlasting, preserve us, and accept this our sacrifice." 299-1

In the voluminous specimens of Aztec prayers preserved by Sahagun, moral improvement, the "spiritual gift," is very rarely if at all the object desired. Health, harvests, propitious rains, release from pain, preservation from dangers, illness, and defeat, these are the almost unvarying themes. But here and there we catch a glimpse of something better, some dim sense of the divine beauty of suffering, some feeble glimmering of the grand truth so nobly expressed by the poet: —

aus des Busens Tiefe strömt Gedeihn
Der festen Duldung und entschlossner That.
Nicht Schmerz ist Unglück, Glück nicht immer Freude;
Wer sein Geschick erfüllt, dem lächeln beide.

"Is it possible," says one of them, "that this scourge, this affliction, is sent to us not for our correction and improvement, but for our destruction and annihilation? O Merciful Lord, let this chastisement with which thou hast visited us, thy people, be as those which a father or mother inflicts on their children, not out of anger, but to the end that they may be free from follies and vices." Another formula, used when a chief was elected to some important position, reads: "O Lord, open his eyes and give him light, sharpen his ears and give him understanding, not that he may use them to his own advantage, but for the good of the people he rules. Lead him to know and to do thy will, let him be as a trumpet which sounds thy words. Keep him from the commission of injustice and oppression." 300-1

At first, good and evil are identical with pleasure and pain, luck and ill-luck. "The good are good warriors and hunters," said a Pawnee chief, 300-2 which would also be the opinion of a wolf, if he could express it.

Gradually the eyes of the mind are opened, and it is perceived that "whom He loveth, He chastiseth," and physical give place to moral ideas of good and evil. Finally, as the idea of God rises more distinctly before the soul, as "the One by whom, in whom, and through whom all things are," evil is seen to be the negation, not the opposite of good, and itself "a porch oft opening on the sun."

The influence of these religions on art, science, and social life, must also be weighed in estimating their value.

Nearly all the remains of American plastic art, sculpture, and painting, were obviously designed for religious purposes. Idols of stone, wood, or baked clay, were found in every Indian tribe, without exception; so far as I can judge; and in only a few directions do these arts seem to have been applied to secular purposes. The most ambitious attempts of architecture, it is plain, were inspired by religious fervor. The great pyramid of Cholula, the enormous mounds of the Mississippi valley, the elaborate edifices on artificial hills in Yucatan, were miniature representations of the mountains hallowed by tradition, the "Hill of Heaven," the peak on which their ancestors escaped in the flood, or that in the terrestrial paradise from which flow the rains. Their construction took men away from war and the chase, encouraged agriculture, peace, and a settled disposition, and fostered the love of property, of country, and of the gods. The priests were also close observers of nature, and were the first to discover its simpler laws. The Aztec sages were as devoted star-gazers as the Chaldeans, and their calendar bears unmistakable marks of native growth, and of its original purpose to fix the annual festivals. Writing by means of pictures and symbols was cultivated chiefly for religious ends, and the word *hieroglyph* is a witness that the phonetic alphabet was discovered under the stimulus of the religious sentiment. Most of the aboriginal literature was composed and taught by the priests, and most of it refers to matters connected with their superstitions. As the gifts of votaries and the erection of temples enriched the sacerdotal order individually and collectively, the terrors of religion were lent to the secular arm to enforce the rights of property. Music, poetic, scenic, and historical recitations, formed parts of the ceremonies of the more civilized nations, and national unity was strengthened by a common shrine. An active barter in amulets, lucky stones, and charms, existed all over the continent, to a much greater extent than we might think. As experience demonstrates that nothing so efficiently promotes civilization as the free and peaceful intercourse of man with man, I lay particular stress on the common custom of making pilgrimages.

The temple on the island of Cozumel in Yucatan was visited every year by such multitudes from all parts of the peninsula, that roads, paved with cut stones, had been constructed from the neighboring shore to the principal cities of the interior. 302-1 Each village of the Muyscas is said to have had a beaten path to Lake Guatavita, so numerous were the devotees who journeyed to the shrine there located. 302-2 In Peru the temples of Pachacamà, Rimac, and other famous gods, were repaired to by countless numbers from all parts of the realm, and from other provinces within a radius of three hundred leagues around. Houses of entertainment were established on all the principal roads, and near the temples, for their accommodation; and when they made known the object of their journey, they were allowed a safe passage even through an enemy's territory. 302-3

The more carefully we study history, the more important in our eyes will become the religious sense. It is almost the only faculty peculiar to man. It concerns him nearer than aught else. It is the key to his origin and destiny. As such it merits in all its developments the most earnest attention, an attention we shall find well repaid in the clearer conceptions we thus obtain of the forces which control the actions and fates of individuals and nations.

FOOTNOTE:

288-1 Waitz, *Anthropologie der Naturvoelker*, i. p. 459.

288-2 Navarrete, *Viages*, iii. p. 415.

288-3 *Relation de Cueba*, p. 140. Ed. Ternaux-Compans.

290-1 La Vega, *Hist. des Incas*, liv. v. cap. 12.

291-1 Morse, *Rep. on the Ind. Tribes*, App. p. 345.

291-2 Ximenes, *Origen de los Indios de Guatemala*, p. 192; Acosta, *Hist. of the New World*, lib. v. chap. 18.

291-3 Joseph de Maistre, *Eclaircissement sur les Sacrifices*; Trench, *Hulsean Lectures*, p. 180. The famed Abbé Lammenaais and Professor Sepp, of Munich, with these two writers, may be taken as the chief exponents of a school of mythologists, all of whom start from the theories first laid down by Count de Maistre in his *Soirées de St. Petersbourg*. To them the strongest proof of Christianity lies in the traditions and observances of heathendom. For these show the wants of the religious sense, and Christianity, they maintain, purifies and satisfies them all. The rites, symbols, and legends of every natural religion, they say, are true and not false; all that is required is to assign them their proper places and their real meaning. Therefore the strange resemblances in heathen myths to what is revealed in the Scriptures, as well as the ethical anticipations which have been found in ancient philosophies, all, so far from proving that

Christianity is a natural product of the human mind, in fact, are confirmations of it, unconscious prophecies, and presentiments of the truth.

292-1 Alfred Maury, *La Magie et l'Astrologie dans l'Antiquité et au Moyen Age*, p. 8: Paris, 1860.

292-2 Waitz, *Anthropologie*, i. pp. 325, 465.

293-1 So says Dr. Waitz, *ibid.*, p. 465.

294-1 Schoolcraft, *Algic Researches*, i. p. 143.

294-2 *L'Homme Américain*, ii. p. 319.

295-1 Brasseur, *Hist. du Mexique*, liv. iii. chaps. 1 and 2.

295-2 Sahagun, *Hist. de la Nueva España*, lib. x. cap. 29.

296-1 Novalis, *Schriften*, i. p. 244: Berlin, 1837.

296-2 Ibid., p. 267.

296-3 *Hist. de la Civilisation en France*, i. pp. 122, 130.

297-1 *Narrative of J. R. Jewett among the Savages of Nootka Sound*, p. 121.

297-2 *Rel. de la Nouv. France*, An 1636, p. 109.

297-3 Ibid., An 1670, p. 99.

299-1 Geronimo de Ore, *Symbolo Catholico Indiano*, chap, ix., quoted by Ternaux-Compans. De Ore was a native of Peru and held the position of Professor of Theology in Cuzco in the latter half of the sixteenth century. He was a man of great erudition, and there need be no hesitation in accepting this extraordinary prayer as genuine. For his life and writings see Nic. Antonio, *Bib. Hisp. Nova*, tom. ii. p. 43.

300-1 Sahagun, *Hist. de la Nueva España*, lib. vi. caps. 1, 4.

300-2 Morse, *Rep. on the Ind. Tribes*, App. p. 250.

302-1 Cogolludo, *Hist. de Yucathan*, lib. iv. cap. 9. Compare Stephens, *Travs. in Yucatan*, ii. p. 122, who describes the remains of these roads as they now exist.

302-2 Rivero and Tschudi, *Antiqs. of Peru*, p. 162.

302-3 La Vega, *Hist. des Incas*, lib. vi. chap. 30; Xeres, *Rel de la Conq. du Pérou*, p. 151; *Let. sur les Superstit. du Pérou*, p. 98, and others.

INDEX